Oracle Identity and Access Manager 11*g* for Administrators

Administer Oracle Identity and Access Management:
Installation, configuration, and day-to-day tasks

Atul Kumar

PUBLISHING

BIRMINGHAM - MUMBAI

Oracle Identity and Access Manager 11g for Administrators

First published: September 2011

Production Reference: 1160911

Published by Packt Publishing Ltd.
Livery Place
35 Livery Street
Birmingham B3 2PB, UK.

ISBN 978-1-84968-268-8

www.packtpub.com

Cover Image by Stanford Murray (stanmoore@live.com)

Credits

Author
Atul Kumar

Reviewers
Brad Tumy

Grant Allen

Jom John

Peter Stomenhoff

Acquisition Editor
Rukshana Khambatta

Development Editor
Rukshana Khambatta

Technical Editors
Joyslita D'souza

Jenecia Menezes

Copy Editors
Neha Shetty

Laxmi Subramanian

Project Coordinator
Zainab Bagasrawala

Proofreader
Dan McMahon

Indexer
Rekha Nair

Graphics
Valentina D'silva

Production Coordinator
Shantanu Zagade

Cover Work
Shantanu Zagade

About the Author

Atul Kumar is an Oracle ACE and co-founder of Focusthread. Within the partnership, he works as a Consultant/Technical Architect. He has more than 11 years of experience working on Oracle Database, Oracle Applications DBA, and Fusion Middleware including Oracle Identity and Access Management. He is the technical architect, designing and implementing complex systems with high availability and disaster recovery. Atul Kumar also maintains a famous website http://onlineAppsDBA.com dedicated to Oracle Apps DBAs covering a vast range of Oracle products including Oracle E-Business Suite, OID, OVD, OAM, OIM, SSO, WebLogic, SOA, WebCenter, UCM, OHS, and Fusion applications.

He is the author of another book, *Oracle EBS R12 integration with OID and OAM for SSO*, a step-by-step guide to installing and integrating OID/OAM with E-Business Suite R12.

He prefers to spend his free time with his lovely daughter and family. He holds a Bachelor's degree in Mechanical Engineering from the University of Rajasthan and a Post Graduate Diploma from IIIT, India.

I would like to thank the Focusthread team and Anil Passi for providing servers and for their help with installation and testing setup. I would like to thank the PacktPub team. The Acquisition Editor, Rukshana; Project Coordinator Zainab; and Technical Editors, Jenecia and Joyslita for their invaluable advice and guidance.

Brad Tumy, Peter Stomenhoff, Jom John, Grant Allen, and Neha Mittal did a great job as technical reviewers; reading, commenting, and improving the book.

I would also like to thank my colleagues Ryan Davies and Neha Mittal for the technical discussions and their input in the book.

About the Reviewers

Brad Tumy is a senior Identity and Access Management architect for Tumy Technology, Inc., a company that Brad founded in 2008. Brad has over 16 years of Information Technology experience supporting the United States federal government and a variety of commercial customers. Brad specializes in designing and implementing solutions for Federation, Single Sign-On (SSO), strong authentication, and directory services. Prior to starting his own company, Brad worked for Oracle's National Security Group where he supported several agencies within the intelligence community and within the Department of Defense. Brad is a regular contributor to the Identity and Access community through his blog (`http://blog.tumy-tech.com`) and on Twitter (`http://www.twitter.com/brad_tumy`). Brad and his wife Kara live in Frederick, Maryland and have two children, Maggie and Ethan.

Grant Allen has worked in the Information Technology field for nearly 20 years, specializing in relational database management systems from a variety of vendors. For the past decade, he has worked in the Asia-Pacific region and Europe as a principal database consultant and enterprise architect for several organizations, and he now works in the database field for Google. Grant is the author of *Beginning DB2*, and lead author of *Oracle SQL Recipes* and *The Definitive Guide to SQLite*.

Jom John is the Oracle Practice Lead for IDMWorks (`www.idmworks.com`). IDMWorks helps clients solve complex business issues with custom solutions, more efficient processes, and deep industry knowledge. Their consultants gather, analyze, assess, and use information from across the enterprise to create value in all aspects of their customer's organization. Jom has worked in the Information Technology and Security profession with experience in architecting and deploying Access and Identity Management solutions, LDAP Directories, Single/Reduced Sign-On (SSO), RBAC (Role-Based Access Control), as well as custom-built security and technology frameworks.

Peter Stomenhoff has more than 17 years of experience in architecting and building enterprise-scale systems for numerous global organizations and various levels of governments in both the U.S. and Europe. He first got involved with what we now call Oracle Identity Management (IdM) products, many years prior to the start of Oracle's historical acquisition binge in the IdM field as a part of PricewaterhouseCoopers SIS.com group as well as a consultant for other leading IdM SIs. After Oracle became actively involved in the field, Peter joined Oracle and helped establish the new, at the time, Protected Enterprise group within Oracle Consulting. Currently Peter is the IdM Practice Lead at Mythics Consulting, one of the most respected Oracle Platinum Partners, where he specializes in all things including Identity Management, GRC, Privacy, Security, and Oracle Fusion Middleware in general.

As Peter co-chairs the original Oracle IdM Partner Council, he would like to reach out to all the current or future Oracle IdM customers and partners at pstomenhoff@gmail.com or/and at LinkedIN.com. Also, if there are any Oracle Identity Management (IdM), Security/GRC, or Oracle Fusion Middleware-related questions or anything else that he could be of help with, please feel free to contact him and he will do his best to answer your questions or/and he will reach out to the right people within Oracle IdM or the extensive eco-system outside of Oracle.

www.PacktPub.com

Support files, eBooks, discount offers and more

You might want to visit www.PacktPub.com for support files and downloads related to your book.

Did you know that Packt offers eBook versions of every book published, with PDF and ePub files available? You can upgrade to the eBook version at www.PacktPub.com and as a print book customer, you are entitled to a discount on the eBook copy. Get in touch with us at service@packtpub.com for more details.

At www.PacktPub.com, you can also read a collection of free technical articles, sign up for a range of free newsletters and receive exclusive discounts and offers on Packt books and eBooks.

http://PacktLib.PacktPub.com

Do you need instant solutions to your IT questions? PacktLib is Packt's online digital book library. Here, you can access, read and search across Packt's entire library of books.

Why Subscribe?

- Fully searchable across every book published by Packt
- Copy and paste, print and bookmark content
- On demand and accessible via web browser

Free Access for Packt account holders

If you have an account with Packt at www.PacktPub.com, you can use this to access PacktLib today and view nine entirely free books. Simply use your login credentials for immediate access.

Instant Updates on New Packt Books

Get notified! Find out when new books are published by following @PacktEnterprise on Twitter, or the *Packt Enterprise* Facebook page.

This book is dedicated to my wife Khushi, for her unconditional love and support and to my beautiful daughter Kashish for keeping mummy occupied and me entertained.

Table of Contents

Preface

Oracle Identity and Access Manager 11g for Administrators covers the complete process of installing, configuring, and managing Oracle Access Manager (OAM) and Oracle Identity Manager (OIM). This book covers everything an administrator needs during and after an Oracle Identity and Access Management implementation.

This book covers all aspects of the Oracle Identity and Access Management life cycle from an administrator's point of view. It starts with an introduction to Oracle's Identity and Access Management products, touching all the products which are part of the Oracle Identity Management Suite. It then covers installation and the configuration of multiple OAM/OIM servers in clusters for resilience and high availability for production deployments, creating identity and access management schemas, and configuring Identity Manager and Access Manager in detail. The book then dives into OAM components, WebGate Installation/Configuration, Single Sign-On, Session Management, OIM navigation, and integration with Oracle Internet Directory and Microsoft Active Directory using OIM Connectors. Towards end it touches high level steps to integrate OAM with E-Business Suite and Fusion Middleware (OBIEE, UCM, WebCenter) for Single Sign-On(SSO). Finally, the book covers the important key topic for IDAM management that is logging and auditing in OIM/OAM, including the configuration of a dedicated database for auditing.

What this book covers

Chapter 1, Oracle Identity Management Overview and Architecture, covers various Identity Management components, WebLogic server and goes into detail about the architecture of Oracle Access Manager and Oracle Identity Manager 11g.

Chapter 2, Installing Oracle Identity and Access Manager, focuses on installing and configuring Oracle WebLogic server, Oracle Access Manager, and Oracle Identity Manager both single node and on multiple machines (Active-Active cluster) for high-availability.

Chapter 3, IDAM Directory Structure and files, discusses important environment variables, key files, and directories for Oracle Identity and Access Administration.

Chapter 4, Start-up Shutdown IDAM, covers starting up and shutting down of Oracle Access Manager/Oracle Identity Manager with various options to start services such as command line or console. This chapter also covers Node Manager in WebLogic, which monitors OAM/OIM services.

Chapter 5, OAM Administration and Navigation, covers the OAM Administration console (a browser-based tool) including login/logout, policy and system configuration tabs. This chapter also covers steps to register a WebGate instance both from command-line utility (Remote Registration Tool) and through a graphical user interface (OAM Administration console).

Chapter 6, OAM Policy Component and Single Sign-On, covers OAM Policy Components, that is, Application Domain, Authentication and Authorization Schemes, Host Identifiers, Resource Types and Cookies. This chapter also covers login flow in applications protected by OAM Single Sign-On. The chapter ends with real-time requirement and then step-by-step configuration of Access Manager Application Domain.

Chapter 7, OAM Session Management, focuses on Session Management in OAM 11*g* including various session data stores such as in-memory local cache, in-memory distributed cache managed by Oracle Coherence, and configuring separate database to store session data. This chapter also covers user session life cycle states such as ACTIVE, INACTIVE, and EXPIRED.

Chapter 8, Install and Configure OAM Agents, covers OAM Agents and instructions to install and configure 11*g*/10*g* Webgates with Oracle HTTP Server 11*g*.

Chapter 9, OIM Navigation – Administration and Design Console, covers various interfaces to Oracle Identity Manager that is Administrative and User console, SPML Web Service, and Design console. It also discusses various Administrative and User Consoles such as authenticated and un-authenticated self service, administration and advanced administration consoles.

Chapter 10, OIM Connectors Installation and Configuration, covers Oracle Identity Manager Connector, provisioning and reconciliation, types of connectors, and predefined connectors for various it systems such as Oracle, Microsoft and SAP. It also focuses on installation and configuration of predefined connectors for Microsoft Active Directory User Management, Oracle Internet Directory, and Oracle e-Business Suite User Management.

Chapter 11, OIM Configuration and Tasks, focuses on common Oracle Identity Manager configuration and key tasks such as generating WebLogic Full Client, managing files using MDS utility, OIM password policy, purging the cache, managing OIM configuration, and updating the OIM Server name, port or password.

Chapter 12, OAM Integration with Fusion Middleware and EBS R12, discusses Fusion Middleware security concepts such as Users, groups, roles, authentication and identity assertion provider, and integration of Oracle Fusion Middleware applications such as WebCenter and OBIEE. It also covers integration of Oracle e-Business Suite with Oracle Access Manager.

Chapter 13, Logging and Auditing for OIM/OAM, covers logging in Oracle Access manager and Oracle Identity Manager. This chapter also focuses on ODL framework including steps on how to change logging level, log properties such as file name, log rotation method, and much more. This chapter also covers auditing in OAM and OIM.

Appendix, covers frequently asked questions for Oracle Identity Manager and Oracle Access Manager such as how to find version/port numbers or how to install patches. This appendix also cover basic troubleshooting or common issues reported on the Internet, including suggested fixes.

What you need for this book

This book is complete in itself; you can pick and read at your leisure. To fully utilise and better understand this book, our recommendation is that you install and configure IDAM software on a Windows or Unix machine; you will need to install the Database, WebLogic, and IDAM software. This software is available on the Oracle Technology Network and can be downloaded after registering on `http://otn.oracle.com`.

Who this book is for

If you are a security architect, IDAM or database administrator looking to carry out administration tasks correctly, beginning with installation and configuration, then this book is for you.

Conventions

In this book, you will find a number of styles of text that distinguish between different kinds of information. Here are some examples of these styles, and an explanation of their meaning.

Code words in text are shown as follows: "OAM Configuration Data is stored in a file-based repository that is an XML file (oam-config.xml) containing all OAM-related system configuration data."

A block of code is set as follows:

```
inventory_loc=oui_inventory_directory
inst_group=oui_install_group
```

Any command-line input or output is written as follows:

```
$MW_HOME/oracle_common/common/bin/pack.sh -domain=$MW_HOME/user_projects/
domain/base_domain/ -template=/tmp/IDAMOIMDomain.jar -template_name="OAM
Domain" -managed=true
```

New terms and **important words** are shown in bold. Words that you see on the screen, in menus or dialog boxes for example, appear in the text like this: "Click on **Next** when Progress is 100 percent on **Configuration Progress** screen."

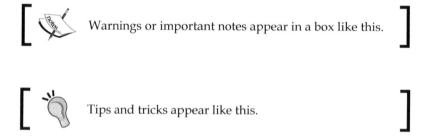

Warnings or important notes appear in a box like this.

Tips and tricks appear like this.

Reader feedback

Feedback from our readers is always welcome. Let us know what you think about this book—what you liked or may have disliked. Reader feedback is important for us to develop titles that you really get the most out of.

To send us general feedback, simply send an e-mail to feedback@packtpub.com, and mention the book title via the subject of your message.

If there is a book that you need and would like to see us publish, please send us a note in the **SUGGEST A TITLE** form on www.packtpub.com or e-mail suggest@packtpub.com.

If there is a topic that you have expertise in and you are interested in either writing or contributing to a book, see our author guide on www.packtpub.com/authors.

Customer support

Now that you are the proud owner of a Packt book, we have a number of things to help you to get the most from your purchase.

Errata

Although we have taken every care to ensure the accuracy of our content, mistakes do happen. If you find a mistake in one of our books—maybe a mistake in the text or the code—we would be grateful if you would report this to us. By doing so, you can save other readers from frustration and help us improve subsequent versions of this book. If you find any errata, please report them by visiting http://www.packtpub. com/support, selecting your book, clicking on the **errata submission form** link, and entering the details of your errata. Once your errata are verified, your submission will be accepted and the errata will be uploaded on our website, or added to any list of existing errata, under the Errata section of that title. Any existing errata can be viewed by selecting your title from http://www.packtpub.com/support.

Piracy

Piracy of copyright material on the Internet is an ongoing problem across all media. At Packt, we take the protection of our copyright and licenses very seriously. If you come across any illegal copies of our works, in any form, on the Internet, please provide us with the location address or website name immediately so that we can pursue a remedy.

Please contact us at copyright@packtpub.com with a link to the suspected pirated material.

We appreciate your help in protecting our authors, and our ability to bring you valuable content.

Questions

You can contact us at questions@packtpub.com if you are having a problem with any aspect of the book, and we will do our best to address it.

1

Oracle Identity Management: Overview and Architecture

Oracle Identity Management products can be categorized in following components, providing services of Identity/Access management, governance, and directory services:

- **Identity Administration**: Oracle Identity Manager (OIM)
- **Access Management**: Oracle Access Manager (OAM), Oracle Identity Federation (OIF), Oracle Enterprise Single Sign-On (eSSO), Oracle Adaptive Access Manager (OAAM), Oracle Entitlement Server (OES), Oracle OpenSSO Fedlet, and Oracle OpenSSO Security Token Service
- **Identity & Access Governance**: Oracle Identity Analytics (OIA)
- **Directory Services**: Oracle Internet Directory (OID), Oracle Directory Server Enterprise Edition (ODSEE), and Oracle Virtual Directory (OVD)
- **Platform Security Services**: Oracle Platform Security Services (OPSS), Oracle Authorization Policy Model (OAPM), and Oracle Web Services Manager (OWSM)
- **Operations Management**: Oracle Identity Navigator (OIN) and Oracle Enterprise Manager Management pack for Identity management

This chapter provides an overview of Oracle Identity Management products, including:

- WebLogic server
- Identity Manager and Access Manager components
- Architecture of Oracle Access Manager and Oracle Identity Manager

Oracle Identity Management overview

In this section I'll briefly cover the following identity and access manager products:

- **Oracle Identity Manager (OIM)**: It is an identity lifecycle management software that includes provisioning, reconciliation and administration tools. Oracle Identity Manager comes as part of Identity Management and Access Management Software.

- **Oracle Access Manager (OAM)**: It is an access management software and recommended single sign-on solution. Oracle Access Manager comes as part of Identity Management and Access Management Software.

 Currently there are two single sign-on solutions from Oracle – 10g Oracle Application Server Single Sign-On (OSSO) and Oracle Access Manager (OAM) Single Sign-On.

- **Oracle Identity Federation (OIF)**: It is a multi-protocol federation software, used to share identities across enterprises, partners, and vendors. Oracle Identity Federation simplifies the process of enabling a federated single sign-on.

- **Oracle Enterprise Single Sign-On (eSSO)**: It is an access management software which provides authentication and single sign-on across all enterprise resources, including desktops, client-server, and host-based mainframe applications:

- **Oracle Adaptive Access Manager (OAAM)**: It is a strong and proactive authentication and, real-time fraud prevention software. Oracle Adaptive Access Manager comes as part of Identity Management and Access Management software.

- **Oracle Entitlement Server (OES)**: It is a fine-grained entitlements management solution that provides authorization services for enterprise applications:

- **Oracle Identity Analytics (OIA)**: It provides identity analytics, dashboards, and compliance features that monitor, analyze, and govern user access.

- **Oracle Internet Directory (OID)**: It is a LDAP v3 compliant directory with meta-directory capabilities.

- **Oracle Directory Server Enterprise Edition (ODSEE)**: Formerly called the Sun Directory Server, this is a directory server ideally suited for heterogeneous environments.

- **Oracle Virtual Directory (OVD)**: It virtually aggregates identity information from multiple identity sources (directory server or databases) and presents a real-time unified view, thus eliminating the need to synchronize or move identity data across multiple sources.

- **Oracle Platform Security Services (OPSS)**: It is a portable, integrated, enterprise-grade platform for Java applications. Java EE and Java SE applications can use OPSS. OPSS is installed/configured by default with Fusion Middleware components including OIM and OAM.

- **Oracle Authorization Policy Model (OAPM)**: It is a J2EE application to manage authorization policy for applications that use Oracle Platform Security Services.

- **Oracle Web Services Manager (OWSM)**: It is a J2EE application designed to define and implement web services security in heterogeneous environments. OWSM is available both as a standalone product and as part of the SOA suite.

- **Oracle Identity Navigator (OIN)**: It is an administrative portal which acts as a launch pad for Oracle Identity Management components. It allows access to all identity management consoles from a single page.

- **OEM Grid Control Management pack for Identity Management**: Proactively manages performance, availability, and service levels for identity and access management services.

Identity Administration	Access Management	Directory Services
OIM	OAM, OIF, eSSO OAAM, OES	OID, ODSEE OVD
IDENTITY GOVERNANCE - OIA		
OPSS, OWSM		
MANAGEMENT - OIN, OEM Pack for IDAM		

 There are two parts to 11*g* Identity Management Suite – Identity Management 11*g* which includes OID, OVD, OIF, and OHS; and Identity and Access Management 11*g* which includes OAM, OIM, OAAM, OAPM, and OIN.

WebLogic Server overview

WebLogic Server is a J2EE application server on which both Oracle Identity Manager (OIM) and Oracle Access Manager (OAM) are deployed. The following diagram and sections cover the WebLogic domain and the key WebLogic components respectively:

- WebLogic Server Domain
- WebLogic Admin Server
- WebLogic Managed Server
- WebLogic Cluster
- Weblogic JDBC Datasource
- Node Manager

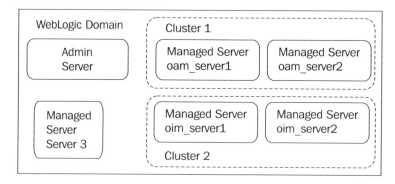

- **WebLogic Server Domain**: WebLogic server domain is logical grouping of resources and services. It contains Admin Server, Managed server, JDBC data Sources, Java Messaging Server, and coherence.

- **WebLogic Administration (Admin) Server**: Administration server is a WebLogic server that maintains configuration data for a domain. There is always one and only one administration server in a Weblogic domain.

- **WebLogic Managed Server**: Any WebLogic server other than the Admin server is called a Managed server. When you configure both OAM and OIM in same domain, domain creation creates three Managed servers one for OAM (`oam_server1`); the second for OIM (`oim_server1`); and the third for SOA (`soa_server1`).

These are default names used by the domain configuration utility and can be changed to something else.

- **WebLogic Cluster**: WebLogic cluster is a group of WebLogic Servers (Admin or Managed) that work together to provide high availability and scalability for applications. WebLogic Servers within a cluster can run on the same machine or on different machines. WebLogic Cluster comprised of just Managed Server is also known as Managed Server Cluster.

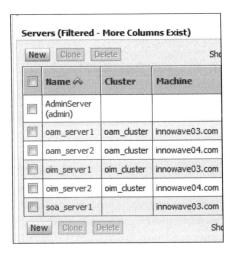

The previous screenshot shows a WebLogic domain consisting of one Admin server, five Managed servers, and two clusters. Managed servers `oim_server1` and `oim_server2` are deployed in a cluster named `oim_cluster` while Managed servers `oam_server1` and `oam_server2` are deployed in second cluster, named oam_cluster. Finally, the domain also contains a fifth managed server (`soa_server1`) that is not in a cluster.

 WebLogic domain files are stored under `$DOMAIN_HOME` which by default is the directory `user_projects/ domain/base_domain/`

- **WebLogic JDBC Datasource**: WebLogic uses JDBC data sources to connect to databases. JDBC resources are deployed to servers or clusters within a domain. Application deployed on servers (Admin/Managed server) can then use the deployed JDBC data source to a connect to database. The following screenshot represents default JDBC data sources created after creating a domain with OIM (including SOA) and OAM.

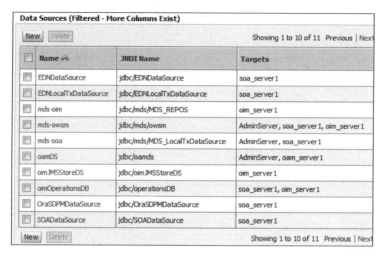

Data Sources (Filtered - More Columns Exist)

New Delete   Showing 1 to 10 of 11 Previous | Next

	Name ⌃	JNDI Name	Targets
☐	EDNDataSource	jdbc/EDNDataSource	soa_server1
☐	EDNLocalTxDataSource	jdbc/EDNLocalTxDataSource	soa_server1
☐	mds-oim	jdbc/mds/MDS_REPOS	oim_server1
☐	mds-owsm	jdbc/mds/owsm	AdminServer, soa_server1, oim_server1
☐	mds-soa	jdbc/mds/MDS_LocalTxDataSource	AdminServer, soa_server1
☐	oamDS	jdbc/oamds	AdminServer, oam_server1
☐	oimJMSStoreDS	jdbc/oimJMSStoreDS	oim_server1
☐	oimOperationsDB	jdbc/operationsDB	soa_server1, oim_server1
☐	OraSDPMDataSource	jdbc/OraSDPMDataSource	soa_server1
☐	SOADataSource	jdbc/SOADataSource	soa_server1

New Delete   Showing 1 to 10 of 11 Previous | Next

- **Node Manager**: Node manager is a Java utility that runs as a separate process from WebLogic server and allows common operational tasks for a Managed server. Node Manager can also be configured to automatically restart the Admin or Managed servers in case of unplanned outage, and is used to start/stop Managed servers from the WebLogic console. Use of Node Manager in OIM/OAM deployment is optional.

Oracle Access Manager overview & architecture

Oracle Access Manager (OAM) provides centralized, policy-driven services for authentication, single sign-on (SSO), and identity assertion. The following diagram shows the Oracle Access Manager Component Architecture:

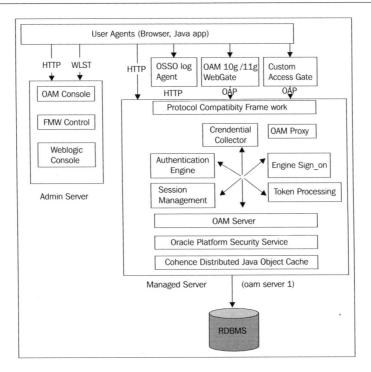

- **User Agents**: These include Web servers, Java applications, and Web service applications with OAM agents (10*g*/11*g* WebGates, OSSO, AccessGate). Client accesses the OAM Administration Console server (a.k.a OAM Console) via HTTPs.

- **Protocol Compatibility Framework**: It interfaces with agents a.k.a. Policy Enforcement Points (PEP) such as 10*g*/11*g* WebGate, mod_osso agents, and custom Access Gates.

- **OAM Server**: It provides shared service for access and includes Authentication Engine, Single Sign-On Engine, Session Management, Authorization Service, and Token Processing.

- **Oracle Platform Security Service (OPSS)**: Oracle Access Manager including WebLogic server relies on OPSS for authentication, authorization, credential store, Audit Framework, and identity service.

- **Protected Resources**: These include the application or webpage which you wish to protect by OAM agents (10*g*/11*g* WebGates, OSSO, AccessGate). OAM agents act as plug-ins between user agents and the OAM server (a.k.a Access Server). OAM 10*g*/11*g* WebGate and AccessGate communicate with the OAM server (Access server) with the help of a proprietary protocol – Oracle Access Protocol (OAP). Oracle as Single Sign-On (OSSO) 10*g* Agent communicates with OAM server on HTTPs.

- **OAM Administration Console**: OAM administration console is a Web application deployed on WebLogic's Administration server that is used to manage and configure OAM server, authentication/authorization policies, and OAM Agents. Some configuration can also be achieved via WebLogic Scripting Tool (WLST) commands.

 OAM Console 11*g* replaces OAM Policy domain component in OAM 10*g*.

- **Coherence Distributed Object Cache**: It is used to propagate configuration changes and session information between OAM servers in high-availability deployments. Coherence is installed as part of WebLogic installation as shown in the following screenshot:

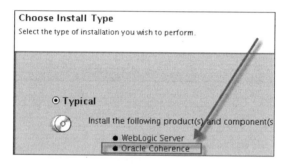

- **FMW Grid Control**: It is a Java application (/em) deployed on a WebLogic Admin server and used to manage logging in Oracle Access Manager. It is also used for monitoring status, performance management, and to enable/disable logging or diagnostics.

- **WebLogic Scripting Tool (WLST)**: It is a command-line tool used to configure and manage Oracle Access Manager from the command line.

  WLST commands for OAM are limited and do not support all configuration/management features of OAM.

- **Data Store (File, LDAP and RDBMS)**: OAM requires data stores for:
    a. User/Identity Store
    b. OAM policy and session data
    c. OAM configuration data

  By default in OAM 11*g*:

    ° User Identity Store is WebLogic's embedded LDAP server.

It is recommended that you change OAM's primary identity store from WebLogic's embedded LDAP server to an enterprise LDAP server.

° OAM policy data is stored in the database under OAM schema configured during Repository Creation Utility (RCU). In previous versions, the OAM policy store could be an LDAP. In 11*g* it must be an RDBMS.

° OAM configuration data is stored in a file-based repository, specifically an XML file (`oam-config.xml`) containing all OAM-related system configuration data.

Oracle Access Manager server-side components

There are two main runtime components to OAM, the Administration Console, and the Server. Here's what they do:

- **Oracle Access Manager Administration Console** (a.k.a Oracle Access Manager Admin server or in short OAM Console) runs on WebLogic Admin server and is used to manage OAM server properties, create policies, define agents, and manage user sessions. You can access OAM Administration Console using the URI `/oamconsole` on the Admin server.

- **Oracle Access Manager Server** is a runtime engine used to provide shared services for access such as Authentication/Authorization service, session management, token processing, and single sign-on. OAM Server runs on one of WebLogic's Managed servers, such as `oam_server1`.

Oracle Identity Manager overview & architecture

Oracle Identity Manager 11*g* is a Java application deployed on Oracle WebLogic server for identity and user provisioning. Oracle Identity Manager (OIM) 11*g* provides user administration, password management, workflow and policy, audit and compliance management, user provisioning and organization, and role management functionalities.

Oracle Identity Manager architecture

Oracle Identity Manager is a three tier J2EE application that consists of – presentation tier, business services tier, and data tier.

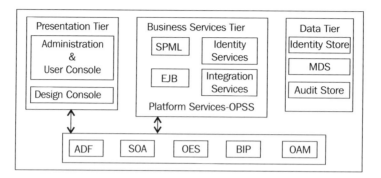

Presentation tier

OIM Presentation tier consists of two type of clients, Oracle Identity Manager Administrative & User Console, and Oracle Identity Manager Design Console.

- **Oracle Identity Manager Administrative and User Console**: It is a thin client that is accessible via a web browser. The console provides self-service and delegated administration features.

- **Oracle Identity Manager Design Console**: It is a thick (Java) client which is installed on a client machine. The console provides system configuration and development capabilities, and connects directly to Business Service Tier.

Business Services tier

OIM Business tier is implemented as an Enterprise Java Beans (EJB) application, and includes the following services:

- **Core Services**: User management, provisioning and reconciliation.

- **API Services**: SPML and EJB APIs. It allows custom clients to integrate with OIM using API.

- **Integration Services**: Adapter factory, connector framework, generic technology connector, and remote manager.

- **Platform Services**: Request management, authorization service, entity manager, and scheduler service.

Data tier

OIM Data tier consists of a repository or database, which manages and stores OIM data and metadata. Data stored in OIM database consists mainly of:

- **Entity Data**: Users, roles, organizations, role membership, and resources
- **Transactional Data**: Requests, approval and provisioning workflow instances, and human tasks
- **Audit Data**: Request history, user profile history

Oracle Identity Manager components

Oracle Identity Manager consists of the following components:

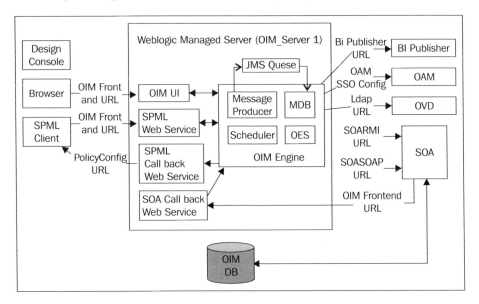

- **OIM Server**: It is a Java EE application that is stored on a WebLogic Managed server and uses a database to store runtime and configuration data. OIM server includes a Quartz-based scheduler (for job scheduling), Oracle Entitlement Server (OES) microkernel for authorization checks, Message Driven Beans (MDB), and a message producer.
- **Design Console**: It is a thick client (Java Application) that runs on the client machine and connects to the OIM business tier directly. The console provides system configuration and development capabilities.

- **External Interfaces**: OIM Server is exposed to external users/systems via following services:
    - ° **SOA**: OIM server connects to SOA Managed server over RMI (using SOA RmiURL) to invoke SOA EJBs. OIM connects to SOA web services using SOAP (using SOA SoapURL). SOA Managed server connects to OIM using the SOA Callback web service (using OimFrontendURL).
    - ° **SPML Client**: SPML client connect to OIM using the SPML web service (via OimFrontEndURL), whereas OIM server connect to SPML client using the SPML callback web service (via PolicyConfigURL) .
    - ° **Browser**: End users access OIM servers via web browser using the OIM User Interface (UI) component (via OimFrontEndURL).
    - ° **BI Publisher**: OIM connects to BI publisher for all reporting features (via BIPublisher URL).
    - ° **OVD Server**: When LDAPSych is enabled, OIM connects to LDAP server via OVD (Oracle Virtual Directory).
    - ° **OAM Server**: OIM integrates with OAM for single sign-on configuration.
- **Remote Manager**: It is a component that runs on a target system and provides the network and security layers required to integrate OIM with applications that do not have network-aware APIs.
- **Database**: OIM uses a database to store runtime, user, and configuration data. Configuration information is stored in MDS schema, whereas runtime and user information is stored in OIM schema.

Summary

In this chapter, we discussed an overview of Oracle Identity Management 11*g*. We also briefly covered the various Identity Management components, WebLogic server and the architecture of Oracle Access Manager and Oracle Identity Manager 11*g* in detail.

In the next chapter, we are going to install Oracle WebLogic and Oracle Identity Management 11*g*. We will also cover Identity and Access Management High Availability deployment (Active-Active Cluster) for resilience and performance.

2

Installing Oracle Identity and Access Manager

Oracle Identity Manager (OIM) and **Oracle Access Manager (OAM)** are part of Oracle Fusion Middleware 11*g* R1. The starting release number for these two products is 11.1.1.3.0 and then 11.1.1.5.0. **Oracle Service Oriented Architecture (SOA)** suite (another product from Oracle Fusion Middleware Family) is used by **Oracle Identity Manager (OIM)** for workflow capabilities of BPEL and Human Workflow hence before configuring Oracle Identity Manager, SOA suite must be installed.

In this chapter we will cover:

- Installation of Oracle Fusion Middleware, Repository Creation Utility, Oracle SOA Suite, and Oracle Identity and Access Management (Oracle Identity Manager and Oracle Access Manager) 11*g* R1
- Configuring Oracle Identity Manager and Oracle Access Manager installation in high-availability (Active-Active) deployment

Installation overview

The following diagram illustrates the high-level overview of **Oracle Identity and Access Management (IDAM)** installation flow. As shown in the following figure Oracle Identity and Access Management (Oracle Identity Manager and Oracle Access Manager) installation consists of seven main steps:

- Creating database schemas
- Installing WebLogic server
- Installing Identity and Access Management software
- Installing SOA Suite
- Applying SOA Suite patchset
- Configuring IDAM software and creating WebLogic domain
- Configuring Oracle Identity Manager

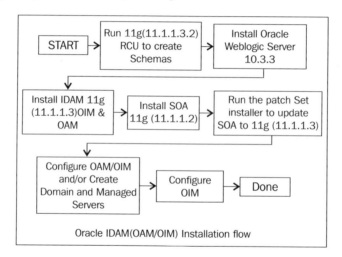

Oracle IDAM(OAM/OIM) Installation flow

1. **Create database schemas**: The installation of IDAM products require availability of database. This is used to store metadata of OIM, and for auditing and configuring OIM/OAM. This database must be up and running, and does not have to be on the same system where you are installing the Oracle Identity and Access Management (IDAM) components. It must be compatible with Repository Creation Utility (RCU), which is used to create the schemas necessary for your Oracle Identity and Access Management (IDAM) components. Supported databases are Oracle Database and Microsoft SQL Server; for a full list of certified databases, see http://www.oracle.com/technetwork/middleware/ias/downloads/ fusion-requirements-100147.html#BABFDFDD

Repository Creation Utility (RCU) is a Java tool to create database schema for Oracle Identity and Access Management Components. RCU can be run from any Windows/Linux machine, either the same one hosting the database or any machine connected to the database server through a network. Repository Creation Utility must be of version 11.1.1.3.2 or higher.

 RCU is available only on 32-bit Linux and Windows platforms. There is no need to install a database client on the machine from where you are running RCU (RCU comes with database client tools.)

2. **Install WebLogic server**: WebLogic server is a J2EE application server on which **Oracle Identity** and **Access Management** products (**OIM & OAM**) run. As shown in the following screenshot, when you install the WebLogic server it will create an **Oracle Middleware** home directory; Oracle Identity and Access Management Products are required to be installed under this Oracle Middleware home directory.

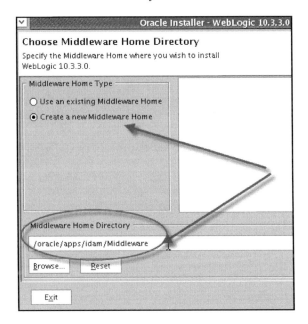

3. **Install Identity and Access Management server**: After the schemas and Oracle WebLogic server are installed, you are ready to install your Oracle Identity and Access Management products (OIM and OAM).

Oracle Identity and Access Management (IDAM) software is available at Oracle Technology Network (OTN) `http://www.oracle.com/technetwork/middleware/downloads/oid-11g-161194.html`. You will also see Identity Management 11.1.1.2 and 11.1.1.3. Do not select these as they are for Oracle Internet directory, Oracle Virtual directory, and Oracle Identity Federation. Select Oracle Identity and Access Management (11.1.1.3)

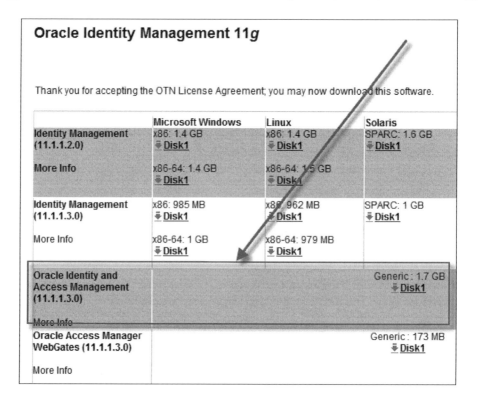

When you install Oracle Identity and Access Management, make sure to install it under `Middleware Home` (directory you created during WebLogic server installation). This will create a directory like **Oracle_IDM1** (as shown in the following screenshot) which will be your ORACLE_HOME directory for Oracle Identity and Access Management Components:

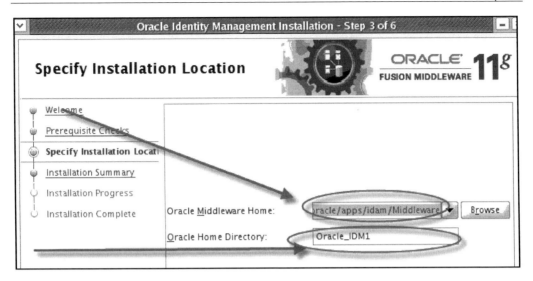

4. **Install Oracle SOA Suite 11.1.1.2.0**: Oracle SOA Suite (Human Workflow and Tasklists component) is used by Oracle Identity Manager 11*g* component. You must install SOA 11.1.1.2.0 under `Middleware Home` (directory you created during WebLogic server installation). This will create a directory like **Oracle_SOA1** (as shown in the following screenshot) which will be your ORACLE_HOME directory for SOA Suite:

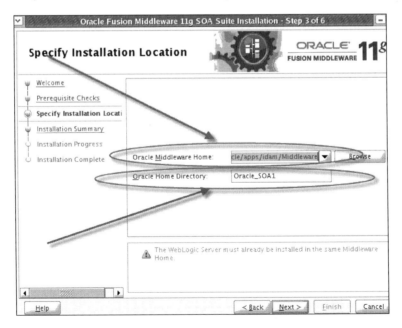

SOA Suite is required for OIM server only. If you are installing OAM only, then SOA Suite is not required.

5. **Update Oracle SOA Suite to 11.1.1.3.0**: Oracle Identity Manager 11.1.1.3.0 requires SOA Suite 11.1.1.3.0, so you must upgrade SOA Suite 11.1.1.2.0 to SOA 11.1.3.0. You must apply the update to the same directory that has SOA 11.1.1.2.0 installed, that is, Oracle_SOA1.

 SOA Suite 11.1.1.2.0 is a complete piece of software; version 11.1.1.3.0 is a patch set only. SOA 11.1.1.3.0 patch set should be applied on existing base software such as SOA 11.1.1.2.0

6. **Configure IDAM and create domain**: After IDAM and SOA suite are installed, you must configure them using Configuration Wizard (`config.sh` for Unix and `config.cmd` for Windows) to create WebLogic domain, Administration server, and various Managed servers.

 `config.sh/cmd` is found a few levels under `Middleware Home`; to create the domain to run Oracle IDAM (OIM & OAM) you must run it from `IDAM_ORACLE_HOME/common/bin`, that is, `$MW_HOME/Oracle_IDM1/common//bin` for Unix and `%MW_HOME%\Oracle_IDM1\common\bin` for Windows.

7. **Configure Oracle Identity Manager**: Configure Oracle Identity Manager server by running `config.sh/config.cmd` (for Unix/Windows) from `IDAM ORACLE_HOME/bin`, that is, `Oracle_IDM1/bin/config.sh` for Unix and `Oracle_IDM1\bin\config.cmd` for Windows.

Installation types

This section covers various installation types for Oracle Identity and Access Management (Oracle Identity Manager and Oracle Access Manager) 11*g*R1.

Interactive versus Silent Install

In interactive Install, Installer prompts you questions such as your `Middleware Home` location, Identity Management Oracle Home Location, and administrator username/password.

In silent install, you supply a response to the question in advance by providing a response file to the Installer. In silent mode, graphical output is not displayed and no input is required from user during install time. A silent install is performed by using the `-silent` flag on the command line with the installer. For example:

- To install the WebLogic server in silent mode:

  ```
  <executable_name> -mode=silent -silent_xml=path_to_silent.xml
  ```

- To install IDAM in silent mode:

  ```
  <executable_name> -silent -response <response_file>
  ```

Collocated versus Distributed install

In Collocated Install all Identity and Access Management (IDAM) components such as Oracle Identity Manager, Oracle Access Manager, Fusion Middleware Enterprise Manager Control, or Oracle Access Manager administration console are deployed on a single machine.

In Distributed Install Identity and Access Management (IDAM) components are distributed on more than one machine. You install WebLogic server (which creates `Middleware Home`) and Oracle Identity Manager component (which creates `ORACLE_HOME`) on all machine parts of distributed installation but configure a specific component (Access Manager or Identity Manager) targeted to different machines, you then use `pack & unpack` commands to configure these machines.

Single instance versus Multiple instance (cluster) install

In Single Instance, you create one server of each identity management component, such as one managed server for Oracle Access Manager and one managed server for Oracle Identity Manager. Single Instance installation is default configuration.

In Multiple Instance, you create two or more managed servers in *cluster* for Oracle Identity Manager similarly you create two or more managed server in *cluster* for Oracle Access Manager.

For more information on managed servers, admin servers and clusters refer to section *WebLogic server overview* from *Chapter 1, Oracle Identity Management: Overview and Architecture*.

In the 11.1.1.3 version of Oracle Access Manager (OAM) there can only be one cluster with two or more managed servers in a single WebLogic domain. Oracle Access Manager administration console is deployed on a WebLogic administration server and there can be only one active administration server in a WebLogic domain at any given time.

Things good to know for IDAM Installation

The following are a few things that are important while installing IDAM, including WebLogic server and RCU:

- There are two installers for Oracle Identity Management 11*g* R1 (11.1.1). Initially Identity Management 11 g R1 (11.1.1.1.0) included products such as Oracle Internet Directory (OID), Oracle Directory Integration Platform (DIP), Oracle Virtual Directory (OVD), and Oracle Identity Federation (OIF). Then came 11*g* R1 (11.1.1.2.0) as a full version for the same products as mentioned previously, that is, OID, DIP, OVD, and OIF. Then came 11*g* R1 PS2 (11.1.1.3.0) as patchset only for the same products as mentioned previously, that is: OID, DIP, OVD, and OIF. As part of 11.1.1.3.0 came base Oracle Identity and Access Management products such as Oracle Identity Manager (OIM), Oracle Access Manager (OAM), Oracle Adaptive Access Manager (OAAM), Oracle Identity Navigator (OIN), and Oracle Authorization Policy Manager (OAPM).

- If you are installing IDAM on a 64-bit machine then first install certified 64-bit JDK on the machine then use `weblogic` jar file to install 64-bit WebLogic.

- WebLogic version 10.3.3 is also known as WebLogic 11*g* R1.

- SOA Suite is only required if you are installing Oracle Identity Manager. Ignore the SOA Suite and the Oracle Identity Manager sections if you want to install just Oracle Access Manager Component of Oracle Identity and Access Management.

- Oracle SOA Suite base release is 11.1.1.2.0 whereas 11.1.1.3.0 is a patch set, so you must first install the base SOA release, that is, 11.1.1.2.0 and then patch SOA to 11.1.1.3.0.

- You must run RCU 11.1.1.3.2 or higher to create schema, as OIM and OAM related schemas are available on RCU 11.1.1.3.2 and higher version.

- Install Oracle Identity and Access Management (IDAM) software, and WebLogic Software and SOA Suite using the same user account on your operating system.

- `$ORACLE_HOME/bin/config.cmd` (`config.sh` on Unix) is for configuring Oracle Identity Manager where as `$ORACLE_HOME/common/bin/config.cmd` (`config.sh` on Unix) is for creating WebLogic domain (admin and managed servers) for Oracle Identity and Access Management Component.

- Repository Creation Utility (RCU) log files are stored under `$RCU_SOFTWARE/rcu/log/logdir<YYYY>-<MM>-<DD>_<HH>-<MM>/`.

- Identity and Access Management Installation log files are stored under `<oraInventory_location>/oraInventory/logs/install<YYYY>-<MM>-<DD>_<HH>-<mm>-<ss>.log`, where `oraInventory_location` varies by operating system (OS):

  - Windows uses `C:\Program Files\oracle`
  - Linux/Unix uses `/etc/oraInst.loc`
  - Solaris uses `/var/opt/oracle/oraInst.loc`

Installing Oracle Identity and Access Management

This section covers steps in detail to install Identity and Access Management such as system requirements (memory, CPU, disk, packages, and temp space), loading schema, installing SOA Suite and IDAM Suite, and configuring components.

1. **Check system requirements**:

   The first step in Oracle Identity Management installation is to check system requirements such as minimum disk space, memory requirement, system libraries, and packages.

   - For the latest Oracle Identity and Access Management certification matrix (list of certified OSs) check the following link: `http://www.oracle.com/technetwork/middleware/id-mgmt/identity-accessmgmt-11gr1certmatrix-161244.xls`

   - Check memory requirement for:
     - WebLogic administration server running OAM administration server console: 750 MB.
     - WebLogic managed server running Oracle Access Manager server: 720 MB.
     - WebLogic managed server running Oracle Identity Manager server: 720 MB.
     - WebLogic managed server running Oracle SOA Suite: 720 MB.

- Check disk requirement: Oracle Identity Manager (including SOA Suite), and Oracle Access Manager including domain, requires a minimum of 5.0 GB.

These memory and disk requirements are for a development environment. For a production environment, follow proper capacity planning based on the number of user transactions.

- CPU speed: At least 300 MHz.
- Temp space: At least 270 MB.
- Swap space: At least 500 MB.
- Open file limit: At least 4096.
- Packages for Unix/Windows: For list of required packages on Linux x86/x86-64, Solaris Sparch 64, HP-UX, and AIX, check:

  ```
  http://www.oracle.com/technetwork/middleware/ias/
  downloads/fusion-requirements-100147.html#BABGBCIG
  ```

2. **Install Database for Oracle Identity and Access Management**:

   Oracle Database and Microsoft SQL Server are the supported databases for Oracle Identity and Access Management 11*g*. Use vendor database installation instructions to set up a database for Oracle Identity and Access Management Repository.

For Oracle Identity Management 11*g* you must configure your database to use AL32UTF8 character set encoding.

At the time of publishing this book IBM DB2 Database is not supported for Oracle Identity Management Schema.

3. **Run Repository Creaion Utility to create schemas**: Repository Creation Utility is available only on 32-bit x86 Linux and 32-bit Microsoft Windows Operating System platforms. You can run RCU from these machines to connect to any certified versions of Oracle, or Microsoft SQL Server database, in order to create the schemas required by Fusion Middleware components.

   Note the following key points for schema creation:

   - If you are creating schemas on an Oracle database, you must use a user with SYSDBA privileges such as SYS.

- ° Oracle Identity Management 11*g* only supports schemas in a byte-mode database. The `nls_length_semantics` initialization parameter on the database where the schemas reside must be set to `BYTE`.

- ° For Microsoft SQL Server, the database's `read_committed_snapshot` option must be turned on.

- ° For Microsoft SQL Server, the database must be configured to use case-sensitive collation.

Start RCU from `<RCU_SOFTWARE>/rcuHome/bin`:

- ° For Windows: `rcu.bat`
- ° For Unix: `./rcu`

The following screenshots are for RCU on Linux:

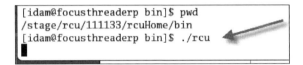

As shown next, you have two options:

- ° **Create**: To create IDAM schema
- ° **Drop**: To drop an existing IDAM schema

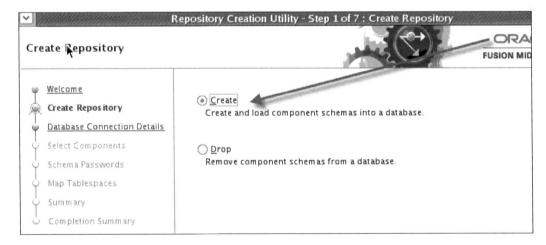

Enter your database details on the next screen:

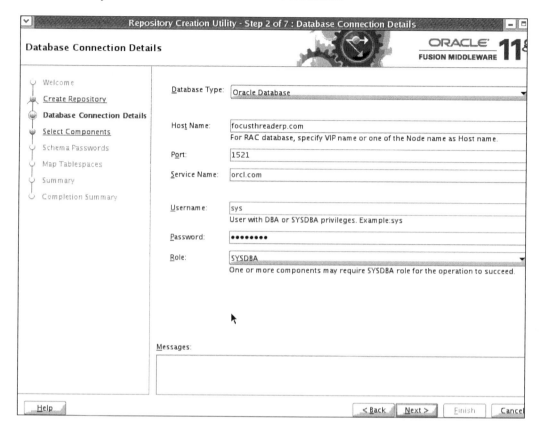

 Make sure you connect using **sys** user or user with *sysdba* privileges.

Select the following Schemas: Metadata Services (XXX_MDS), Audit Services (XXX_IAU), Oracle Identity Manager (XXX_OIM), Oracle Access Manager (XXX_OAM), SOA Infrastructure (XXX_SOAINFRA), and User Messaging Service (XXX_ORASDPM).

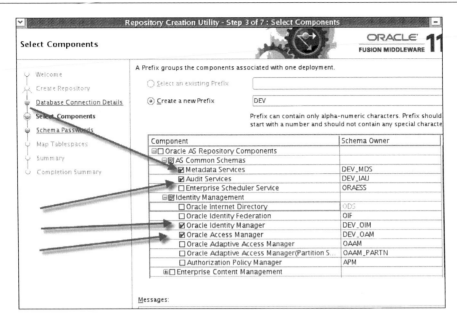

Next, scroll down and select **SOA Infrastructure** and **User Messaging Service** components as shown in the following screenshot:

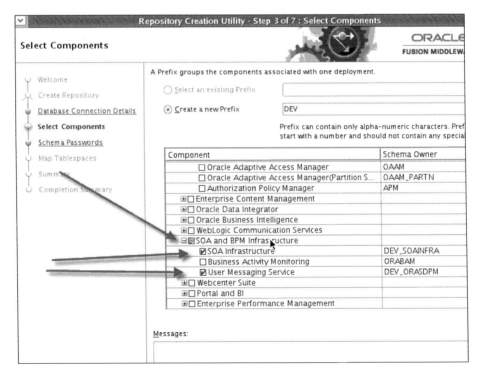

On the next screen select a password for database schemas. For production environments, for security reasons it is recommended to use different passwords for schemas.

Finally, make sure that you get status as "**Success**" for all components.

4. **Install Oracle WebLogic 10.3.3 server**: Use the following steps to install the WebLogic server:

   ° Create operating system user and group. Use operating system command to create a group and user to install WebLogic. Use that same user to install Identity and Access Management software.

   ° Start WebLogic installer:

   ° For 32-bit Windows: `wls_win32.exe`

   ° For 32-bit Unix: `./wls_linux32.bin`

   ° For 64-bit Windows:
   `<JAVA_HOME>/bin/java -jar wls_generic.jar`

   ° For 64-bit Unix:
   `<JAVA_HOME>/bin/java -d64 -jar wls_generic.jar`

(Replace `JAVA_HOME` with the JDK already installed on the machine.)

   ° Click **Next**.

   ° Select "**Create a new Middleware Home**" and enter location of your `Middleware Home` directory (hereafter referred to as `MW_HOME`).

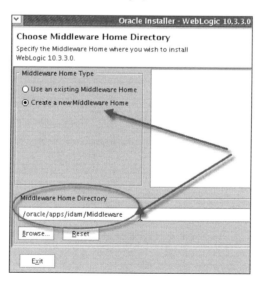

- On the next screen, select **Install Type** as **Typical** and ensure that you get **Weblogic Server** and **Oracle Coherence** under **Install the following product(s) and component(s)**. If you don't see these two components listed, then use the WebLogic Installer which comes with Oracle Coherence. Oracle Coherence is used for caching and session/configuration replication across managed servers in high-availability deployments.

- Leave the default values for the next screen, that is, Product Installation Directories. Installer will create two folders under Middleware Home (MW_HOME) :

    wlserver_10.3 also known as WebLogic Home (WL_HOME)

    coherence_3.5 also known as Coherence Home (COHERENCE_HOME).

- Click **Next** to start WebLogic installation.

- Click **Finish** on the **Installation Complete** screen to finish installation.

Installing IDAM 11.1.1.3

 Install Identity and Access Management Software using the same user account that installing WebLogic server was installed with.

Go to the directory where you have unzipped Oracle Identity and Access Management (IDAM) 11.1.1.3 and start IDAM installation from Disk1 using:

- `setup.exe -jreLoc <JDK_Location>` for Windows
- `./runInstaller -jreLoc <JDK_Location>` for Unix

```
[idam@focusthreaderp Disk1]$ ./runInstaller -jreLoc /oracle/apps/idam/Middleware
/jdk160_18
Starting Oracle Universal Installer...

Checking if CPU speed is above 300 MHz.    Actual 2833 MHz    Passed
Checking Temp space: must be greater than 150 MB.    Actual 79705 MB    Passed
Checking swap space: must be greater than 512 MB.    Actual 101040 MB    Passed
Checking monitor: must be configured to display at least 256 colors.    Actual 6
5536    Passed
Preparing to launch Oracle Universal Installer from /tmp/OraInstall2010-10-03_06
-29-17AM. Please wait ...[idam@focusthreaderp Disk1]$ Log: /oracle/apps/upgrade/
oatest/oraInventory/logs/install2010-10-03_06-29-17AM.log
```

Where JDK_Location is a top-level directory for JDK installation. When you install a 32-bit WebLogic server, the installer automatically installs two JDKs under Middleware Home (MW_HOME):

- Sun JDK under jdk160_<XX>

- JRocket JDK under jrockit_160_XX_RXX.X.X-XXX

Use any one of these two JDK locations. For 64-bit machines, use the 64-bit JDK directory already installed on your machine.

```
[idam@focusthreaderp Disk1]$ pwd
/stage/idam/11113/Disk1
[idam@focusthreaderp Disk1]$ ls
doc  install  runInstaller  setup.exe  stage
[idam@focusthreaderp Disk1]$ ./runInstaller -jreLoc /oracle/apps/idam/Middleware
/jrockit_160_17_R28.0.0-679
Starting Oracle Universal Installer...

Checking if CPU speed is above 300 MHz.   Actual 2833 MHz    Passed
Checking Temp space: must be greater than 150 MB.   Actual 79766 MB    Passed
Checking swap space: must be greater than 512 MB.   Actual 101040 MB    Passed
Checking monitor: must be configured to display at least 256 colors.   Actual 6
5536    Passed
```

The installer will run all prerequisite checks like Operating System Packages, kernel parameters, and memory, and will report any missing dependency. Fix any issues reported on this screen or click on **Next** if all checks are complete successfully.

On the next screen specify the Oracle Middleware Home and Oracle Home (for IDAM) directories:

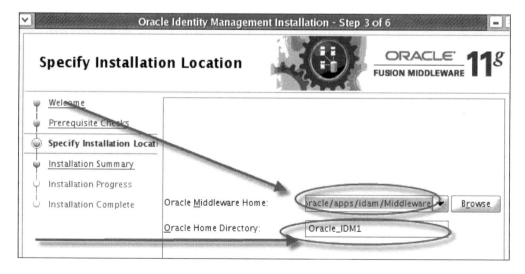

Click on the **Install** button to install Oracle Identity and Access Management Component.

Click on the **Finish** button after installation.

Installing SOA Suite 11.1.1.2.0

Start SOA suite installation from Disk1 of SOA 11.1.1.2.0 software:

- For Windows: `setup.exe -jreLoc <JDK_Location>`

- For Unix: `./runInstaller -jreLoc <JDK_Location>`

Where `JDK_Location` is top-level directory for JDK installation. When you install a 32-bit WebLogic server, the installer automatically installs two JDK under Middleware Home (`MW_HOME`):

- Sun JDK under `jdk160_<XX>`

- JRocket JDK under `jrockit_160_XX_RXX.X.X-XXX`

Use any one of these two JDK locations. For 64-bit machines, use the 64-bit JDK directory already installed on your machine.

```
[idam@focusthreaderp Disk1]$ ls
doc  install  runInstaller  setup.exe  stage
[idam@focusthreaderp Disk1]$ ./runInstaller -jreLoc /oracle/apps/idam/Middleware
/jdk160_18
Starting Oracle Universal Installer...

Checking if CPU speed is above 300 MHz.   Actual 2823 MHz    Passed
Checking Temp space: must be greater than 150 MB.   Actual 70667 MB    Passed
Checking swap space: must be greater than 500 MB.   Actual 100971 MB   Passed
Checking monitor: must be configured to display at least 256 colors.   Actual 6
5536    Passed
Preparing to launch Oracle Universal Installer from /tmp/OraInstall2010_10-03_05
-56-20PM. Please wait ...
```

On the next screen the installer will check all system prerequisites such as OS version, kernel parameter, OS packages/service packs, and memory.

Click **Next**, and enter **Oracle Middleware Home** (MW_HOME) and **Oracle Home Directory** for SOA Suite.

SOA Suite Oracle Home directory should be different from Identity Management Oracle Home.

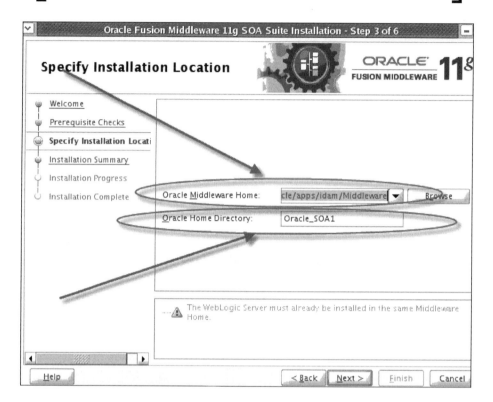

Click on the **Install** button in the next screen to start installation.

Click on the **Next** button and then the **Finish** button to finish installation.

Upgrading SOA Suite to 11.1.1.3.0

 SOA 11.1.1.3.0 is a patch set only. Install it on an existing 11.1.1.2.0 `Oracle_Home` for SOA Suite.

Start SOA Suite Patchset Installation by running `setup.exe` (Windows) or run the installer (Unix) from Disk1 of SOA 11.1.1.3.0 software:

- For Windows: `setup.exe -jreLoc <JDK_Location>`
- For Unix: `./runInstaller -jreLoc <JDK_Location>`

Where `JDK_Location` is a top-level directory for JDK installation. When you install 32-bit WebLogic server, the installer automatically installs two JDKs under `MW_HOME`:

- Sun JDK under `jdk160_<XX>`

- JRocket JDK under `jrockit_160_XX_RXX.X.X-XXX`

Use any one of these two JDK locations. For 64-bit machines, use the 64-bit JDK directory already installed on your machine.

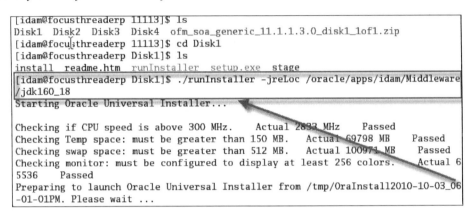

```
[idam@focusthreaderp 11113]$ ls
Disk1  Disk2  Disk3  Disk4  ofm_soa_generic_11.1.1.3.0_disk1_1of1.zip
[idam@focusthreaderp 11113]$ cd Disk1
[idam@focusthreaderp Disk1]$ ls
install  readme.htm  runInstaller  setup.exe  stage
[idam@focusthreaderp Disk1]$ ./runInstaller -jreLoc /oracle/apps/idam/Middleware
/jdk160_18
Starting Oracle Universal Installer...

Checking if CPU speed is above 300 MHz.    Actual 2833 MHz    Passed
Checking Temp space: must be greater than 150 MB.    Actual 69798 MB    Passed
Checking swap space: must be greater than 512 MB.    Actual 100971 MB    Passed
Checking monitor: must be configured to display at least 256 colors.    Actual 6
5536    Passed
Preparing to launch Oracle Universal Installer from /tmp/OraInstall2010-10-03_06
-01-01PM. Please wait ...
```

Install SOA 11.1.1.3.0 Patchset under the same directory (`Oracle_SOA1` default directory) in which you installed the SOA 11.1.1.2.0 software.

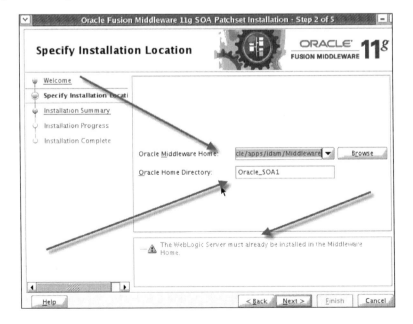

On the next screen click on the **Install** button to start the SOA 11.1.1.3.0 patchset.

After installation click on the **Finish** button to finish the SOA 11.1.1.3.0 patchset.

Configuring Identity and Access Management and creating your WebLogic domain

Start Oracle Identity and Access Management configuration by running `config.sh` (Unix) a `config.bat` (Windows) from `ORACLE_HOME/common/bin directory` where `ORACLE_HOME` is the root directory for IDAM:

- For Windows: `<ORACLE_HOME_for_IDAM>\common\bin\config.bat`
- For Unix: `<ORACLE_HOME_for_IDAM>/common/bin/config.sh`

```
[idam@focusthreaderp bin]$ pwd
/oracle/apps/idam/Middleware/Oracle_IDM1/common/bin
[idam@focusthreaderp bin]$ ls
config.cmd  pack.cmd  setHomeDirs.cmd  setWlstEnv.cmd
config.sh   pack.sh   setHomeDirs.sh   setWlstEnv.sh
[idam@focusthreaderp bin]$ ./config.sh
```

Select **create a new WebLogic domain** on the next screen.

On the next screen select the following product:

- **Oracle Identity Manager – 11.1.1.3.0 [Oracle_IDM1]**
- **Oracle Access Manager with database Policy Store – 11.1.1.3.0 [Oracle_IDM1]**

 In OAM 10*g*, policy and configuration are stored in the LDAP server, where as in OAM 11*g* configuration is stored in a file-based repository (`oam-config.xml`) and policy in database-based repository.

Following products will automatically get selected:

- **Oracle SOA Suite – 11.1.1.0 [Oracle_SOA1]**
- **Oracle Enterprise Manager – 11.1.1.0 [oracle_common]**
- **Oracle WSM Policy Manager – 11.1.1.0 [oracle_common]**
- **Oracle JRF – 11.1.1.0 [oracle_common]**

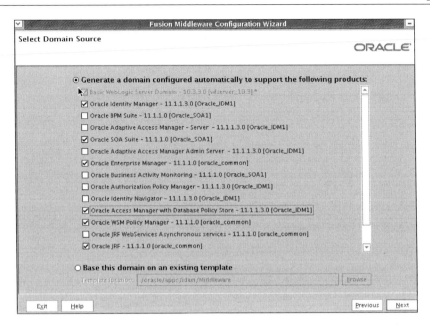

On the next screen select **Domain name**, **Domain location** and **Application location**. (domain directory contains runtime files such as log file, configuration file, and so on.)

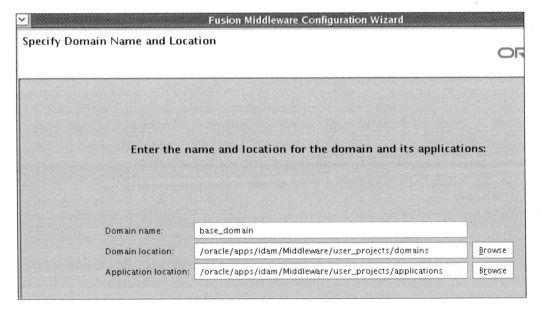

The following screenshot shows the **Configure Administrator User Name and Password** screen:

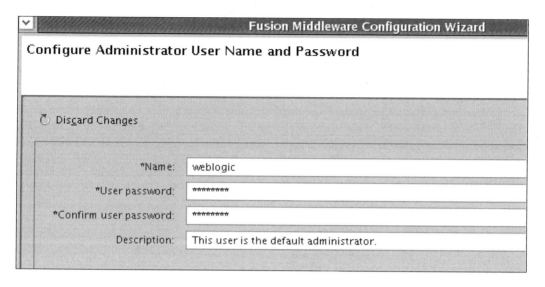

 The WebLogic username is hardcoded in the Oracle Identity Manager application. If you use a different username then you can change the WebLogic administrator server username for OIM using Enterprise Manager. Refer to the Appendix Section http://download. oracle.com/docs/cd/E14571_01/install.1111/e12002/ common002.htm#BABHACAI

In the next screen select a **WebLogic Startup Mode**, that is, **Development Mode** or **Production Mode**.

 For the difference between development mode and production mode check: http://download.oracle.com/docs/cd/E14571_01/ web.1111/e13814/wls_tuning.htm#PERFM175

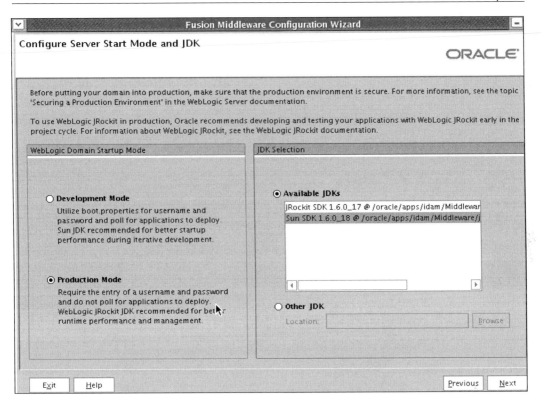

On the next screen, configure the JDBC component of Oracle Identity and Access Management by selecting:

- **Vendor**: Database vendor name, that is, Oracle or Microsoft SQL Server
- **DBMS/Service**: Database service name used to connect to database
- **Host Name**: Name of machine where database is running
- **Port**: Database listener port

- **Schema Password**: If you have selected different password schemas, then select one schema name at a time and enter passwords; else select all schemas and enter password

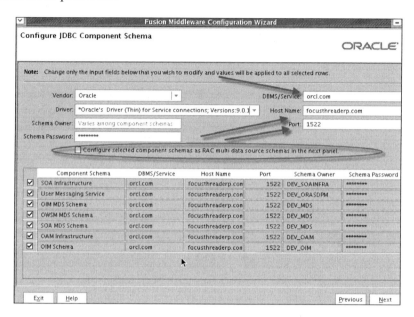

On the next screen, the installer will validate the schema name and version by running SQL:

```
SQL>SELECT 1 FROM SCHEMA_VERSION_REGISTRY WHERE OWNER=(SELECT USER
FROM DUAL) AND MR_TYPE='OIM' AND VERSION='11.1.1.3.0';
```

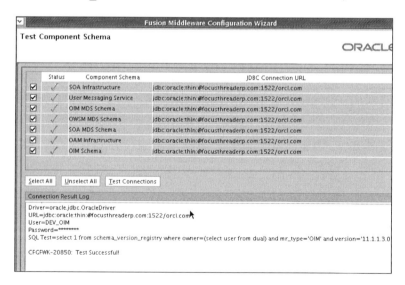

Click **Next** on the **Select Optional Configuration** screen. This screen is used if you are planning to configure IDAM in high-availability deployment (to define cluster) or if you want to change any default setting such as port number, server name, and JMS file store

Click **Next** on the **Configuration Summary** screen.

When progress reaches 100 percent, click on **Done** to finish Oracle Identity and Access Management Configuration (domain creation).

Configuring Oracle Identity Manager server

Start Oracle Identity Manager server configuration by running `config.sh` (Unix) and `config.bat` (Windows) from `ORACLE_HOME/bin directory` where `ORACLE_HOME` is for Identity and Access Management:

- For Windows: `<ORACLE_HOME_for_IDAM>\bin\config.bat`
- For Unix: `<ORACLE_HOME_for_IDAM>/bin/config.sh`

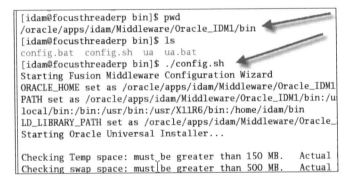

```
[idam@focusthreaderp bin]$ pwd
/oracle/apps/idam/Middleware/Oracle_IDM1/bin
[idam@focusthreaderp bin]$ ls
config.bat  config.sh  ua  ua.bat
[idam@focusthreaderp bin]$ ./config.sh
Starting Fusion Middleware Configuration Wizard
ORACLE_HOME set as /oracle/apps/idam/Middleware/Oracle_IDM1
PATH set as /oracle/apps/idam/Middleware/Oracle_IDM1/bin:/u
local/bin:/bin:/usr/bin:/usr/X11R6/bin:/home/idam/bin
LD_LIBRARY_PATH set as /oracle/apps/idam/Middleware/Oracle_
Starting Oracle Universal Installer...

Checking Temp space: must be greater than 150 MB.   Actual
Checking swap space: must be greater than 500 MB.   Actual
```

Select **OIM Server** from the **Oracle Identity Manager** component list and click **Next**:

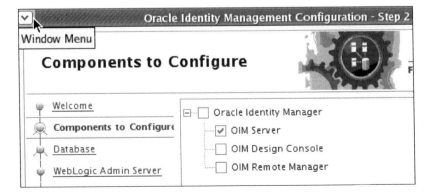

Provide a connect string where OIM and MDS schemas exists. These schemas were created earlier in this chapter using Repository Creation Utility (RCU):

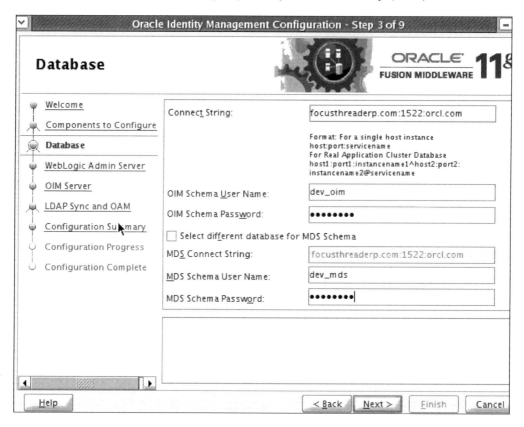

Ensure that WebLogic admin server is running at this stage by checking the admin server start-up process. For more on How to start admin server or How to check if admin server is running refer to *Chapter 4, IDAM Start-up/Shutdown*.

You can add WebLogic admin URL in format
`t3://<weblogicHost>:<admin_port>` or
`http://<weblogicHost>:<admin_port>`.

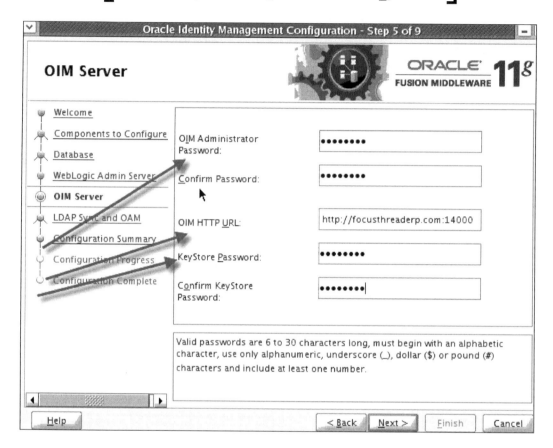

Make a note of the **OIM Administrator Password** as this password will be used to login to Oracle Identity Manager Design console.

 The username for the OIM administrator is XELSYSADM.

On the next screen, LDAP Sync and OAM, uncheck all options and click Next. Enable LDAP sync and Enable Identity Administration Integration with OAM are required for OIM-OAM integration where as Configure BI Publisher is required for reporting in OIM. These integration can be configured at later stage.

> LDAP Sync requires two additional components, Oracle Internet Directory (OID) and Oracle Virtual Directory (OVD).

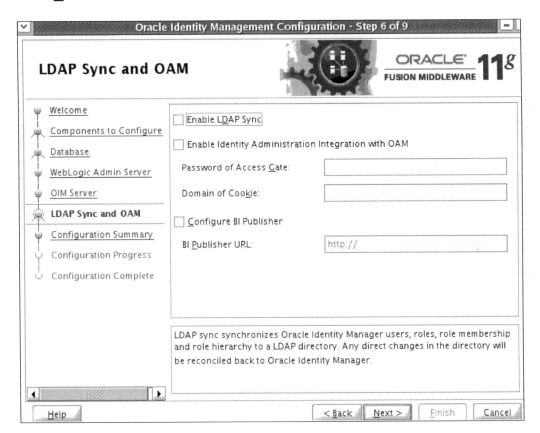

Click on **Next** when progress reaches 100% on **Configuration Progress** screen.

Click **Finish** on the **Configuration Complete** screen to finish the Oracle Identity Manager Configuration.

Starting Services and testing URLs

After installation and configuration of Oracle Identity and Access Manager components, all Services are down. Use the following steps to start WebLogic admin server and managed servers (SOA server, OIM server, and OAM server) to start IDAM services. For detailed Start-Up options check *Chapter 4, IDAM Start-up/Shutdown.*

- Start admin server:

  Start admin server using the command-line utility:

  ○ On Unix: $DOMAIN_HOME/bin/startWebLogic.sh

  ○ On Windows: %DOMAIN_HOME%\bin\startWebLogic.bat

- Start Oracle Identity Manager server:

  ○ On Unix: $DOMAIN_HOME\bin\startManagedWebLogic.sh oim_server1 t3://<adminServerHost>:<admin_server_port>

  ○ On Windows: %DOMAIN_HOME%\bin\startManagedWebLogic.bat oim_server1 t3://<adminServerHost>:<admin_server_port>

- Start Oracle SOA server:

  ○ On Unix: $DOMAIN_HOME\bin\startManagedWebLogic.sh soa_server1 t3://<adminServerHost>:<admin_server_port>

  ○ On Windows: %DOMAIN_HOME%\bin\startManagedWebLogic.bat soa_server1 t3://<adminServerHost>:<admin_server_port>

- Start Oracle Access Manager server:

  ○ On Unix: $DOMAIN_HOME\bin\startManagedWebLogic.sh oam_server1 t3://<adminServerHost>:<admin_server_port>

  ○ On Windows: %DOMAIN_HOME%\bin\startManagedWebLogic.bat oam_server1 t3://<adminServerHost>:<admin_server_port>

http://<serverName>:<admin_server_port>/console is to check if WebLogic console is configured and running.

http://<serverName>:<admin_server_port>/em is to check if Fusion Middleware Control is configured and running.

http://<serverName>:<admin_server_port>/oamconsole is to check if Oracle Access Manager console is configured and running.

http://<serverName>:<oim_server_port>/oim is to check if Oracle Identity Manager is configured and running.

http://<serverName>:<soa_server_port>/soa-infra is to check if SOA Suite is configured and running.

`http://<serverName>:<oam_server_port>/oam` is to check if Oracle Access Manager server is configured and running.

The default `admin_server_port` is `7001`, `soa_server_port` is `8001`, for `oim_server_port` it is `14000`, and `oam_server_port` is `14100`.

Installing for high availability

The following diagram shows a sample Oracle Fusion Middleware 11*g* Oracle Identity Management high-availability (HA) architecture. This architecture includes an application tier (OAM/OIM), and a data tier (database).

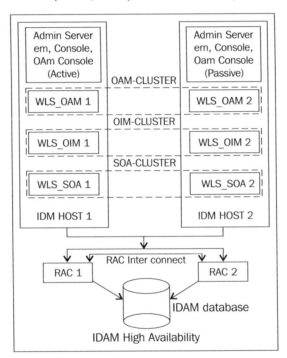

The application tier includes the IDMHOST1 and IDMHOST2 computers.

On IDMHOST1, following installations have been performed:

- An Oracle Access Manager Access server instance has been installed in the `WLS_OAM1` managed server.

- An Oracle Identity Manager server instance has been installed in the `WLS_OIM1` managed server.

- An Oracle SOA server instance has been installed in the `WLS_SOA1` managed server.

- A WebLogic administration server has been installed. The administration server is a singleton application running OAM console and Fusion Middleware Control. Under normal operations, this is the *active* administration server.

On IDMHOST2, the following installations have been performed:

- An Oracle Access Manager Access server instance has been installed in the WLS_OAM2, managed server. WLS_OAM1 on IDMHOST1 and WLS_OAM2 on IDMHOST2 are configured as OAM_CLUSTER cluster.

- An Oracle Identity Manager server instance has been installed in the WLS_OIM2 managed server. WLS_OIM1 on IDMHOST1 and WLS_OIM2 on IDMHOST2 are configured as OIM_CLUSTER cluster.

- An Oracle SOA server instance has been installed in the WLS_SOA2 managed server. WLS_SOA1 on IDMHOST1 and WLS_SOA2 on IDMHOST2 are configured as SOA_CLUSTER cluster.

- A WebLogic administration server has been installed. Under normal operations, this is the *passive* administration server. If admin server on IDMHOST1 becomes unavailable, then admin server on IDMHOST2 will become active.

 In HA deployment, Oracle SOA Suite requires a shared file system to store transactional logs (TLOGS) and Java Messaging Server (JMS) Persistence Store, so that SOA server running on different machines can access same file system.

Prerequisites for Oracle IDAM high-availability configuration

In order to deploy Oracle Identity and Access Management in a high-availability configuration, consider the following key points:

- Oracle Home for identity management must be the same across all nodes. For example, if Oracle Home on IDMHOST1 is /u01/oracle/Middleware/Oracle_IDM then Oracle Home on IDMHOST2 must also be /u01/oracle/Middleware/Oracle_IDM.

- SOA Suite component requires a shared file system for TLOGS and JMS as Persistence Store.

- It is recommended to use a hardware load balancer to distribute client traffic to the pool of available OIM/OAM servers. The load balancer must be able to detect service and node failures and to stop directing traffic to failed nodes. It should also have ability to maintain sticky connections to components based on cookies or URLs.

> Oracle Identity Manager can be deployed on an Oracle RAC database, but Oracle RAC failover is not transparent for Oracle Identity Manager in this release. If an Oracle RAC failover occurs, end users may have to resubmit their requests.
>
> Oracle Identity Manager always requires that at least one of the nodes in the SOA cluster be available. If the SOA cluster is not available, end user requests will fail. Oracle Identity Manager does not retry for a failed SOA call. Therefore, the end user must retry when a SOA call fails.

Installing and Configuring IDAM for high-availability

Use the following steps to install and configure IDAM in Active-Active mode:

1. Install the Oracle WebLogic server 10.3.3 on IDMHOST1 and IDMHOST2 (Install WebLogic on the same path on each server.)

2. Install Oracle Identity and Access Management server 11.1.1.3 on IDMHOST1 and IDMHOST2.

3. Install Oracle SOA Suite 11.1.1.2.0 on IDMHOST1 and IDMHOST2.

4. Upgrade Oracle SOA Suite to 11.1.1.3.0 on IDMHOST1 and IDMHOST2.

5. Create a virtual IP address such as `adminvh.mycompany` on IDMHOST1.

6. Create domain for the administration server:

   ○ Run Configuration Wizard on IDMHOST1:

   Unix: `$MW_HOME/oracle_common/common/bin/config.sh`

   Windows: `%MW_HOME%\oracle_common\common\bin\config.bat`

   ○ Select **Create a New WebLogic Domain**.

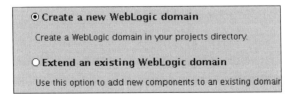

○ Select **Oracle Enterprise Manager – 11.1.1.0[oracle_common]** and **Oracle JRF – 11.1.1.0 [oracle_common]**.

○ On **Optional Screen** select **Administration Server** and **Managed Servers, Clusters and Machines**:

- On the **Configure Admin Server** screen, change **Listen address** to VIP address, that is, **adminvh.mycompany.com**.

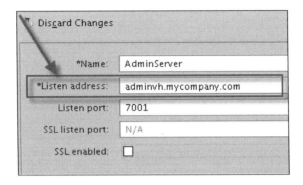

- Leave all other fields at their default values, and click **Create domain**.

7. Extend the domain (created in step 6) to include Oracle Access Manager 11*g*:

- Run Configuration Wizard on IDMHOST1 again.
  Unix: $MW_HOME/oracle_common/common/bin/config.sh
  Windows: %MW_HOME%\oracle_common\common\bin\config.bat.
- Select **Extend an existing WebLogic domain**.
- Select the name of the domain you created previously in Step 6.
- Select **Oracle Access Manager with Database Policy Store – 11.11.3.0 [Oracle_IDM1]**.

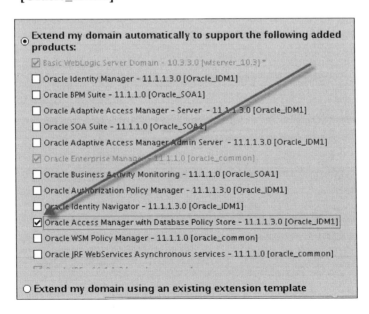

  °   On the **Configure JDBC Data Sources** screen, select the data source **OAM Infrastructure** and select **Configure selected data sources as RAC multi data sources**.

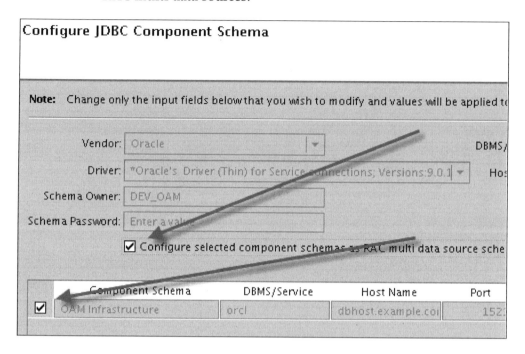

  °   Enter RAC database connection details.

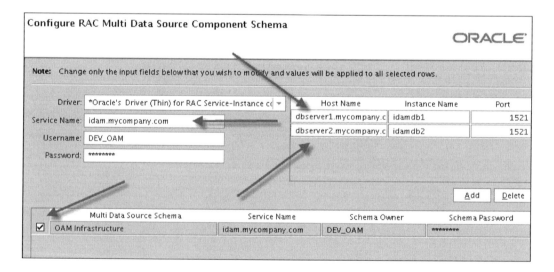

- ° On the **Optional Configuration** screen select **Managed Servers, Clusters and Machines**.

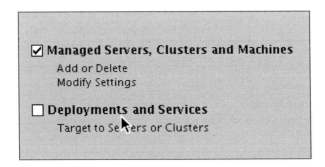

- ° On the **Configure Managed Server** screen, create two managed servers: WLS_OAM1 on **Listen address** IDMHOST1 and **Listen port** 14100, and WLS_OAM2 on **Listen address** IDMHOST2 and **Listen port** 14100.

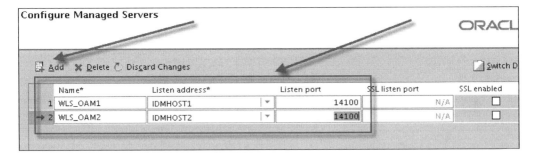

- ° On the next screen create a cluster by clicking **Add**. Here the **Name** is OAM_CLUSTER and **Cluster messaging mode** is unicast:

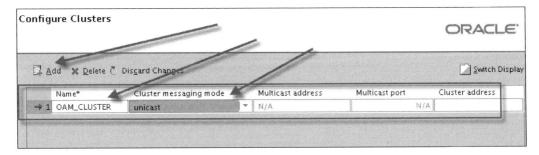

      °   On the next screen, assign managed server **WLS_OAM1** and **WLS_OAM2** to **OAM_CLUSTER**:

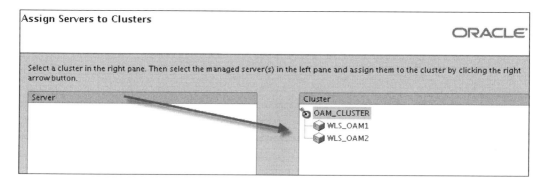

      °   Select **Machine** if your managed servers are running on Windows. For managed servers running on Unix, select **Unix Machine** and then click **Add**.

      °   Create two machines `idmhost1.mycompany.com` and `idmhost2.mycompany.com`:

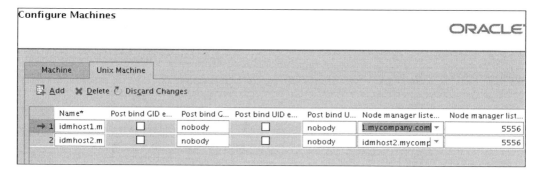

- ○ Assign **AdminServer** and **WLS_OAM1** to **idmhost1.mycompany.com**, and **WLS_OAM2** to **idmhost2.mycompany.com** as shown in the following screenshot:

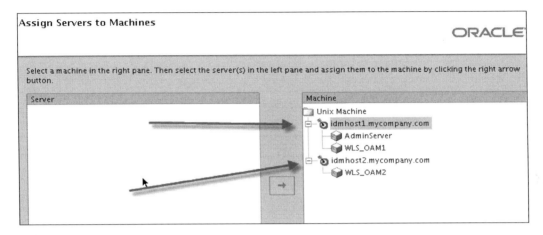

- ○ On the **Configuration Summary** screen, click **Extend** to extend the domain.

8. Propagate domain changes from the IDMHOST1 server to the IDMHOST2 server using the `pack` and `unpack` commands.

    - ○ Run the `pack` command on IDMHOST1. (Replace `$MW_HOME` with full path to Middleware Home.)

    ```
    $MW_HOME/oracle_common/common/bin/pack.sh -domain=$MW_HOME/
    user_projects/domain/base_domain/ -template=/tmp/IDAMDomain.
    jar -template_name="OAM Domain" -managed=true
    ```

    - ○ The previous command will create a file called `IDAMDomain.jar` in the `/tmp` directory. Copy this file to IDMHOST2.

    - ○ Run the `unpack` command on IDMHOST2:

    ```
    $MW_HOME/oracle_common/common/bin/unpack.sh -domain=$MW_
    HOME/user_projects/domain/base_domain -template=/tmp/
    IDAMDomain.jar -overwrite_domain=true -app_dir=$MW_HOME/
    user_projects/applications/base_domain
    ```

○ Start admin server on IDMHOST1 and access **WebLogic Console |
   Servers** to see managed server and cluster:

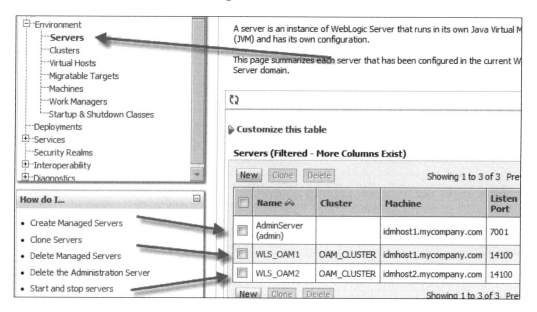

9. Extend the domain to configure Oracle Identity Manager and SOA Suite:

   ○ Run Configuration Wizard on IDMHOST1 again
      Unix: $MW_HOME/oracle_common/common/bin/config.sh
      Windows: %MW_HOME%\oracle_common\common\bin\config.bat

   ○ Select **Extend an existing WebLogic domain**.

   ○ Select the domain name which you created previously in Step 6.

   ○ Select **Oracle Identity Manager – 11.1.1.3.0 [Oracle_IDM1]**. (Note:
      Oracle SOA Suite – 11.1.1.0 [Oracle_SOA1] and **Oracle WSM Policy
      Manager – 11.1.1.0 [oracle_common]** are selected automatically).

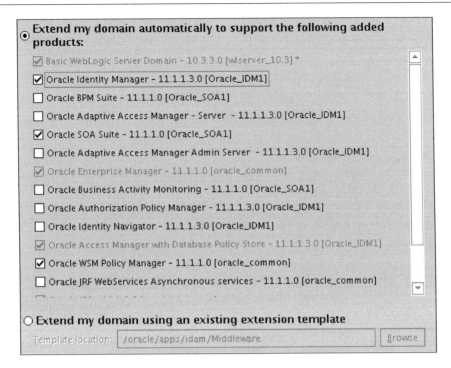

○ On the **Configure JDBC Data Sources** screen, select all schemas and then select **Configure selected data sources as RAC multi data sources**.

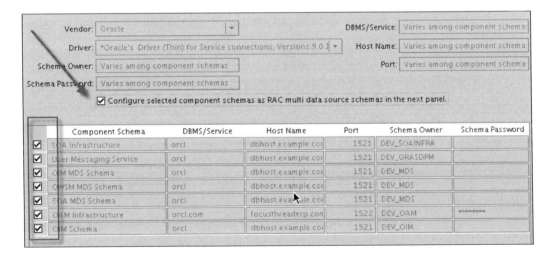

      ° On the **Optional Configuration** screen select **JMS Distributed Destination** and **Managed Servers, Clusters and Machines**.

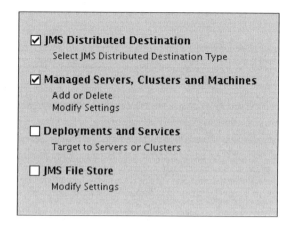

      ° On the **JMS Distributed Destination** screen, ensure that all the JMS system resources are configured as uniform distributed destinations (UDD).

      ° Click **OK** when you get a warning like:

"CFGFWK-40915: At least one JMS system resource has been selected for conversion to a Uniform Distributed Destination (UDD). This conversion will take place only if the JMS System resource is assigned to a cluster Click OK on the Override Warning box."

      ° On the **Configure Managed Server** screen, create four new managed servers (two managed servers **WLS_OAM1** and **WLS_OAM2** should already be there from the previous extension)

      ° **WLS_OIM1** on **Listen address IDMHOST1** and **Listen port 14000**, and **WLS_OIM2** on **Listen address IDMHOST2** and **Listen port 14000**

○ **WLS_SOA1** on **Listen address IDMHOST1** and **Listen port 8001,**
and **WLS_SOA2** on **Listen address IDMHOST2** and **Listen
port 8001**

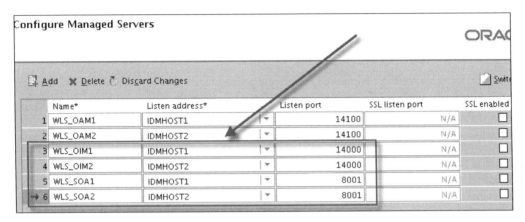

○ On the next screen, create two new clusters by clicking on **Add** (one
cluster **OAM_CLUSTER** should already be there from the previous
domain extension).

○ **OIM_CLUSTER**: Set **Cluster messaging mode** as **unicast**.

○ **SOA_CLUSTER**: Set **Cluster messaging mod**e as **unicast**.

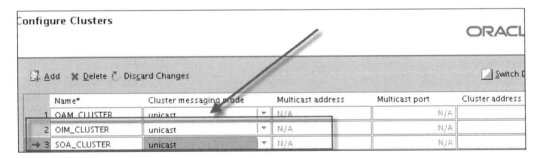

  ○   On the next screen, assign managed servers **WLS_OIM1** and
    WLS_OIM2 to **OIM_CLUSTER**, and **WLS_SOA1** and **WLS_SOA2**
    to **SOA_CLUSTER**. (**OAM_CLUSTER** should already be there from
    the previous domain extension.)

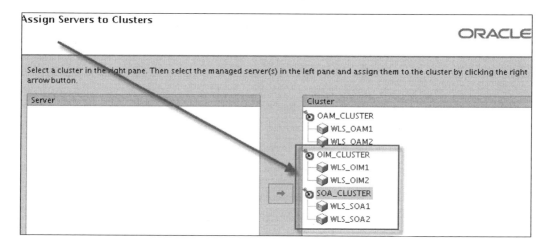

  ○   Select **Machine** if your managed servers are running on Windows.
    For managed server running on Unix, select **Unix Machine.** You
    should already see two machines (**idmhost1** and **idmhost2**) from
    the previous domain extension.

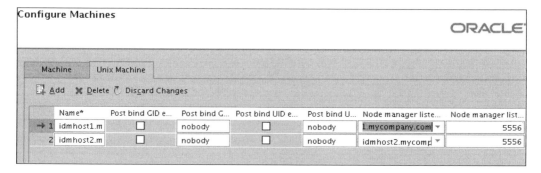

  ○   Assign **WLS_O1M1** and **WLS_SOA1** to idmhost1.mycompany.com,
    and **WLS_OIM2** and **WLS_SOA2** to idmhost2.mycompany.com.
    (admin server, **WLS_OAM1**, and **WLS_OAM2** should already be
    assigned to machines from the previous domain extension.)

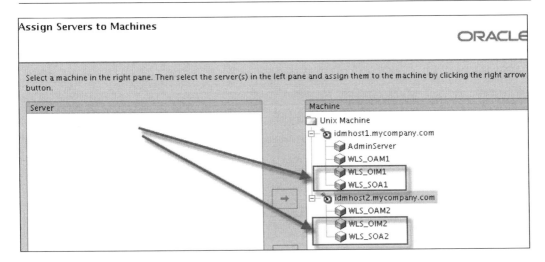

Assign Servers to Machines

ORACLE

Select a machine in the right pane. Then select the server(s) in the left pane and assign them to the machine by clicking the right arrow button.

- ○ On **Configuration Summary** screen, Click **Extend** to extend the domain.

10. Configure Oracle Identity Manager by running `$IDM_ORACLE_HOME/bin/config.sh` as shown earlier in the *Configuring Oracle Identity Manager server* section.

11. Propagate domain changes from IDMHOST1 server to IDMHOST2 server using the `pack` and `unpack` commands.

    - ○ Run the following `pack` command on IDMHOST1 (replace `$MW_HOME` with full path to Middleware Home):

        ```
        $MW_HOME/oracle_common/common/bin/pack.sh -domain=$MW_
        HOME/user_projects/domain/base_domain/ -template=/tmp/
        IDAMOIMDomain.jar -template_name="OAM Domain" -managed=true
        ```

    - ○ The previous command will create a file called `IDAMOIMDomain.jar` in the `/tmp` directory. Copy this file to IDMHOST2.

    - ○ Run `unpack` command on IDMHOST2:

        ```
        $MW_HOME/oracle_common/common/bin/unpack.sh -domain=$MW_
        HOME/user_projects/domain/base_domain -template=/tmp/
        IDAMOIMDomain.jar -overwrite_domain=true -app_dir=$MW_HOME/
        user_projects/applications/base_domain
        ```

° Restart admin server on IDMHOST1 and access **WebLogic Console |
Servers** to see managed servers and clusters

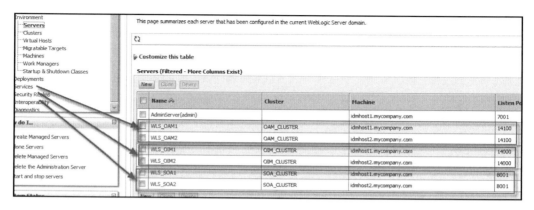

° Update Coherence Configuration for SOA managed server under
startup tab. **Environment | Servers | WLS_SOA1 | Server Start**
and enter the following text in a single line under **Argument**:

For **WLS_SOA1** add the following text in a single line under
Arguments:

```
-Dtangosol.coherence.wka1=idmhost1.mycompany.com -Dtangosol.
coherence.wka2=idmhost2.mycompany.com -Dtangosol.coherence.
localhost=idmhost1.mycompany.com
```

° For **WLS_SOA2** add the following text in single a line under
Arguments

```
-Dtangosol.coherence.wka1=idmhost1.mycompany.com -Dtangosol.
coherence.wka2=idmhost2.mycompany.com -Dtangosol.coherence.
localhost=idmhost2.mycompany.com
```

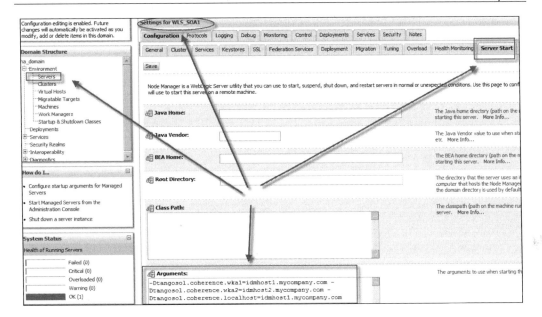

 Coherence by default uses Port 8089.

° Configure Shared JMS persistence store.

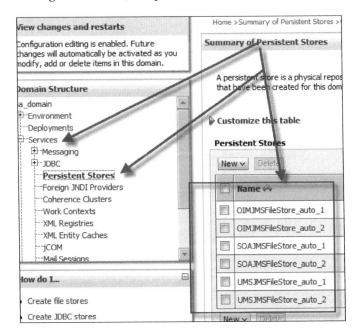

- ° Configuring a default persistence store for Transaction Recovery can be done using the steps at: `http://download.oracle.com/docs/cd/E14571_01/core.1111/e12035/oim.htm#CFHJCIHE`

- ° Start OIM and SOA sever on both IDMHOST1 and IDMHOST2.

Silent installation

A silent installation eliminates the need to monitor the Oracle Identity Management installation process, because no graphical output is displayed and no input by the user is required.

To perform a silent Oracle Identity Management installation, you invoke the installer with the `-silent` flag and provide a response file from the command line. The response file is a text file containing variables and parameter values which provide answers to the installer prompts.

Silent installation steps

The following are the steps for silent installation:

1. Create your inventory location:

   - ° For Windows, create a registry key and value as `HKEY_LOCAL_MACHINE / SOFTWARE / Oracle / inst_loc = C:\Program Files\Oracle\Inventory`

   - ° For Unix, create `oraInst.loc` as follows:

     ```
     inventory_loc=oui_inventory_directory
     inst_group=oui_install_group
     ```

   Replace `oui_inventory_directory` with the location in which you wish to create the inventory, and replace `oui_install_group` with the group of the user installing Identity Management.

2. Create response file:

Response files are text files used during silent installation to pass parameters to the installer. A sample response file is located under:

- ° `$IDAM_SOFTWARE/Disk1/stage/Response` on Unix
- ° `$IDAM_SOFTWARE\Disk1\stage\Response` on Windows

Other methods to create a response file: When you use the Oracle Identity Management Installation Wizard to install the software for the first time, you can save a summary of your installation in a response file. This will create a response file for that specific product. Save the response files for Oracle SOA Suite 11.1.1.2.0 installation, SOA 11.1.1.3.0 patchset, and IDAM 11.1.1.1.3.0 installation.

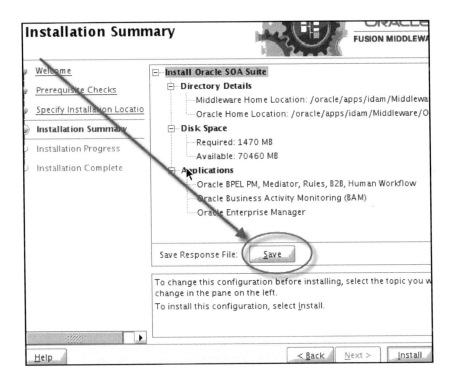

Creating Response Files for Oracle Identity Manager Configuration: When you use the Oracle Identity Manager configuration wizard to configure Oracle Identity Manager server, Design console, or Remote Manager for the first time, you can save a summary of your configuration in a response file.

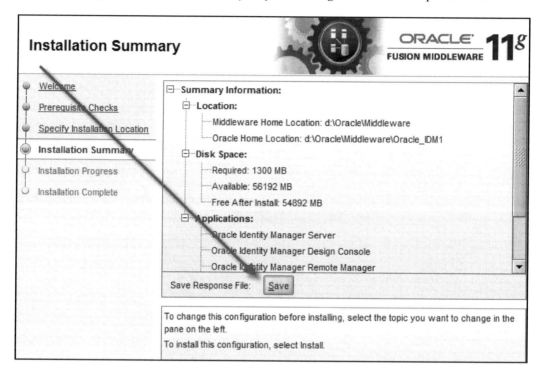

3. Perform silent installation:

    ° On Unix `./runInstaller -silent -response FILE`
        replace FILE with the location of your response file

    ° On Windows `setup.exe -silent -response FILE`
        replace FILE with the location of your response file

Deinstalling/Uninstalling

Oracle Identity and Accesss Management 11*g* installation consists of three ORACLE_HOMEs (for more information on Oracle_Home check *Chapter 3, IDAM Directory Structure and Files*.) Here are few useful points while Deinstalling or Uninstalling Oracle Identity Management:

- Use runInstaller (or `setup.exe` on windows) with option deinstall to deinstall software
- The deinstaller attempts to remove the Oracle Home directory from which it was started
- oraInventory is required for removing instance and Oracle Home
- Deinstalling Oracle Identity Management does not remove any WebLogic domains that you have created—it only removes the software in the Oracle Identity Management Oracle Home directory

Deinstalling/Uninstalling Oracle Identity Management Home

Deinstall Oracle Identity Management Home using:

- For Unix: `./runInstaller -deinstall`
- For Windows: `setup.exe -deinstall`

Deinstalling/Uninstalling Oracle Common Home

Deinstall Oracle Common Home using:

- On Unix: `./runInstaller -deinstall -jreLoc FULL_PATH_TO_JRE_ DIRECTORY`
- On Windows: `setup.exe -deinstall -jreLoc FULL_PATH_TO_JRE_ DIRECTORY`

Summary

We have discussed Installation of Oracle Fusion Middleware, including Oracle Identity Manager and Oracle Access Manager Products. We also covered installation of Oracle Identity Manager (OIM) and Oracle Access Manager (OAM) in an Active-Active (high-availability) cluster.

In the next chapter, we are going to cover the directory structure and the most important files of Oracle Identity and Access Management (OIM and OAM).

3

IDAM Directory Structure and Files

In this chapter we will cover file systems, including key files and directories used in Identity and Access Management (IDAM). We will cover the following topics in this chapter:

- Environment variables
- Directory structure
- Important files for OAM & OIM

Common environment variables

This section covers common environment variables and top-level directories used in Identity and Access Management:

- Middleware Home: `MW_HOME`
- WebLogic Home: `WL_HOME`
- Coherence Home: `COHERENCE_HOME`
- Oracle Home for IDAM: `IDAM ORACLE_HOME`
- Oracle Home for common: `COMMON ORACLE_HOME`
- Oracle Home for SOA: `SOA ORACLE_HOME`
- Domain Home: `DOMAIN_HOME`

Middleware Home

Middleware Home is a top-level directory, created during WebLogic installation and contains all the Oracle Home, WebLogic server, Coherence server, and optionally WebLogic domains. Middleware Home is represented by %MW_HOME% (Windows) or $MW_HOME (Unix). Middleware Home can reside on local file systems or on a remote shared disk accessible to the server. The following screenshot lists files and directories created under Middleware Home after WebLogic installation. The directory /oracle/apps/oamoim/mw_home represents MW_HOME

The following table explains directory content of Middleware Home (MW_HOME):

Directory/File	Description
jdk[version]	Contains software for Sun JDK.
jrockit_[version]	Contains software for JRockit JDK.
Logs	Contains a history file, which has information about installation and uninstallation for the Middleware Home directory.
Modules	Contains the modules installed in the Home directory.
Utils	Contains utilities that are used to support the installation, for example to apply patches in WebLogic using BSU (BEA Smart Update).
wlserver_version	The WebLogic server home directory as explained above.
coherence_version	The Coherence home directory as explained above.
.home	Contains the location of Middleware Home directory.
ocm.rsp	This response file contains information about the Oracle Configuration Manager (OCM) installation.
registry.xml	This registry file contains record of all WebLogic products installed along with product-related information such as version number, patch set level, patch level, and location of the product installation directories.

Directory/File	Description
registry.dat	An encrypted version of the registry.xml file.
domain-registry.xml	Contains the location of all domains currently registered with this WebLogic server installation. Whenever you add a new domain, it is registered in this file.
Oracle_IDM1	The Oracle Identity and Access Management Server home directory as explained above.
Oracle_SOA1	The Oracle SOA Server home directory as explained above.
user_projects	Contains domain and applications configured using config.sh or config.cmd.

 Directories marked with * i.e jdk[version] and jrockit_[version] are created only with the binary of WebLogic and not created if you use the jar version of the WebLogic installer.

WebLogic Home

WebLogic Home is represented by %WL_HOME% (Windows) or $WL_HOME (Unix) and created during WebLogic installation under Middleware Home. In the following screenshot, WebLogic Home is represented by directory /oracle/apps/oamoim/mw_home/wlserver_10.3. WebLogic Home contains files required to run the WebLogic Server.

```
[idam11g@innowave03 wlserver_10.3]$ pwd
/oracle/apps/oamoim/mw_home/wlserver_10.3
[idam11g@innowave03 wlserver_10.3]$ ls
bugsfixed   common   inventory   L10N   server   sip   uninstall
[idam11g@innowave03 wlserver_10.3]$
```

Coherence Home

This directory is represented by %COHERENCE_HOME% (Windows) or $COHERENCE_HOME (Unix). Coherence Home is created during WebLogic Installation under $MW_HOME. The following screenshot lists files and directories created under COHERENCE_HOME. The directory /oracle/apps/oamoim/mw_home/coherence_3.5 represents Coherence Home where 3.5 is the coherence version.

```
[idam11g@innowave03 coherence_3.5]$ pwd
/oracle/apps/oamoim/mw_home/coherence_3.5
[idam11g@innowave03 coherence_3.5]$ ls
bin   inventory   lib   product.xml   uninstall
[idam11g@innowave03 coherence_3.5]$
```

IDAM Oracle Home

This directory is represented by %ORACLE_HOME% (Windows) or $ORACLE_HOME (Unix) and contains IDAM software. It is created during IDAM software installation under $MW_HOME. It must be created under MW_HOME and can use the default name Oracle_IDM1 or any other name assigned during IDAM software installation.

The following screenshot lists files and directories created under ORACLE_HOME. In the screenshot, directory /oracle/apps/oamoim/mw_home/Oracle_IDM1 represents ORACLE_HOME. There can be multiple Oracle Homes in Middleware Home (MW_HOME), for instance one for IDAM, a second for SOA (Oracle_SOA1), and a third for a web server Oracle_WT1. IDAM Oracle Home contains software including OAM and OIM.

```
[idam11g@innowave03 Oracle_IDM1]$ pwd
/oracle/apps/oamoim/mw_home/Oracle_IDM1  ◄━━━━━━━━━━━
[idam11g@innowave03 Oracle_IDM1]$ ls
apm            designconsole     modules         OPatch        server
asdmeofftool   diagnostics       oam             oraInst.loc   upgrade
bin            install.platform  oam             oui
cfgtoollogs    inventory         oinav           rda
common         jlib              oneoffpatches   remote_manager
[idam11g@innowave03 Oracle_IDM1]$
```

Common Oracle Home

This directory is represented by %COMMON_ORACLE_HOME% (Windows) or $COMMON_ORACLE_HOME (Unix), and contains binary and library files such as those required for Java Required Files (JRF) and Fusion Middleware Control (/em). It also contains the BSU (BEA Smart Update) tool for applying WebLogic patches. This directory is created during IDAM software installation under $MW_HOME in the directory oracle_common. The following screenshot lists files and directories created under COMMON_ORACLE_HOME. In the screenshot, /oracle/apps/oamoim/mw_home/oracle_common represents COMMON_ORACLE_HOME. There can only be one Common Oracle Home (oracle_common) in a Middleware Home (MW_HOME).

```
[idam11g@innowave03 oracle_common]$ pwd
/oracle/apps/oamoim/mw_home/oracle_common  ◄━━━━━━━━━━━
[idam11g@innowave03 oracle_common]$ ls
admin                     clone             inventory  oraInst.loc  util
adminserver_registration  common            jdk        oui          webcenter
atgpf                     diagnostics       jlib       rcu          webservices
BC4J                      doc               lib        rda
bin                       hapowertools      modules    soa
bpm                       install           network    sysman
cfgtoollogs               install.platform  OPatch     uix
[idam11g@innowave03 oracle_common]$
```

Some patches applied using opatch are specifically for `oracle_common`. In such cases set `ORACLE_HOME` to the `oracle_common` directory and use "opatch apply" to patch Common Oracle Home.

SOA Oracle Home

This directory, represented by `%ORACLE_HOME%` (Windows) or `$ORACLE_HOME` (Unix) contains SOA software required for Oracle Identity Manager (OIM). Oracle Home for SOA is created during SOA software installation under `MW_HOME`, and can use the default name `Oracle_SOA1` or any other name assigned during SOA software installation. The following screenshot lists files and directories created under `SOA ORACLE_HOME`. In the screenshot, directory `/oracle/apps/oamoim/mw_home/Oracle_SOA1` represents `SOA ORACLE_HOME`.

```
[idam11g@innowave03 Oracle_SOA1]$ pwd
/oracle/apps/oamoim/mw_home/Oracle_SOA1
[idam11g@innowave03 Oracle_SOA1]$ ls
bam              common           inventory    OPatch        soa         webcenter
BC4J             communications   jdk          oraInst.loc   uddi
bin              diagnostics      jlib         oui           uix
bpm              doc              lib          rcu           upgrade
cfgtoollogs      install.platform modules      rda           util
[idam11g@innowave03 Oracle_SOA1]$
```

 SOA Suite is required only for OIM. If you are only installing OAM server, then SOA is not required.

Domain Home

This directory, represented by `%DOMAIN_HOME%` (Windows) or `$DOMAIN_HOME` (Unix) contains configuration and runtime files required for WebLogic Domain. This directory is created during WebLogic Domain creation under the default location `$WL_HOME/user_projects/domains/base_domain`, but can be created at any other place including outside `MW_HOME`. In the following screenshot, directory `/oracle/apps/oamoim/mw_home/user_projects/domains/base_domain` represents `DOMAIN_HOME`.

```
[idam11g@innowave03 base_domain]$ pwd
/oracle/apps/oamoim/mw_home/user_projects/domains/base_domain
[idam11g@innowave03 base_domain]$ ls
autodeploy       logs             SOAJMSFileStore
bin              ngamui.log       startManagedWebLogic_readme.txt
config           OIMJMSFileStore  startWebLogic.sh
console-ext      output           sysman
edit.lok         pending          tmp
fileRealm.properties security     UMSJMSFileStore
init-info        servers
lib              soa
[idam11g@innowave03 base_domain]$
```

The following table explains, directory content of Domain Home (DOMAIN_HOME):

File/Directory	Description
Autodeploy	When the Oracle WebLogic server instance is running in development mode, it automatically deploys any application or module that you place in this directory.
Bin	The start-up and shutdown scripts are maintained in this directory.
bin\setDomainEnv.sh	Script that the environment variables.
bin\startWebLogic.sh	Script that starts the WebLogic Admin server.
bin\stopWebLogic.sh	Script that stops the WebLogic Admin server.
bin\startManagedWebLogic.sh	This script starts the WebLogic Managed servers such as oim_server1 and oam_server1.
bin\stopManagedWebLogic.sh	Script that stops the WebLogic Managed server such as oim_server1 and oam_server1.
Config	This directory contains WebLogic Domain configurations.
config\config.xml	The main WebLogic domain configuration file, which contains the name of the domain, Admin server, Managed server, port and so on. Most of the configurations which you edit from WebLogic console are stored in this configuration file.
config\jdbc	This directory contains JDBC connection details to connect from WebLogic server to database.
config\jms	This directory contains JMS details used in the OIM and SOA server.
config\fmwconfig	This is the main configuration directory for Fusion Middleware products like OAM, OIM, and SOA.
Security	This directory holds the security-related files required by all WebLogic servers, that is SerializedSystemIni.dat and security files required only by Admin server (DefaultAuthorizerInit.ldift, DefaultAuthenticatorInit.ldift, DefaultRoleMapperInit.ldift).
Servers	This directory contains one subdirectory per WebLogic server that is AdminServer, oam_server1, oim_server1 or soa_server1.

File/Directory	Description
`servers\<serverName>\logs`	This directory contains log file for specific WebLogic server. If there are issues in the servers such as Admin server, OIM server, or OAM server then check logs under this directory. This is one of the key directories used during troubleshooting.
`servers\<serverName>\ security\boot.properties`	This file contains encrypted username and password used during server start-up.
`OIMJMSFileStore, SOAJMSFileStore, UMSJMSFileStore`	These are default JMS stores for OIM, SOA, and UMS respectively.

Key files/Directories used by both OAM & OIM server:

File/Directory	Description
`DOMAIN_HOME/config/ fmwconfig/ system- jazn-data.xml & jps- config.xml`	This is the Policy Store, for role definition. In a high availability environment, it is recommended to move Policy Store to an external LDAP server such as OID.
`DOMAIN_HOME/config/ fmwconfig/cwallet.sso`	This is the file used as the credential store. In a high availability environment, it is recommended to move Policy Store to an external LDAP server such as OID.
`DOMAIN_HOME/config/ fmwconfig/servers /<server_name> / logging.xml`	This file is used to store logging configuration.
`DOMAIN_HOME/config/ fmwconfig/servers/ <server_name> /dms_ config.xml`	This file is used to store Dynamic Monitoring System (DMS) configuration.

Key Files/Directories for OAM server:

File/Directory	Description
`DOMAIN_HOME/config/ fmwconfig/ oam- configuration.xml`	The key OAM configuration file which contains all OAM configurations such as OAM server port, identity stores, webgate servers, and any configuration changes you make via OAMConsole.
`DOMAIN_HOME/config/ fmwconfig/ oam-policy.xml`	The OAM server main configuration file, which contains instance-specific information like the OAM proxy server, OAM server hostname, port, Application Domains and so on.
`DOMAIN_HOME/config/ fmwconfig/ .oamkeystore`	This file is used for storing symmetric and asymmetric keys.
`DOMAIN_HOME/config/ fmwconfig/ component_ events.xml`	This file is used for audit definition.
`IDAM ORACLE_HOME/oam/ server/rreg`	Directory that contains files required for Remote Registration Utility (RREG) to register OAM Agents (WebGates & osso_agents).
`IDAM ORACLE_HOME/oam/ server/oim-intg/schema`	These are LDIF files used for OID schema extension for OIM/OAM Integration.

Key Files/Directory for OIM server:

File/Directory	Description
`oim-config.xml` (stored in database under MDS)	The OIM configuration file that contains OIM server configuration and is stored in the database.
`DOMAIN_HOME/config/ fmwconfig/.xldatabasekey`	Keystore that stores the database encryption key.
`DOMAIN_HOME/config/ fmwconfig/ default_keystore.jks`	The default JKS keystore.
`DOMAIN_HOME/config/ fmwconfig/xlserver.crt`	The OIM server certificate file.
`IDAM ORACLE_HOME/ bin/config.sh`	Script for configuring Oracle Identity Manager.
`IDAM ORACLE_HOME/ server/ldap_config_util`	This directory contains files used during LDAP synchronization with OIM.
`IDAM ORACLE_HOME/ designconsole`	This directory contains files related to the OIM Design console.
`IDAM ORACLE_HOME/ remotemanager`	This directory contains files related to Remote Manager.

if you want to configure a second OID domain against an existing OIM database (used in a different OIM domain) then copy `cwallet.so`, `default_keystore.jks`, and `xlserver.crt` from the first WebLogic Domain to the second WebLogic Domain under `$DOMAIN_HOME/config/fmwconfig`.

Summary

In this chapter we discussed the important environment variables, key files, and directories for Oracle Identity and Access Administration. Note that the environment variables discussed in this chapter should be set manually, as IDAM does not provide any script to automate this.

In the next chapter we are going to cover steps to start-up and shutdown IDAM.

4

Start-up Shutdown IDAM

Oracle Identity and Access Management (IDAM) components are Java applications deployed on WebLogic Server with database as repository. Consider the following components when starting and stopping an Oracle Identity and Access management server:

1. One and only one Admin server
2. One or more SOA Suite Managed servers
3. One or more OIM Managed servers
4. One or more OAM Managed servers
5. Database server used as repository for Oracle Identity and Access Management
6. Node Manager per machine (optional component)
7. External LDAP server as User store (optional component)

 Oracle Access Manager's default identity store is an embedded LDAP server (shipped as part of WebLogic server). It is recommended to configure Oracle Access Manager's Identity Store to external LDAP server, such as Oracle Internet directory or Microsoft Active directory.

In this chapter we will cover:

- Start-up/Shutdown order
- Start-up/Shutdown Oracle IDAM
- Tools to assist in the process

Start-up/Shutdown order

Oracle identity management servers and their databases must start/stop in an order. For startup, the database and database listener must be started first and then the OAM, SOA, and OIM servers. For shutdown OAM, OIM, and SOA must be stopped first and then the database and database listener. The following diagram shows the flowchart for start-up:

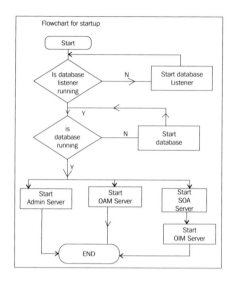

The next diagram shows the flowchart for shutdown:

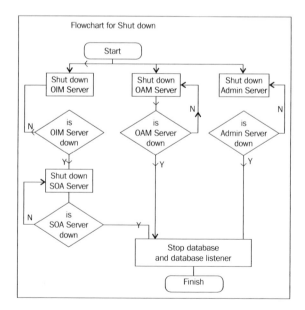

Starting IDAM server

This section contains steps to start the default IDAM server configuration that is, the Oracle Database, WebLogic Admin server, and WebLogic Managed server (soa_server1, oim_server1, and oam_server1).The commands in the following section assume that the hostname of the machine is focusthread, the admin server port is 7001, and managed server names for SOA, OIM, OAM are soa_server1, oim_server1, and oam_server1 respectively.

> 7001 is WebLogic's default Admin server port which the installer will assign during domain configuration. If 7001 is in use by another process during domain configuration then the installer will use the next available port, that is 7002.

> If you are not sure about the port used by Weblogic server's Admin and Managed servers (OAM, OIM and SOA), you can verify it from the configuration file $DOMAIN_HOME/config/config.xml.

1. Starting Database and Listener containing IDAM schema
   - Set ORACLE_HOME to the directory in which database server is installed, ORACLE_SID to database SID, and PATH to include $ORACLE_HOME/bin.
   - Start database listener and database:

     ```
     $ORACLE_HOME/bin/lsnrctl start
     $ORACLE_HOME/bin/sqlplus "/as sysdba"
     SQL> startup
     SQL> exit
     ```

   To check which database (Server Name, SID, Port) is used by the IDAM server check the configuration file $DOMAIN_HOME/config/jdbc/*.xml.

2. Start WebLogic Admin server.

   ```
   cd $MW_HOME\user_projects\domains\<DOMAIN_NAME>
   ```

   Windows: bin/startWebLogic.cmd

   Unix: bin\startWebLogic.sh

3. To start Admin or Managed server in the background on Windows, create a service or for Unix use nohup, like this: nohup ./startWebLogic.sh &:

```
[idam@focusthreaderp bin]$ ls
nodemanager          service_migration    startManagedWebLogic.sh  stopWebLo
secureWebLogic.sh    setDomainEnv.sh      startWebLogic.sh
server_migration     setSOADomainEnv.sh   stopManagedWebLogic.sh
[idam@focusthreaderp bin]$ pwd
/oracle/apps/idam/Middleware/user_projects/domains/base_domain/bin
[idam@focusthreaderp bin]$ ls
nodemanager          service_migration    startManagedWebLogic.sh  stopWebLo
secureWebLogic.sh    setDomainEnv.sh      startWebLogic.sh
server_migration     setSOADomainEnv.sh   stopManagedWebLogic.sh
[idam@focusthreaderp bin]$ ./startWebLogic.sh
***********************************************************
** Setting up SOA specific environment...
***********************************************************
EXTRA_JAVA_PROPERTIES= -da:org.apache.xmlbeans...
```

4. Wait for Admin server to start properly. In Admin server log file at $DOMAIN_HOME/servers/AdminServer/logs/AdminServer.log check server status as **RUNNING mode** and **listening on <IP:port>** as shown in the next screenshot:

```
<Oct 5, 2010 9:46:20 PM BST> <Notice> <Server> <BEA-002613> <Channel "Default[6]
" is now listening on 127.0.0.1:7001 for protocols iiop, t3, ldap, snmp, http.>
<Oct 5, 2010 9:46:20 PM BST> <Notice> <Server> <BEA-002613> <Channel "Default[2]
" is now listening on 172.16.160.1:7001 for protocols iiop, t3, ldap, snmp, http
.>
<Oct 5, 2010 9:46:20 PM BST> <Notice> <Server> <BEA-002613> <Channel "Default[4]
" is now listening on fe80:0:0:0:250:56ff:fec0:1:7001 for protocols iiop, t3, ld
ap, snmp, http.>
<Oct 5, 2010 9:46:20 PM BST> <Notice> <Server> <BEA-002613> <Channel "Default[3]
" is now listening on fe80:0:0:0:21c:f0ff:fe0c:351a:7001 for protocols iiop, t3,
ldap, snmp, http.>
<Oct 5, 2010 9:46:20 PM BST> <Notice> <WebLogicServer> <BEA-000329> <Started Web
Logic Admin Server "AdminServer" for domain "base_domain" running in Production
Mode>
<Oct 5, 2010 9:46:20 PM BST> <Notice> <WebLogicServer> <BEA-000365> <Server stat
e changed to RUNNING>
<Oct 5, 2010 9:46:20 PM BST> <Notice> <WebLogicServer> <BEA-000360> <Server star
ted in RUNNING mode>
```

5. Start WebLogic Managed server (soa_server1, oim_server1 and oam_server1).

   cd $MW_HOME\user_projects\domains\<DOMAIN_NAME>

   Windows: **bin/startManagedWebLogic.cmd <managed_server_name> <admin_url>**

   Unix: **bin\startManagedWebLogic.sh <managed_server_name> <admin_url>**

- ° To Start SOA Suite Managed server:

  Windows: `bin/startManagedWebLogic.cmd soa_server1 http://focusthread:7001`

  Unix: `bin\startManagedWebLogic.sh soa_server1 http://focusthread:7001`

- ° To Start OIM Managed server:

  Windows: `bin/startManagedWebLogic.cmd oim_server1 http://focusthread:7001`

  Unix: `bin\startManagedWebLogic.sh oim_server1 http://focusthread:7001`

- ° To Start OAM Managed server:

  Windows: `bin/startManagedWebLogic.cmd oam_server1 http://focusthread:7001`

  Unix: `bin\startManagedWebLogic.sh oam_server1 http://focusthread:7001`

Stopping default IDAM installation

This section contains steps to stop the default IDAM Installation; that is, Oracle Database, WebLogic Admin Server, and WebLogic Managed Server (`soa_server1`, `oim_server1` and `oam_server1`). The commands in the following section assumes that the `hostname` of the machine is `focusthread`, the `admin server` port is `7001`, the username/password for administrator user is weblogic/welcome1, and the managed server names are `soa_server1`, `oim_server1`, and `oam_server1` respectively.

It is recommended that you create the file `boot.properties` under `$DOMAIN_HOME/servers/<server_name>/security/` so that you don't have to provide username and password manually. This file should contain two lines:

```
USERNAME=<weblogic_user_name>
PASSWORD=<weblogic_user_password>
```

 WebLogic server will encrypt the `boot.properties` file during next start-up.

1. Stop WebLogic Managed Server wls_soa1, wls_oim1, and wls_oam1

   `cd $MW_HOME\user_projects\domains\<DOMAIN_NAME>`

   Windows: `bin/stopManagedWebLogic.cmd <managed_server_name>`
   `<admin_url> <username> <password>`

   Unix: `bin\stopManagedWebLogic.sh <managed_server_name>`
   `<admin_url> <username> <password>`

   a. To Stop SOA Suite Managed server:

      Windows: `bin/stopManagedWebLogic.cmd soa_server1`
      `http://focusthread:7001 weblogic welcome1`

      Unix: `bin\stopManagedWebLogic.sh soa_server1`
      `http://focusthread:7001 weblogic welcome1`

   b. To stop OIM Managed server:

      Windows: `bin/stopManagedWebLogic.cmd oim_server1`
      `http://focusthread:7001 weblogic welcome1`

      Unix: `bin\stopManagedWebLogic.sh oim_server1`
      `http://focusthread:7001 weblogic welcome1`

   c. To stop OAM Managed server:

      Windows: `bin/stopManagedWebLogic.cmd oam_server1`
      `http://focusthread:7001 weblogic welcome1`

      Unix: `bin\stopManagedWebLogic.sh oam_server1`
      `http://focusthread:7001 weblogic welcome1`

    If you do not want to supply username/password during start/stop then use the `boot.properties` file.

2. Stop WebLogic Admin server.

   `cd $MW_HOME\user_projects\domains\<DOMAIN_NAME>`

   Window: `bin/stopWebLogic.cmd`
   Unix: `bin\stopWebLogic.sh`

3. Stop Database and Listener containing IDAM schema.

   a. Set the `ORACLE_HOME`, `ORACLE_SID` and `PATH` (include `$ORACLE_HOME/bin`).

   b. Stop Database Listener and Database as:

      ```
      $ORACLE_HOME/bin/lsnrctl stop
      $ORACLE_HOME/bin/sqlplus "/as sysdba"
      SQL> shutdown immediate
      SQL> exit
      ```

Configure Node Manager

Node Manager is a utility in Oracle WebLogic server which can start, stop, and restart Managed server or Administration server remotely. When Admin Server/Managed server are managed using Node Manager, and if the OS instance is rebooted, WebLogic server (Admin or Managed) returns to the state it was in, prior to reboot (started or stopped). In order for Node Manager to start Managed servers properly, follow these steps:

1. Define Machine for all Managed servers.

   Login to WebLogic server console (`http://serverName:AdminPort` where default Admin server port is `7001`) and check if Machine is defined or not (If not define a Machine) by clicking on **Machines** and then the **New** button:

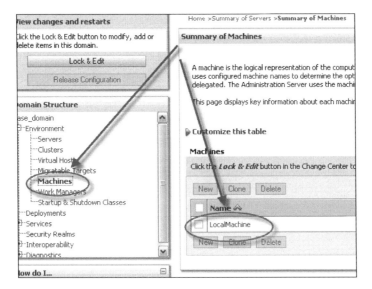

You can use any name for Machine, but the Node Manager IP and the port defined for this machine should be matched with the Node Manager running on the server. For example for machine `LocalMachine` if the Node Manager server name is focusthread and the Node Manager port is 5556 then start the node manager on listen address focusthread and on port 5556.

2. Assign a Machine to a Managed server.

   Log in to WebLogic server console and click on **Servers**. In the right panel click on the server you wish to assign to a Machine (like **oam_server1**, **oim_server1** or **soa_server1**). Select Machine Name from the drop-down menu in front of **Machine**:

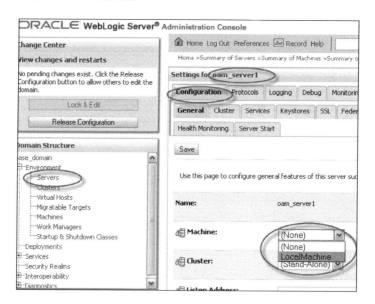

3. Change Node Manager Properties file to use script to start Managed server.

   Node Manager uses the script (`startWebLogic.cmd`/`startWebLogic.sh`) which already has `classpath` configured, to start OIM, OAM, or SOA Managed server. Configure Node Manager to restore servers to their last known state after a reboot or in case of WebLogic server crash by setting the property `CrashRecoveryEnabled`. Change `StartScriptEnabled`, `StopScriptEnabled`, and `CrashRecoveryEnabled` from `false` to `true` in the Node Manager Properties file (`$WL_HOME/common/nodemanager/nodemanager.properties`), then restart Node Manager.

 `Nodemanager.properties` is created when Node Manager is first started.

4. Start Node Manager by running the script or by configuring services (mentioned in the next section):

Windows: `cd $WL_HOME\server\bin`
`startNodeManager.cmd`

Unix: `startNodeManager.sh`

5. Restart Admin server for changes to take effect.

Configure Node Manager as a service

It is recommended to configure Node Manager as a service. This way, it will start automatically after a Server reboot.

Configure Node Manager as a service on Windows

To configure the Node Manager on Windows carry out the following steps:

1. Take a backup of `$WL_HOME\server\bin\installNodeMgrSvc.cmd`, then add `set NODEMGR_HOST=<machineName>` (Replace `<machineName>` with the name of your Windows machine).

 This change is required so that the Node Manager listens on the actual machine IP rather than localhost (127.0.0.1)

2. Run `$WL_HOME\server\bin\installNodeMgrSvc.cmd`. This command will create the Windows service **Oracle WebLogic NodeManager** as shown in the next screenshot:

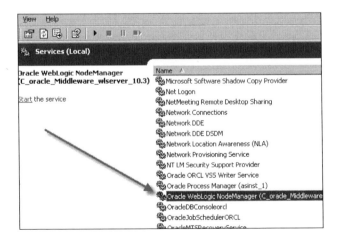

Uninstall Node Manager service from Windows

If you wish to uninstall Node Manager service from Windows:

1. Open command prompt.
2. Set environment variables by running:

    `%WL_HOME%\server\bin\setWLSEnv.cmd`

3. Run service uninstall command:

    `%WL_HOME%\server\bin\uninstallNodeMgrSvc.cmd`

Configure Node Manager as a service on Unix/Linux

WebLogic server does not provide a script to install/uninstall the Node Manager daemon process. Node Manager should be configured as part of start-up process using rc scripts or xinetd service.

To configure Node Manager as an xinetd service, follow Oracle documentation at `http://download.oracle.com/docs/cd/E12839_01/web.1111/e13740/java_nodemgr.htm#i1069394`

To configure the Node Manager to start with Unix using rc script, create a simple shell script that starts Node Manager under `/etc/init.d`. Then create the symbolic link pointing to this shell script from the right run-level folder. For detailed steps, including an example script, follow `http://weblogicserver.blogspot.com/2010/01/node-manager-as-unix-startup-process.html`

You can also refer to the operating system documentation for instructions on creating a service/daemon.

Options to start/stop IDAM

Oracle Identity and Access Management provides various options such as WebLogic Scripting Tool (WLST) commands, Fusion Middleware Control, or WebLogic Administration console to start/stop its components. This section will cover these start-up/shutdown options in detail:

*   Starting and stopping using WLST command line (Admin server and Managed servers)
*   Starting and stopping using Fusion Middleware Control (only Managed servers)
*   Starting and stopping using WebLogic Server Administration console (only Managed servers)

Start/Stop using WLST commands

You can use WLST commands (shown in the section *Starting default IDAM Installation*) to start the Admin server or the Managed server.

- Use the WLST command to start Admin server.

  Windows: `cd $MW_HOME\user_projects\domains\<DOMAIN_NAME> bin/startWebLogic.cmd`

  Unix: `bin\startWebLogic.sh`

- Use the WLST command to start Managed server.

  `cd $MW_HOME\user_projects\domains\<DOMAIN_NAME>`

  Windows: `bin/startManagedWebLogic.cmd <managed_server_name> <admin_url>`

  Unix: `bin\startManagedWebLogic.sh <managed_server_name> <admin_url>`

Start/Stop using Fusion Middleware Control

Oracle Fusion Middleware Control uses Node Manager to start Managed servers (SOA, OIM and OAM). The following conditions should met in order to start/stop a managed server using Fusion Middleware Control.

- Node Manager should be configured to start the Managed server.
- Node Manager should be running.
- Node Manager must be started with property `StartScriptEnabled=true` (Add this in `$WL_HOME/common/nodemanager/nodemanager.properties`).
- Only Managed servers (SOA, OIM & OAM) can be started using Fusion Middleware Control (for Admin server use WLST commands explained in previous section).
- Ensure that the Admin server is up and running.

To stop Identity and Access Management component using Fusion Middleware Control, follow these steps:

1. Log in to FMW Control URL `http://hostname:port/em` (where `port` is `Admin Server` port, the default value being `7001`)

2. From the navigation pane, expand **WebLogic Domain** | [domain name] | [server name].

3. From the right panel, expand the **WebLogic Server** menu, select **Control**, and use **Start Up / Shut Down**.

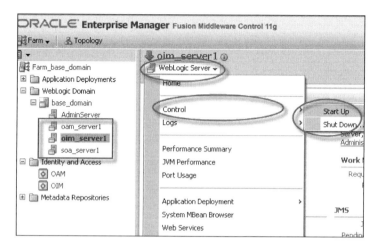

Start/Stop using WebLogic console

Oracle WebLogic console uses Node Manager to start Managed servers (SOA, OIM and OAM). The following conditions should be met in order to start/stop a Managed server using WebLogic console.

- Node Manager should be configured to start the Managed server.
- Node Manager should be running.
- Node Manager must be started with property `StartScriptEnabled=true` (add this in `$WL_HOME/common/nodemanager/nodemanager.properties`).
- Only Managed servers (SOA, OIM & OAM) can be started using WebLogic console.
- Ensure that the Admin server is running.

To start WebLogic Managed servers using the WebLogic console, follow these steps:

1. Login to WebLogic Console `http://hostname:port/em` (where `port` is `Admin Server` port, the default value being `7001`).
2. Click on **Environment | Servers | Control**. Select three managed servers (oam_server1, oim_server1 and soa_server1) and click on **Start**.

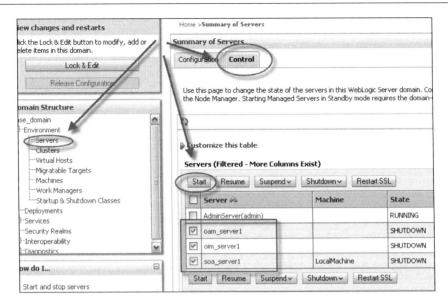

3. To stop running instances select the server that you wish to stop and click on **Shutdown.**

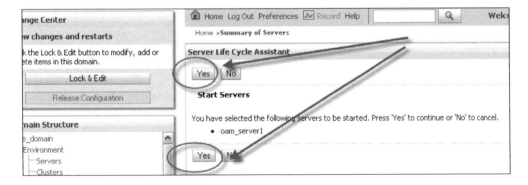

4. Click **Yes** when prompted.

Troubleshooting Start-up

Error 1: If you get an error such as:

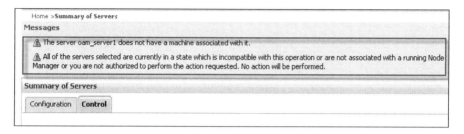

Fix 1: Ensure that you have configured Machines for Managed servers (check the section *Configure Node Manager*).

Error 2: If you get an error such as:

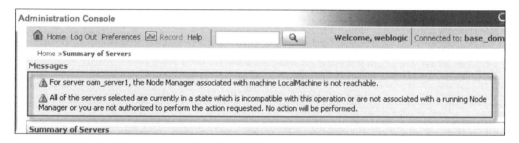

Fix 2: Make sure the Node Manager is up and running.

Things good to know

Note the following points related to starting and stopping of WebLogic server:

1. WebLogic configuration is stored in the XML file `$DOMAIN_HOME/config/config.xml` and contains information such as Admin/Managed server hostname, port, and name of managed server. Check this file to find the information required to start/stop IDAM components.

2. Boot identity file (`boot.properties`) is a text file that contains user credentials for starting and stopping an instance of WebLogic server. For more information on Boot Identity File: `http://download.oracle.com/docs/cd/E12839_01/web.1111/e13708/overview.htm#START128`.

3. Each WebLogic server instance runs in its own JVM. If you are unable to shut down a server instance using the methods described in the previous sections, you can use an operating system command to kill the JVM.

 Killing a java process will do a forceful shutdown of WebLogic server instance.

4. There is no script to stop the Node Manager. If you want to stop the Node Manager use `kill -9 <PID>`

   where `PID` is process ID of Node Manager.

5. If you are using Fusion Middleware Control or WebLogic console to start/stop servers in WebLogic, then Node Manager should be configured and running.

6. WebLogic server log files are located in the following directory: `$DOMAIN_HOME/servers/<servername>/logs`.

Summary

In this chapter we covered command line scripts to start/stop a Identity Management server and various other options to start/stop Identity and Access Management components, such as Fusion Middleware control and WebLogic Console. We also covered using Node Manager to start, stop, and manage servers. In the next chapter we are going to cover Oracle Access Manager administration and navigation.

5

OAM Administration and Navigation

The OAM **Administration console** is a web application running on WebLogic admin server. The console is used to configure the OAM system, which includes adding additional OAM servers, updating server properties, and adding data sources and agents. OAM Administration console is also used to define policy components such as host identifiers, authentication schemes, and application domains.

In this chapter we will cover:

- Accessing OAM Administration console
- Access Manager navigation
- Managing data sources
- Creating OAM server instances
- Registering agents and partner applications using OAM console and Remote Registration Utility (RREG)

Accessing the OA Administration console

As discussed above, OAM Administration console is the web application that runs on WebLogic admin server and is used to configure OAM system properties and policy components. In order to access OAM Administration console, make sure WebLogic's admin server is running. If it isn't, see *Chapter 4, Start-up Shutdown IDAM*).

 OAM Administration Console replaces Policy Manager in OAM 10*g*.

Logging in and out of OAM Administration console

This section describes how to login and logout of OAM Administration console.

1. To login to the console, type the URL `http://servername:port/ oamconsole` where `servername` is the hostname of the server where your WebLogic admin server is running, and `port` is the Admin server port (default is 7001).

 Initially, the LDAP group for the OAM administrator is the same as the LDAP group defined for the WebLogic Server Administration console, that is, *Administrators*.

2. Login with the username/password you created in *Chapter 2*, in the *Configure Identity and Access Management and create WebLogic domain* section.

3. After a successful login, you will land on the **Welcome** page.

4. Click on the **Sign Out** link at the top-right of **Welcome** page to logout from the OAM console.

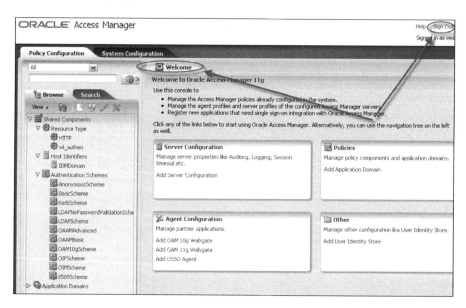

Navigating the OAM Administration console

The OAM Administration console contains two tabs known as **functional-level tabs**, namely Policy Configuration and System Configuration. The **Policy Configuration** tab contains OAM policy model elements such as host identifiers, authentication schemes, and the application domain. The **System Configuration** tab contains elements related to the OAM server configuration such as agents (OAM and OSSO), data sources, and system utilities. Both System Configuration and Policy Configuration tabs are displayed in OAM Administration console in a specific layout.

 To know more about the OAM Policy Model components refer ro *Chapter 6, OAM Policy Component and Single Sign-On.*

The following section covers:

- Console layout
- Policy configuration
- System configuration

Console layout

When you login to OAM console (`http://host:port/oamconsole`), you get the **Welcome** page as shown in the following screenshot:

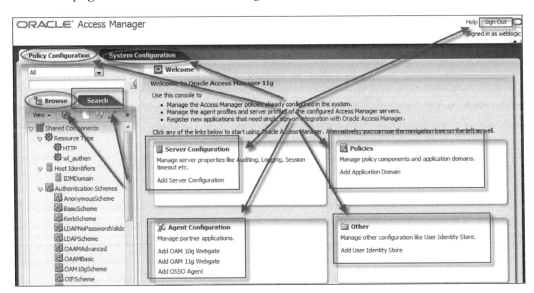

On the **Welcome** page, you get two functional-level tabs Policy Configuration and System Configuration. Under each functional tab there are two sub-tabs **Browse** and **Search**.The **Browse** tab presents a quick-browse view of that specific functional tab. The **Search** tab can be used to search for a specific element within a functional tab.

Just under the **Browse** and **Search** tabs there is a tool bar that contains tools such as view, refresh, create, duplicate, edit, and delete.

Policy configuration

The following screenshot shows OAM Administration console with the **Policy Configuration** tab selected. The search controls appears below the functional-level tabs. The navigation tree for this tab is identified by the **Browse** tab which is located just below the search controls.

Just below the Browse tab, you will see the toolbar (view, add, edit, refresh) to manage policy (application domain and shared component configuration).

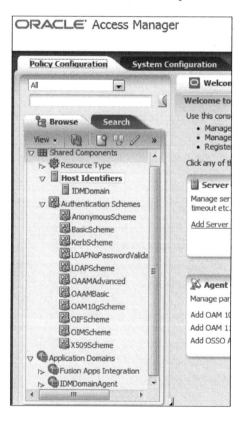

System configuration

The **System configuration** tab is used to manage (create, delete, view, edit) agents, servers, data sources, authentication modules, and system utilities. The following screenshot shows OAM Administration console with the System Configuration tab selected. Search controls appear below the functional-level tabs. The navigation tree for the **System Configuration** tab is identified by the **Browse** tab which is located just below the search controls.

Just below the Browse tab, you will see the tool bar (action, view, refresh, create, edit, delete) which is used to manage the system configuration, that is agents, server instances, data sources, or session management.

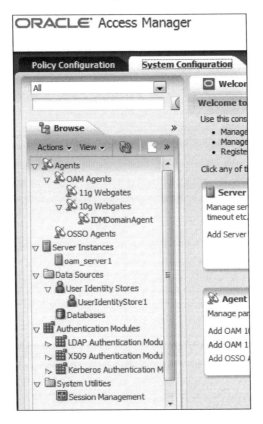

The next screenshot shows the common properties for server `oam_server1` on the right side panel.

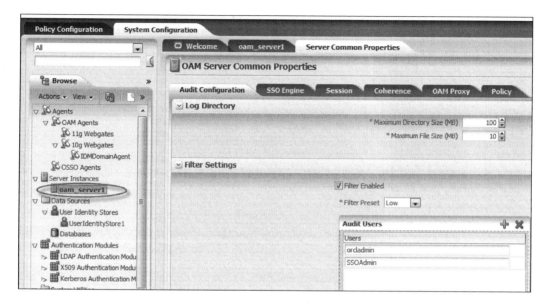

Data sources

OAM uses the following data sources:

- User Identity store
- OAM policy and session data store
- OAM configuration data store
- Security key and Java key store

User Identity store

The **User Identity store** is a centralized LDAP store in which user data and administrators are stored. By default, (`UserIdentityStore1`) for OAM is an embedded LDAP server which comes as part of WebLogic server. This default User Identity store is created by the installer during OAM server installation.

> WebLogic server provides an embedded LDAP server to store WebLogic's users and groups. This is not recommended as OAM's identity store in a production environment; instead, use an enterprise-level embedded LDAP server such as OID, IBM Directory server, or Microsoft Active Directory.

In OAM 11.1.1.3, it is possible to configure multiple identity stores but only one of them (designated as primary identity store) can be used for authentication.

From OAM 11.1.1.5 onwards, multiple identity stores can be used for authentication. Also, there is one identity store set as `System Store`, and one `Default Store`. The store designated as `System Store` contains users and groups for OAM's Access System Administrator role. `Default Store` is used by Oracle Secure Token Service (STS - another product introduced with OAM 11.1.1.5). If you have multiple identity stores configured in OAM 11.1.1.5, then one of them can be set as system store and another one as default identity store, or the same identity store can be set as both system store and default identity store.

This section covers:

- How to access User Identity store?
- How to create User Identity store?
- How to set a User Identity store as Primary?
- Important points for using User Identity Store

How to access User Identity Store?

To access the User Identity store in 11.1.1.3, login to the OAM Administration console. Select the **System Configuration** tab. Expand **Data Sources | User Identity Stores**.

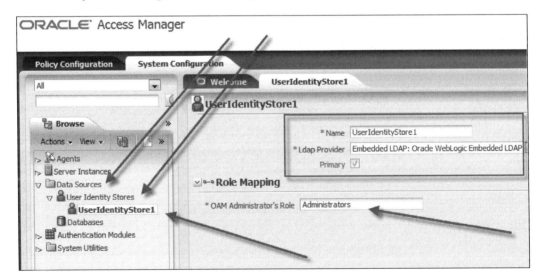

To access the User Identity store in 11.1.1.5, login to the OAM Administration console. Select the **System Configuration** tab. Select **Common Configuration** and expand **Data Sources | User Identity Stores**.

How to create User Identity Store?

To create a new User Identity store from OAM Administration console, follow these steps:

1. Login to the OAM Administration console. Select the **System Configuration** tab. Expand **Data Sources | User Identity Stores.** From **Browse**, click on the **Actions** drop-down menu and click on **Create**.

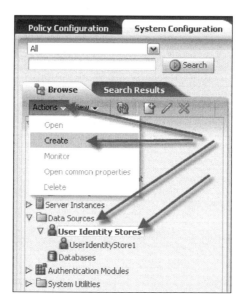

2. On the right-hand panel enter a name for your new User Identity store. From the **LDAP Provider** select the LDAP server where your users are stored such as OID, AD, OVD, or IPlanet as shown in the next screenshot.

> For a list of LDAP servers certified to work with OAM, refer to the certification matrix: http://www.oracle.com/technetwork/middleware/id-mgmt/identity-accessmgmt-11gr1certmatrix-161244.xls.

3. In **Role Mapping** select the role which will define the OAM Administrator's role. Default value is Administrators.

A user who is a member of a group mapped to OAM's administrator role should be used to login to OAM console or utility such as RREG (Remote Registration).

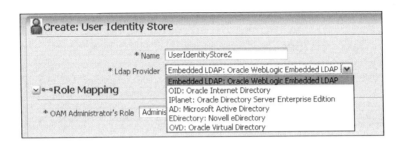

4. Enter LDAP provider details such as:

   ° **LDAP URL**: The LDAP server URL where users are stored. Enter a value in the format `ldap://<ldapserver>:<ldapport>` (Replace `ldap` with `ldaps//` for LDAP servers running on SSL and use SSL port for `ldapport`).

   ° **Principal**: The LDAP server user used to connect to LDAP server.

   ° **Credential**: The password used to connect to the LDAP server.

   ° **User Search Base**: The top level container under which OAM server can search for users.

   ° **Group Search Base**: The top level container under which OAM server can search for groups.

   ° **User Name Attribute**: OAM will compare the username with this attribute of the user in the LDAP server, and will compare the password with `userPassword` attribute of LDAP server. If these two match then authentication is considered successful by OAM.

5. Click on **Test Connection** to test if connection is successful. You should get a message that says **Connection to the User Identity Store successful!**.

If the connection fails then check whether the LDAP server and port are correct and running. If there is a firewall between the OAM server and the LDAP server then check the LDAP port (3060 in above example) is open across the firewall. Ensure that the data defined in Principal, User/Group Search Base is correct.

6. Click on **Apply** to save changes.

How to set a User Identity Store as Primary?

To set a particular User Identity (UI) store as your primary identity store:

Login to the OAM console. Select the **System Configuration** tab. Expand **Data Sources | User Identity Stores**. Select the UI store that you want to set as primary.

Only one UI store can be set as primary at any given time in version 11.1.1.3.

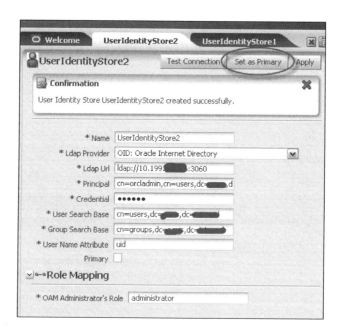

Important points when using stores

Important points when working with UI stores are:

1. It is possible to configure multiple UI stores in OAM.

2. Only one identity store can be set as the primary UI store at any time.

3. In OAM 11.1.1.3, only the primary UI store can be used to authenticate users attempting to access an OAM-protected resource. From OAM 11.1.1.5 onwards, multiple identity stores can be used to authenticate users attempting to access an OAM-protected resource.

4. In OAM 11.1.1.3, only the primary UI store can be used to authenticate administrators signing to OAM Administration console or any administrative commands for OAM 11*g* in WLST. From OAM 11.1.1.5 onwards, an identity store designated as **system store** is used to store OAM Administration console users).

5. OAM administrators can view, modify, register, or delete UI stores using either OAM Administration console or custom WLST commands.

6. UI store is referenced in authentication modules, which are used in authentication schemes.

OAM policy and session data store

OAM policy data includes authentication modules, authentication and authorization policies, application domains, and rules to protect application. OAM policy data is stored in a database under schema created using Repository Creation Utility (RCU) (See *Chapter 2*, *Run Repository Creation Utility to create Schemas*).

Session data store is distributed in in-memory storage, and contains details about logged-in users. This distributed in-memory session store can be backed up by storing session data in a database. This provides scalability and fault-tolerance.

When you install OAM with *Database Policy Store* template (as shown in the following screenshot) during WebLogic domain creation, it automatically prepares the database to store OAM 11*g* policy and session data.

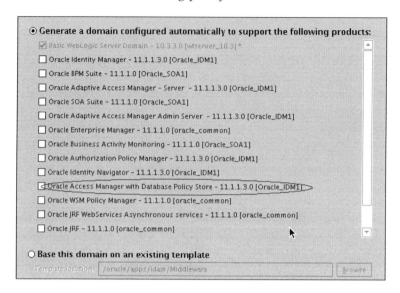

 OAM policy store and session data store can be in a single database or two different databases.

OAM configuration data store

OAM configuration contains all OAM-related system configuration data (such as any UI store added earlier in this chapter). It is contained in an XML file (`oam-config.xml`) stored under $DOMAIN_HOME/config/fmwconfig.

 Do not update `oam-config.xml` directly; use OAM console for any system configuration changes. In high-availability deployments, if the domain directory is not shared across nodes then there is one `oam-config.xml` per server, the files being synchronized on all nodes automatically by WebLogic's Admin server.

Security key and Java key store

OAM agents communicate with the OAM server to determine any (security) policy defined for a given web resource and session information. The data communicated between agents and OAM server is encrypted. OAM uses cryptographic security keys to encrypt this agent traffic and session tokens between the agent and the OAM server. These keys are stored in WebLogic's credential stores in Java Key Store (JKS) format. The store where these keys are stored is also known as **OAM Key Store**.

 OAM Key Store is not available through any console and cannot be viewed or modified.

OAM server registration

When you install OAM server (as shown in *Chapter 2*), it automatically registers the WebLogic Managed server (`oam_server1`) as an OAM Server instance.

To check registered OAM Server instances, login to the OAM console `http://server:port/oamconsole` (default OAM Console port is 7001). Select **System Configuration tab | Server Instances**.

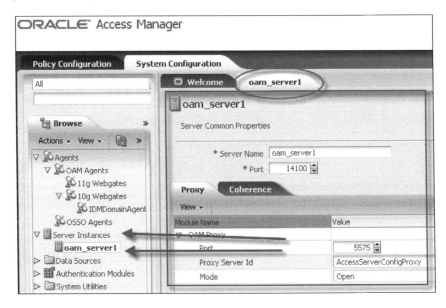

How to add OAM Server Instance?

Multiple OAM servers can be installed and configured under the same WebLogic server domain. These multiple OAM servers can be configured as primary-primary or primary-secondary clusters (to provide resilience and capacity). To add another OAM Server instance to the existing domain with an existing OAM server, follow these steps:

1. Create a new Managed server in WebLogic domain. This can be done either using the WebLogic Scripting Tool (WLST) or using the WebLogic server administration console `http://server:port/oamconsole` (default OAM Console port is 7001). Expand **Environment | Servers**. Click on the **New** button.

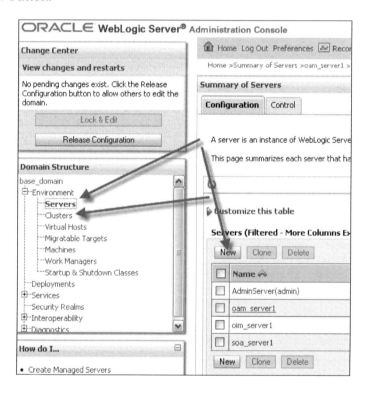

2. After clicking on **New**, enter details of the new OAM server (name, listen port/address) as shown in the following screenshot:

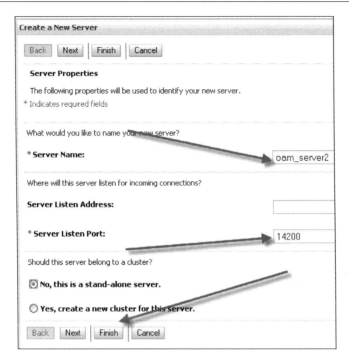

 The port number under Server Listen Port should not be used by any other process on the server. If this port is less than 1024 then an additional step is required on the WebLogic server.

3. On clicking **Finish**, you will see a screen similar to the following screenshot where you can validate the OAM server name and port number.

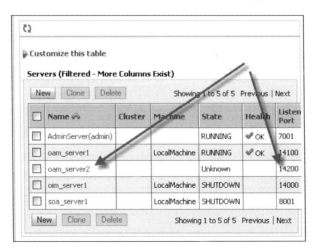

4. Next apply the Oracle Java Required Files (JRF) template. Login to Fusion Middleware Control `http://server:port/em` (default FMW Control port is 7001).

5. Go to **Farm**_<domain_name> | **WebLogic Domain** | <domain_name>. Select the Managed server that was created above (`oam_server2`) and click on **Apply JRF Template**.

The JRF consists of those components not included in default WebLogic server that provide common functionality for OAM/OIM server. JRF files are stored under the `oracle_common` directory (`ORACLE_COMMON_HOME`) under Middleware Home (`MW_HOME`). In the above step, you are attaching JRF files required by OAM server to WebLogic Managed server `oam_server2`.

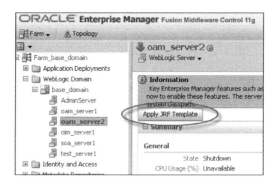

6. Register OAM server instance:

   Login to the OAM server console. Select the **Configuration** tab. Click on **Server Instances**, and from the **Actions** drop-down menu, select **Create**.

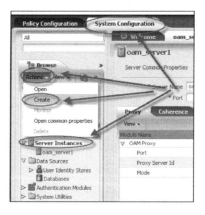

7. Enter details and click on **Apply**.

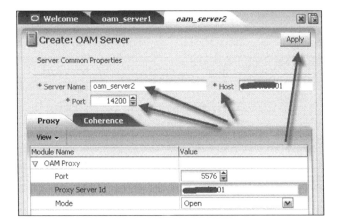

 If you are creating a second OAM server on the same machine, use different OAM-Proxy port than was used by the first OAM server. (In the previous screenshot, **OAM Proxy** port can be seen under the Proxy tab.). After adding the second server, go to **Agents registered** and add it as your primary or secondary OAM server.

Registering OAM agents

OAM agents, also known as **policy-enforcement agents**, act as a filter for HTTP requests. These agents are installed at the web server/apps server level and there are different agents for each web/app server such as OHS, IIS, and EBS for Apache. If there are no pre-built agents available for your App server, then custom agents, known as **AccessGate** can be developed. Agents are of the following types:

1. OAM agents:
   ◦ OAM 11*g* WebGates
   ◦ OAM 10*g* WebGates

2. OSSO agents:
   ◦ mod_osso agent

3. AccessGates:

   These are custom WebGates created using OAM Software Development Kit (SDK)

4. IDMDomainAgent/IAMSuite:

    IDM Domain Agent (11.1.1.3) and IAMSuite (11.1.1.5) provides single sign-on functionality for IDM Administration console.

These agents must be registered with OAM server in order to communicate with it, and to check for any authentication/authorization policy configured when users access a protected resource.

 Registering an agent is also known as registering a partner application or registering a partner application with OAM.

There are two ways to register agents:

1. Registering agents using Administration console
2. Registering agents using command line via the **remote registration tool**

 IDMDomainAgent (in 11.1.1.3) and IAMSuite (11.1.1.5) are registered automatically during OAM installation/ configuration phase.

What happens when registering agent with OAM server

When you register an agent with OAM server (either from Administration console or using the remote registration tool), the following actions take place behind the scenes:

1. One secret key is generated per agent. On the agent machine this key is stored on a local wallet file, whereas on OAM server it is stored in the Java key store.

2. An OAM application domain (**OAM Console | Policy Configuration | Application Domains**) is created with the same name as the agent, and with default authentication and authorization policies.

3. On registering agents using the OAM console, a new directory is created for each agent on the machine hosting the OAM Administration server console (WebLogic Admin server) at $DOMAIN_HOME/output/<Agent_Name>. Copy the generated files from this directory to the agent machines at $WEB_GATE_INSTALL_DIR/webgate/config (for OAM 10*g* & 11*g* WebGate) and $ORACLE_OHS_CONFIG_DIR/osso/ (for the OSSO agent).

4. On the OAM server, a new entry is added in `oam-config.xml` for newly registered agent.

5. On the OAM server, a new entry is added in `oam-policy.xml` for the application domain that is to be protected.

Registering agents using the Administration console

Login to OAM console `http://hostname:port/oamconsole` (where default OAM console port is 7001). Go to **System Configuration**. Select the agent you wish to create (11*g* WebGate, 10*g* WebGate, or OSSO Agent) and from the **Actions** drop-down menu bar, select **Create**.

 10*g* WebGates were initially released for 10*g* OAM server and are available for all standard Web servers such as OHS, HIS, Apache, and IIS. Currently 11*g* WebGate is available only for OHS 11*g*. 10*g* WebGates are compatible with both 10*g* and 11*g* OAM server. WebGates, both 10*g* and 11*g* under OAM 11*g* terminology are also known as **agents**. You may see agents and WebGate used interchangeably in this book and also in Oracle Documentation.

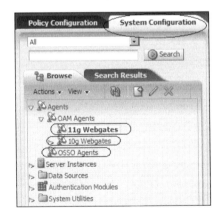

Registering 11*g*/10*g* WebGates using the Administration console

To create OAM agents (10*g*/11*g* WebGate) using the OAM Administration console, follow the given steps:

1. Login to the OAM Administration console and select **System Configuration**.

2.   Select the appropriate OAM agent (11*g* WebGates or 10*g* WebGates) and click the **Create** button on the tool bar.

3.   **Name** is the identifying name of the WebGate agent.

4.   **Base URL** contains the hostname and the port of the computer hosting the web server for which this agent is being installed

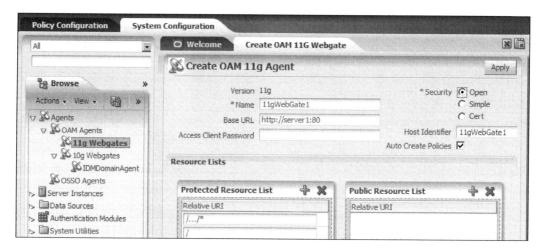

5.   Click on **Apply** to save the agent.

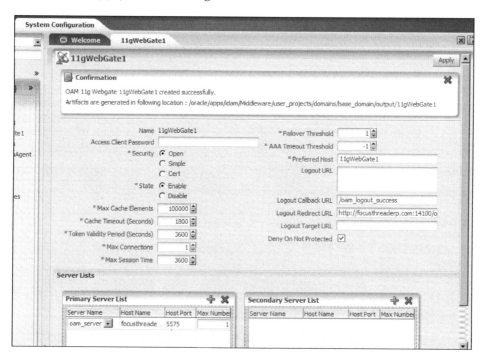

For more information on the parameters mentioned in the 11*g*
WebGate configuration page that is shown in the previous
screenshot, check *Chapter 8, Installing and Configuring OAM Agents.*

6. You will get a confirmation message stating **OAM 11***g* **WebGate**
   <NameofWebGate> **modified successfully**, where <NameofWebGate>
   is the Application domain.

To Create OSSO agents using the OAM Administration console, follow these steps:

1. Login to OAM Administration console and select **System Configuration**.

2. Select the appropriate OSSO agent and click on the **Create** button which is on
   the tool bar.

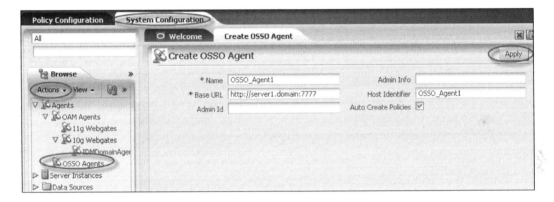

3. Enter the agent name and base URL, and click on **Apply** to save changes.

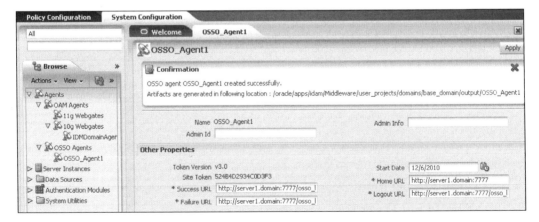

For more information on the parameters mentioned in SSO agent configuration page mentioned above, check *Chapter 8, Installing and Configuring OAM Agents.*

4. You will get a confirmation message saying **OSSO Agent created successfully**.

Registering agents remotely using the command line

Apart from a graphical user interface (the OAM console), OAM also a provides command-line utility for agent registration. This process is also known as **remote registration**. Remote Registration utility (RREG) can be run in one of two modes, either **in-band** registration or **out-of-band** registration. One utility for Remote Registration, **oamreg** (oamreg.bat | oamreg.sh) is available under $ORACLE_HOME/oam/server/rreg.

Remote Registration utility usage

Usage:./oamreg.sh <mode> <input> [prompt_flag] [fusion_configuration_file]

where:

<mode> value: [inband/outofband/validate]

<input> value: Relative path (with respect to OAM_REG_HOME) of Request.xml file. Preferred location: <OAM_REG_HOME>/input/Request.xml

In-band mode example: ./bin/oamreg.sh inband input/Request.xml

Out-of-band request mode example: ./bin/oamreg.sh outofband input/Request.xml

Out-of-band response mode: ./bin/oamreg.sh outofband input/Response.xml

validate mode: ./bin/oamreg.sh validate agentname

This tool can be run in two modes:

- **In-band registration**: Used in a scenario where the web servers on which the agent is installed/configured and the OAM server are managed by the same team or administrator.

- **Out-of-band registration**: Used where the OAM and agent web server are managed by different administrators. Web server administrators generate a response file and submit it to the OAM server administrator. The OAM server administrator then generates a response file using a request file and returns the results to the web server administrator. The web server administrator then runs remote registration utility in out-of-band mode (using response file) to register.

In-band registration

In this mode both the OAM server and web servers (on which OAM agents are installed) are managed by the same administrators. The process of in-band registration is as follows:

1. Download the RREG (`RREG.tar.gz`) from the OAM server `$ORACLE_HOME/oam/server/rreg/client` to the server on which the agent is installed.

2. Untar `RREG.tar.gz` to a suitable location on server hosting the agent.

3. In the `oamreg` script set `OAM_REG_HOME` (pointing to the directory where you have unzipped `RREG.tar`) and `JDK_HOME` (pointing to the Java 1.6 location on the server hosting the OAM agent).

4. Modify `$OAM_REG_HOME/rreg/input/OAMRequest_short.xml` and update values for `serverAddress`, `hostIdentifier`, `agentName`, and `primaryCookieDomain`.

 OAMRequest.xml and OAMRequest_short.xml are sample request files for OAM 10*g* agents; OAM11GRequest_short.xml and OAM11GRequest.xml are for 11g WebGate, and OSSORequest.xml is for OSSO agent.

5. Run the RREG script:

   Linux:

   ```
   $OAM_REG_HOME/rreg/bin/oamreg.sh inband input/OAMRequest_short.xml
   ```

   Windows:

   ```
   %OAM_REG_HOME%\rreg\bi\/oamreg.bat inband input\
     OAMRequest_short.xml
   ```

6. When prompted to **Enter your agent username**, enter a user who is a member of the group that is mapped against the OAM administrator's role in the primary user-identity store (default role is `Administrators` and user is `weblogic`).

7. Select **n** when prompted with:

   Do you want to enter a Webgate password?(y/n)

   Do you want to import an URIs file?(y/n)

8. On successful in-band registration you should get a message saying **Inband registration process completed successfully! Output artifacts are created in the output folder.**

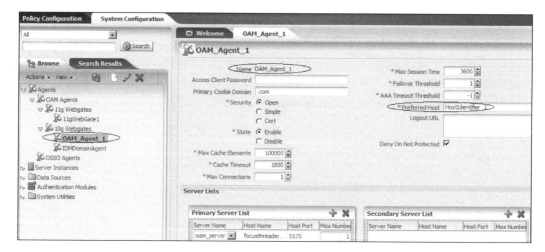

9. Login to the OAM console and verify the OAM agent from the **System Configuration** tab.

Out-of-band registration

In this mode, web servers (on which OAM agents are installed) are managed by different administrators. In out-of-band registration, administrators for these web servers must submit registration request (a **request file**) to the OAM server administrator. After processing the registration request, OAM administrators return a **response file** to the web server administrators, who use it to configure the environment.

The out-of-band registration process is as follows:

1. Download the RREG (RREG.tar.gz) from the OAM server $ORACLE_HOME/ oam/server/rreg/client to your server on which OAM agent is installed.

2. Untar RREG.tar.gz to any location (such as /tmp or any other directory of your choice) on the server hosting the OAM agent.

3. In the oamreg script set OAM_REG_HOME (pointing to the directory where you have unzipped RREG.tar) and JDK_HOME (pointing to the location of Java 1.6 on the server hosting the OAM Agent).

4. The agent server administrators create a request file for the agent using the sample file $OAM_REG_HOME/rreg/input/XXXXXX.xml and submit it to the OAM server administrator.

5. The OAM administrator uses the submitted request file, generates a response file, and returns response file to the agent server administrator.

    Linux:

    ```
    $OAM_REG_HOME/rreg/bin/oamreg.sh outofband input/
      <request_file>.xml
    ```

    Windows:

    ```
    %OAM_REG_HOME%\rreg\bi\/oamreg.bat outofband input\
      <request_file>.xml
    ```

6. When prompted to **Enter your agent username**, enter a user who is a member of the group that is mapped against the OAM administrator's role in the primary UI store (default role is Administrators and user is weblogic).

7. Select **n** when prompted with:
   - ○ **Do you want to enter a Webgate password?(y/n)**
   - ○ **Do you want to import an URIs file?(y/n)**

8. On successful execution of the RREG tool you should get a message saying **Outofband registration (Part 1) completed successfully! Response.xml file is created in input folder.**

```
Enter agent password:                               Do you want to enter a Webgate
password?(y/n):
n
Do you want to import an URIs file?(y/n):
n


--------------------------------------------
Request summary:
OAM Agent Name:OAM_Agent_2
URL String:HostIdentifier_2
Registering in Mode:outofband
Your registration request is being been sent to the Admin server at: http://focu
sthreaderp:7001
--------------------------------------------

Outofband registration (Part 1) completed successfully! Response.xml file is cre
ated in input folder.
[idam@focusthreaderp bin]$
```

9. On the agent server, register the agent using the `<Agent_Name>_Response.xml` file using:

   Linux:

   ```
   $OAM_REG_HOME/rreg/bin/oamreg.sh outofband
   input/<agent_name>_Response.xml
   ```

   Windows:

   ```
   %OAM_REG_HOME%\rreg\bi\/oamreg.bat outofband
   input\<agent_name>_Response.xml
   ```

10. On successful execution of RREG tool using the response file, you should get a message saying **Outofband registration (Part 2) completed successfully! Output artifacts are created in the output folder.**

```
dleware/Oracle_WT1/RREG/rreg/lib/utilities.jar:.
OAM_REG_HOME=/oracle/apps/idam/Middleware/Oracle_WT1/RREG/rreg
------------------------------------------------------------
Welcome to OAM Remote Registration Tool!
Parameters passed to the registration tool are:
Mode: outofband
Filename: /oracle/apps/idam/Middleware/Oracle_WT1/RREG/rreg/input/OAM_Agent_2_Re
sponse.xml
Outofband registration (Part 2) completed successfully! Output artifacts are cre
ated in the output folder.
[idam@focusthreaderp bin]$ 
```

11. Log in to the OAM console and verify the OAM agent from the **System Configuration** tab.

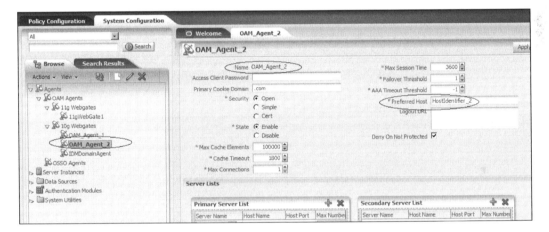

Summary

In this chapter we covered logging in to the OAM Administration console and accessing the **Policy and Configuration** tab. We also discussed various data sources in tOAM, including the creation of user data stores. We then covered steps on how to register new OAM server instances using the OAM console. We finally discussed agents for OAM, registering agents using OAM console, and using the RREG tool.

In the next chapter we are going to cover Policy Model in OAM including domain, resources, policies, authentication/authorization schemes, identifiers and Single Sign-On with OAM.

6

OAM Policy Component and Single Sign-On

The primary function of Oracle Access Manager (OAM) is to provide an access management service (authentication and authorization) including Single Sign-On (SSO) features to all applications protected by OAM. This chapter covers the building blocks of OAM policies and their definition. OAM's Policy component will be followed by SSO flow, cookies, and properties of the SSO engine. Finally, you will see steps to define an application domain. Topics covered in this chapter include:

- OAM policy model components
- Application domain, authentication/authorization schemes, and resources
- Shared components of policy model such as host identifiers, resource types, and authentication schemes
- SSO request flow and cookies
- Example of creating an application domain

Terminology

In this section, we will cover the following OAM's policy components:

- Application domain
- Resources
- Resource type
- Host identifier
- Authentication modules

- Authentication schemes
- Authentication policy
- Authentication policy response
- Authorization policy
- Authorization policy response
- Authorization constraints
- OAM Cookies: OAMAuthnCookie, ObSSOCookie, OAM_REQ, and mod_osso

Application domain

The **application domain** is a logical container for resources and their associated authentication and authorization policies, which dictate who can access these resources. It is the top-level construct of the OAM 11*g* policy model. Application domain is accessible via the OAM Administration console under the **Policy Configuration** tab, as shown in the following screenshot:

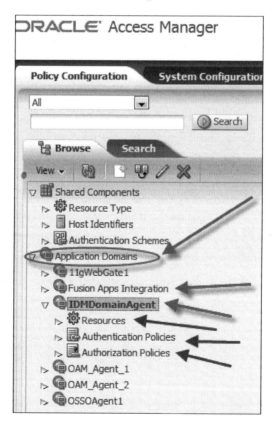

An application domain with basic authentication and authorization policy is automatically created during OAM agent registration. The name of this domain is the same as that of the agent. In the previous screenshot, two application domains **Fusion Apps Integration** and **IDMDomainAgent** are automatically created during OAM installation, whereas others are created during OAM agent registration (as discussed in *Chapter 5, OAM Administration and Navigation*). You can optionally create additional application domains using the OAM Administration console.

Application domains do not have any hierarchical relationship with one another. Each application domain has a unique name. Each application domain can have one or more resources, authentication policies, and authorization policies.

 In OAM 10*g*, the application domain is called the policy domain.

The automatic application domain creation process also creates a **Protected Resource policy** and **Public Resource policy**. Administrators can modify the application domain to add more resources, policies, responses, and authorization constraints.

 Each resource can be protected by only a single authentication policy and single authorization policy.

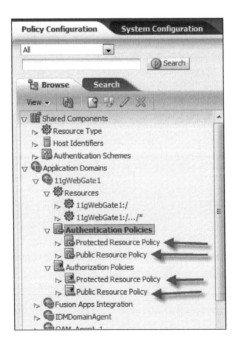

Resource type

A resource is a document, entity, or content stored on the server, which is available to users. Each resource in OAM has a **resource type** that describes the kind of resource to be protected. Each resource has one and only one resource type; a resource type can be assigned to multiple resources. Two resource types, namely **HTTP** and **wl_authen** are automatically created during OAM installation. From OAM 11.1.1.5 onwards, a third resource type **TokenServiceRP** is added for resources representing Token Service Relying Party services. Resource type definitions are organized under Shared components in the **Policy Configuration** tab of the OAM Administration console.

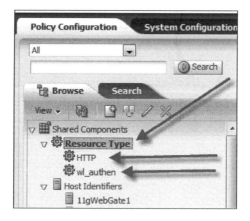

When adding resource to an application domain, a resource type must be selected from a pre-defined list. The resource type **HTTP** is used for resources accessed by HTTP and HTTPS protocols. **wl_authen** can be used with resources deployed in a WebLogic container.

 The name of a resource type cannot match with an existing host identifier and vice versa.

Creating a resource type

Login to the OAM Administration console and select **Policy Configuration**. Then select **Resource Type** under **Shared Components** and click on **Create** button. On the the right-hand panel enter the name and description of the new Resource type and then click on **Apply**.

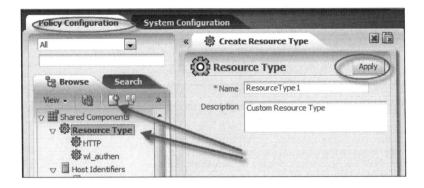

Deleting a resource type

Login to the OAM Administration console and select **Policy Configuration**. Under **Resource Type**, select the name of the resource type
you wish to delete and then click on the **Delete** button.

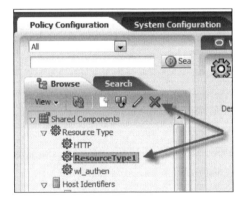

 You cannot remove default resource types **HTTP** and **wl_authen**. If the resource type is in use by one or more resources then it can't be deleted.

Host identifier

A resource hosted on the web server can be accessed by different names, for example, **internal.companyportal.com** is the URL used by employees—which points to a load-balanced proxy, so a request to this URL is actually forwarded to one of several servers hosting the web application. Externally, the same application can be accessed by suppliers with the URL **external.companyportal.com**. The application can also be accessed directly with the URL **server01.companyportal.com**, which is a single machine hosting a web application.

All these various URLs that help access one application are grouped together into the **host identifier**. Host identifiers are created automatically during agent registration or can be created manually using the OAM Administration console. Host identifiers are used while defining HTTP/HTTPS type resources in the application domain.

Creating a host identifier

To manually create a Host Identifier:

1. Login to the OAM Administration console, then from the **Policy Configuration** tab under **Shared Components** select **Host Identifiers**, then click on the **Create** button.

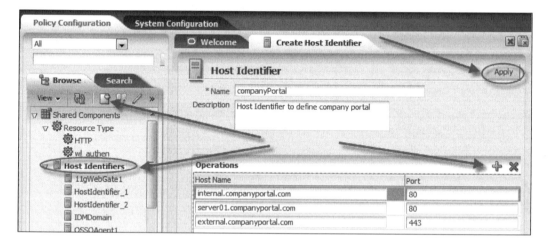

2. Type the name and description of the host identifier and click on the **+** button next to **Operations** to add all the host name: port combinations with which a HTTP/HTTPS resource can be accessed. Click on **Apply** to save.

   ○ **Name**: A unique name to define the host identifier

   ○ **Description**: Optional field that explains the use of the host identifier

   ○ **Operations**: <hostname>:<port> combinations that users might use when accessing the application

 All hostname:port combinations must be unique across all host identifier definitions.

Deleting a host identifier

Each resource of type HTTP/HTTPS in an application domain is associated with a specific host identifier. A deleted host identifier cannot be referenced in any of the resource definitions.

To delete a Host Identifier:

1. Login to the OAM Administration console and from the **Policy Configuration** tab, select **Host Identifiers** in **Shared Components**.

2. Select the name of the host identifier to be deleted and click on the **Delete** button on the toolbar.

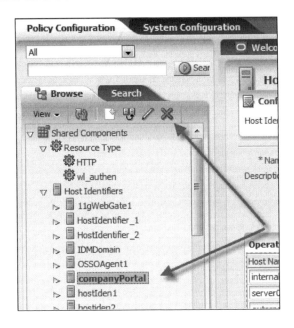

Resources

A **resource** is a document, entity, or content stored on the server that is available to users. Users/Clients access the resource using a particular protocol (for example, HTTP, HTTPS, WebDAV) that is defined by the resource type. Resources are defined within an application domain by using the OAM Administration console.

When the OAM agent is registered, it automatically creates an application domain and two resources, / and /.../*, are also created.

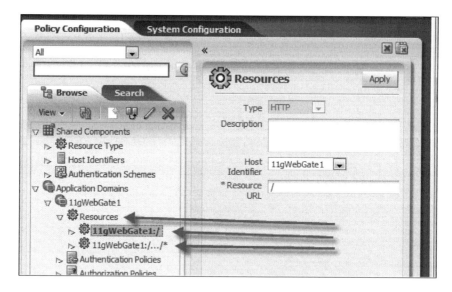

Only resources defined within an application domain can be associated with policies defined for that domain.

Each resource must be unique across application domains.

Authentication modules

Authentication modules are the smallest executable unit of an authentication scheme. Multiple modules are used to create an authentication scheme and are defined under the **System Configuration** tab. Authentication modules come in three pre-configured types, namely LDAP, X509, and Kerberos. New authentication modules can be created from one of these types.

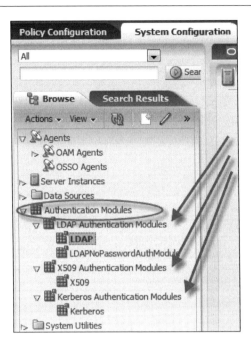

Apart from the authentication modules defined previously, OAM also provides two additional authentication modules, namely, delegate authentication protocol (DAP) and AnonymousModule, which are available to use in the authentication scheme.

- **DAP** used to delegate authentication to a third party such as Oracle Identity Federation (OIF). This module is used in OIFScheme authentication scheme.

- **AnonymousModule** is used in schemes, which allows users to access URLs that you do not want to protect.

Creating a new authentication module

To create a new authentication module, login to the OAM Administration console. Select the **System Configuration** tab and expand **Authentication Modules**. Select the desired module type and click on the **Create** button on the toolbar.

 Authentication modules and schemes are shared components, which can be used across any application domain configured in the OAM server.

Add details of the new authentication module and click on **Apply**.

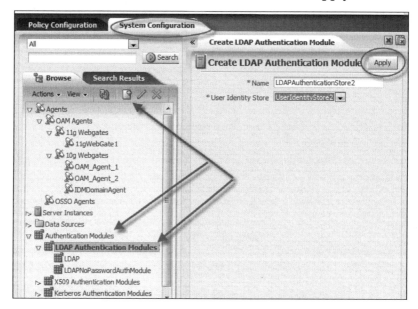

LDAP authentication module details:

- **Name**: Unique name to identify the authentication module.
- **User Identity Store**: The primary UI store that contains the user's credentials required for authentication by this module. LDAP store must be registered with OAM to appear in this list.

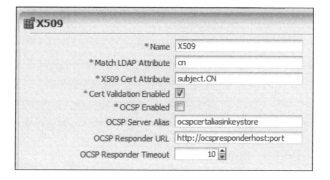

X509 authentication module details:

- **Name**: Unique name to identify the authentication module.
- **Match LDAP Attribute**: Defines the LDAP distinguished name attribute to be used.

- **X509 Cert Attribute**: Defines the certificate attribute to be used to bind the public key.

- **Cert Validation Enabled**: Enables/disables X509 certificate validation.

- **OCSP Enabled**: Enables/disables the Online Certificate Status protocol (OCSP).

- **OCSP Server Alias**: An aliased name for the OCSP responder.

- **OCSP Responder URL**: Provides the URL of the OCSP responder.

- **OCSP Responder Timeout**: Specifies the grace period for users with expired certificates, which enables them to access OAM servers for a limited time before renewing the certificate.

 OCSP Server Alias, **OCSP Responder URL**, and **OCSP Responder Timeout** are required only if **OCSP Enabled** is checked.

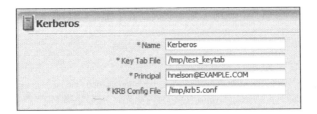

Kerberos authentication module details:

- **Name**: Unique name to identify the authentication module.

- **Key Tab File**: The full pathname to the encrypted, local, on-disk copy of the host's key, required to authenticate to the key distribution center (KDC).

- **Principal**: Identifies the HTTP host for the principal in the Kerberos database, which enables generation of a `keytab` for a host.

- **KRB Config File**: Identifies the path to the configuration file that controls certain aspects of the Kerberos installation. A `krb5.conf` file must exist in the `/etc` directory on each UNIX node that is running Kerberos.

 Change Kerberos `keytab` and `config` file location to a location other than `/tmp`. Location `/tmp` is used only as an example in the previous screenshot.

Deleting a new authentication module

To delete a new authentication module, log in to the OAM Administration console, select the **System Configuration** tab, and expand **Authentication Modules**. Select the authentication module from the desired module type and click the **Delete** button on the toolbar.

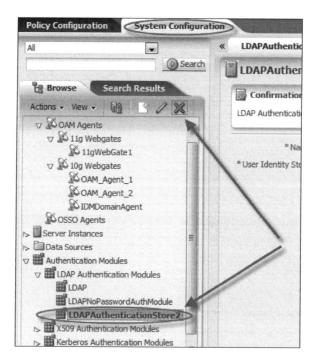

Policy (authentication/authorization) response

Policy response defines the action that must be fulfilled after successful authentication/authorization. Information such as mail, uid, and firstname can be inserted into the session, which can then be used by the application (such as OBIEE, UCM or E-Business Suite) that is using OAM for authentication. OAM administrators can also set URL redirection on success or failure. Authentication responses are set at authentication policy level. OAM supports three types of responses, namely header, session, and cookie.

- **Header**: Sets an HTTP request header for downstream applications using the defined value.

- **Session**: Sets an attribute inside user session, based on defined session variable name and value.

- **Cookie**: Sets a variable name and value (typically set by web agents) inside the authentication session cookie.

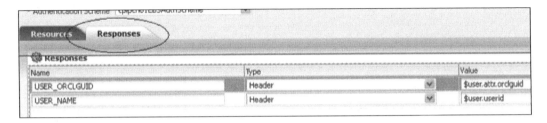

In the previous example, two variables USER_ORCLGUID and USER_NAME of type Header are populated from the orclguid and userid attribute of the authenticated user. These two variables can now be used by the applications integrated with OAM.

Authentication schemes

An **authentication scheme** defines the challenge mechanism, level of trust, and authentication module required to authenticate a user. They are defined globally and can be referenced in authentication policies. OAM comes with some pre-configured authentication schemes and is arranged under **Shared Components** in the **Policy Configuration** tab of the OAM Administration console. Authentication schemes are used in defining authentication policy, which is in turn used to protect the resource defined in the application domain.

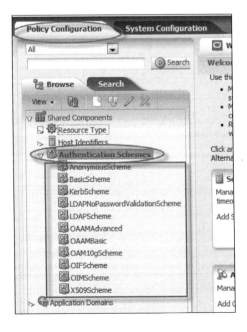

All authentication schemes include same elements such as name, description, authentication level, challenge method, authentication module, and so on. The following screenshot shows the LDAP scheme, which is the default authentication scheme.

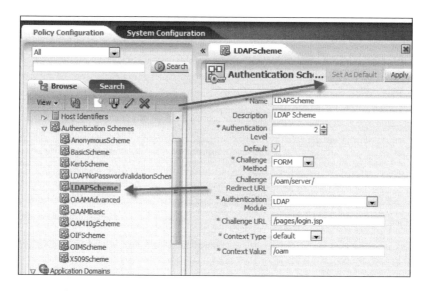

- **Name**: Unique name to identify authentication scheme.

- **Description**: Field to explain the use of this scheme.

- **Authentication Level**: This is the trust level of this authentication scheme. Trust level is expressed as an integer value between 0 (no trust) and 99 (highest level of trust).

- **Default**: This checkbox is enabled for authentication schemes that are not set as default. Only **one** scheme can be set to default. To set another authentication scheme as default, select the scheme (for example, **OAM10gScheme**) and then click on the **Set As Default** button.

- **Challenge Method**: This is the drop-down menu from which one method should be selected from **FORM, BASIC (LDAP), X509 (Certificate), WNA (Windows Native Authentication), NONE, DAP,** or **OAM 10g**. This setting determines the authentication module to be used in the authentication scheme.

- **Challenge Redirect URL**: When a user accesses a protected resource URL, the user is redirected to a server specified in this field. If the authentication challenge is processed by another host, then the name of that host must be defined to be available in the host identifiers list.

- **Authentication Module**: This is the pre-configured authentication module to be used to challenge the user for credentials. The chosen module is based on the challenge method.

- **Challenge URL**: This is the URL the credential collector will redirect to, for credential collection.

- **Context Type**: This is used to build the final URL of the credential collector based on the values `default`, `customWar`, `customHTML`, or `external`. `customWar` and `external` context types require logic within the custom login page to perform the following two tasks:

  ◦ Send back the request ID the page received from the OAM server

  ◦ Submit back to the OAM server the end point, `/oam/server/auth_cred_submit`

- **Context Value**: This is used to build the final URL of the credential collector.

To understand how the credential collector is built using lower-case let's take the example of the authentication scheme mentioned in the previous screenshot where **Challenge URL** is `/pages/login.jsp`, **Context Type** is `default` and **Context Value** is `/oam`. The credential collector URL will therefore be `/oam/pages/login.jsp`.

 The hostname in the **Challenge Redirect** field of an authentication scheme must be defined as a host identifier. Challenge URL, Context Type, and **Context Value** fields are included only in Form, X509, or DAP challenge methods.

Authentication level

Each authentication scheme requires an **authentication level** that defines the strength level of that scheme. The higher this number, the more stringent the scheme, and the more secure the authentication mechanism is. By default, the authentication scheme AnonymousScheme is on level 0; BasicScheme, OIMScheme, and KerbScheme are on level 1; LDAPNOPasswordValidationScheme, LDAPScheme, OAAMAdvanced, OAAMBasic, OAM10gScheme, and OIFScheme are on level 2; and, X509Scheme is on authentication level 5.

OAM's SSO capability enables users to access more than one protected resource or application with a single sign-in. If a user has logged on using an authentication scheme of a specific level, the user can access one or more protected resources of the same or lower authentication level. If an already-authenticated user tries to access a resource protected by a stronger authentication scheme, then he/she will have to re-authenticate using the authentication scheme of a higher authentication level.

To understand authentication level, let's assume *resource1* is protected by authentication scheme 1 with authentication level 1 where as *resource2* is protected by authentication scheme 2 with authentication level 2. If a user initially accesses *resource1* by providing credentials defined in authentication scheme 1 and then later tries to access *resource2*, then the user will again have to provide credentials for authentication scheme 2; whereas if a user, initially authenticated for *resource 2* with authentication level 2, tries to access *resource 1* with authentication level 1 the user will **not** be asked to authenticate again.

Challenge methods

Authentication involves validating the user's identity based on the credentials, which a user must supply when requesting access to a resource. A **challenge method** defines:

- What credentials a user must supply (for example, username/password or certificate)
- Process of gathering credentials over HTTP
- Returning an HTTP response based on the result of credential validation

Challenge methods are used in authentication schemes and OAM provides the following default challenge methods – Form, Basic, X509, WNA, None, DAP, and OAM11*g*.

Form

The **Form** challenge method uses an HTML form with one or more text input fields. In a typical form-based challenge method, the username and password are collected in two textboxes on the form; however, an additional field can be added in the form such as organization. This method uses the LDAP authentication module and the UI store associated with that module. When the user clicks on the **Submit** button of the form, OAM and OSSO agents intercept and process the form data. After validation of credentials collected in the form is done, the user is authenticated.

Basic

The **basic** challenge method is a built-in web server mechanism that requires a user to enter the login ID and password. This method uses the LDAP authentication module and the UI store associated with that module. The credentials supplied are compared to the user's definition in the LDAP directory server.

X509

When using **X509** challenge method, a user's browser must supply an X509 digital certificate over SSL to the OAM server to perform authentication. An X509 challenge uses the X509 authentication module.

WNA

The **WNA** challenge method uses Windows native authentication with Active Directory. This method uses the Kerberos authentication module.

None

The **None** challenge method means users are not challenged and do not need to enter their credentials. This method uses the AnonymousModule authentication module and allows users to access OAM-specific URLs that you do not want to protect.

DAP

The **Delegated Authentication Protocol (DAP)** challenge method is required for OIF scheme (Oracle Identity Federation integration scheme). This mechanism indicates that OAM provides an assertion of the token that it receives, which differs from the standard Form challenge mechanism with the external option.

OAM11*g*

The **OAM11*g*** challenge method is required for the old OAM10*g*Scheme authentication scheme with **LDAPNoPasswordAuthModule** to facilitate trust, when you have OAM 10*g* protecting a domain that also includes an OSSO 10*g* integrated classic application (Portal, Disco, and so on). This new mechanism is created for OAM 10*g* co-existence.

Creating an authentication scheme

To create an authentication scheme, login to the OAM Administration console and click on the **Policy Configuration** tab. Select **Authentication Schemes** under **Shared Components** and click on the **Create** button on the toolbar.

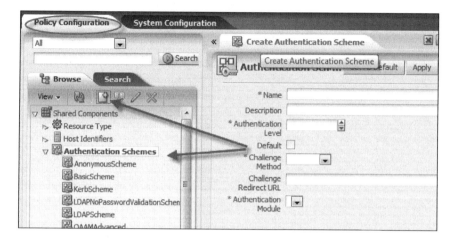

Fill in the Authentication Scheme page.

- **Name**: This is name of the authentication scheme

- **Description**: Description of the authentication scheme

- **Authentication Level**: Authentication level for this authentication scheme

- **Default**: Only one scheme can be set as the default authentication scheme

- **Challenge Method**: Select from one of following challenge methods – **Form, Basic, X509, WNA, None, DAP, OAM10G.** (The selection may vary depending on the challenge method.)

- **Challenge Redirect URL**: The URL of the credential collector

- **Authentication Module**: Depending on the challenge method, select the authentication module from drop-down menu

Deleting an authentication scheme

To delete an authentication scheme, log in to the OAM Administration console and click on the **Policy Configuration** tab. Select the authentication schemes to delete from **Authentication Schemes** navigation under **Shared Components**. Click on the **Delete** button on the toolbar.

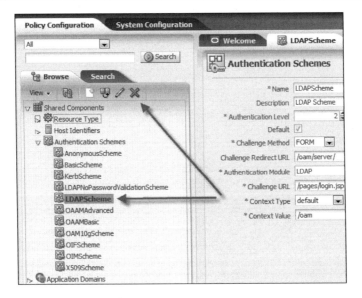

 It is not possible to delete an authentication scheme if it is being used by an existing authentication policy.

Authentication policy

Authentication policy specifies the methodology to be used for authenticating users. Authentication policies are defined for resources in the application domain. A single authentication policy can be defined to protect one or more resources in the application domain. Two default authentication policies, **Protected Resource Policy** and **Public Resource Policy** are automatically created during the agent registration process.

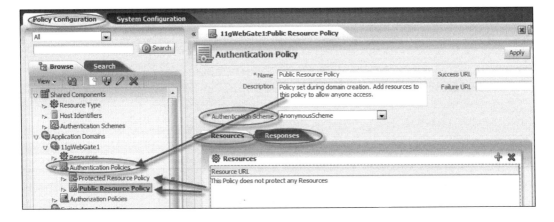

The Authentication policy contains:

- **Authentication Scheme**: This defines how users are authenticated
- **Success URL/Failure URL**: The user is shown something based on the result of the policy evaluation
- **Responses**: This declares optional actions to be taken for OAM's Single Sign-On feature, and provides ability to insert information into a session, cookie or header

Authentication policy response

Authentication response defines the action that must be fulfilled after successful authentication. To create a response, click on the **Responses** tab of the authentication policy and click on **+** button.

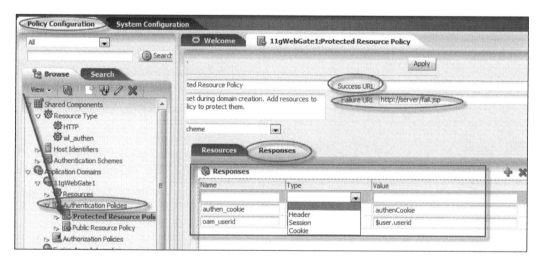

Adding an authentication policy

To create a authentication policy in an application domain:

1. Log in to the OAM Administration console and click on the **Policy Configuration** tab. Under the **Application Domains** navigator, select the **Authentication Policies** area under which this policy needs to be created. Click on the **Create** button on the toolbar to create the authentication policy.

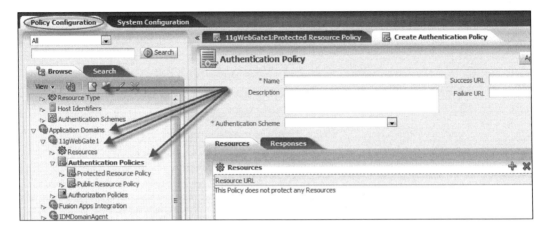

2. Enter the **Name** and **Description**, and select the **Authentication Scheme** of the policy.

3. Type the **Success URL** and **Failure URL**, then click on the **+** button under the **Resources** tab to enter the list of resources to be protected by this authentication policy. To add additional authentication responses, click on **Responses** tab.

Deleting an authentication policy

To delete an authentication policy, log in to the OAM Administration console and click on the **Policy Configuration** tab. Under **Application Domains**, expand the desired application domain and select the authentication policy to be deleted under **Authentication Policies**. Click on the **Delete** button on the toolbar to delete the policy.

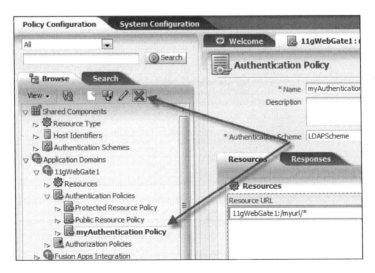

Authorization policy

Authorization is the process of determining if a user has the right to access a requested resource. Authorization policies are defined for resources in the application domain. Two default authorization policies, **Protected Resource Policy** and **Public Resource Policy** are automatically created during agent registration process.

 OSSO agents use only the Authentication Policy and not the Authorization Policies.

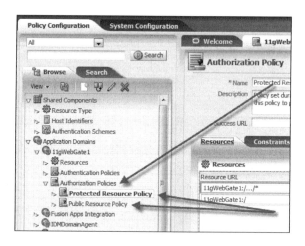

Authorization policy response

Authorization response defines the action that must be fulfilled after a successful authorization. To create a response, click on the **Responses** tab of the **Authorization Policy** and click on the **+** button.

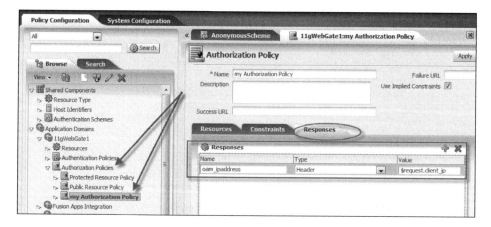

Authorization constraints

An **authorization constraint** is a rule that grants or denies access to a particular resource based on the context of the request. Authorization constraints are applicable specific to an authorization policy. Constraints have a **Type** and a **Class**. Constraint type has values `Allow` or `Deny`, which allows or denies access to the resource. **Constraint Class** consists of `Identity`, `Temporal`, and `IP4 Range`.

Adding an authorization policy

To create an authorization policy in an application domain:

1. Log in to the OAM Administration console and click on the **Policy Configuration** tab. Under the **Application Domains** navigator, select the **Authorization Policies** area under which this policy needs to be created. Click on the **Create** button on the toolbar to create the authorization policy.

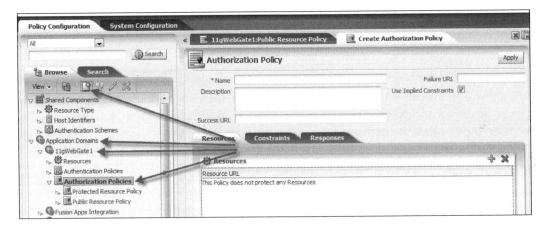

2. Enter a **Name** and **Description** for the authorization policy.

3. Type **Success URL** and **Failure URL** and click on the **+** button under the **Resources** tab to enter the list of resources to be protected by this policy. To add authorization responses, click on the **Responses** tab. To add authorization constraints, click on the **Constraints** tab.

4. Click on the **+** button and then enter the **Name** and select the **Class** and **Type** of the constraint. Based on the type of the class selected (**IP4 Range, Identity,** or **Temporal**), add details under the **Constraints : Details** section.

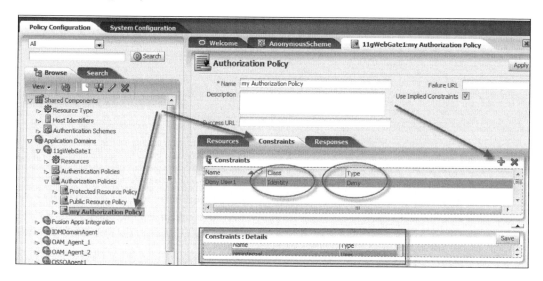

Deleting an authorization policy

To delete an authorization policy, log in to the OAM Administration console and click on the **Policy Configuration** tab. Under **Application Domains**, expand the desired application domain and select the authorization policy to be deleted under **Authorization Policies**. Click on the **Delete** button on the toolbar to delete the policy.

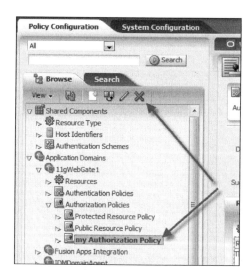

OAM SSO

Single Sign-On (SSO) allows users to log in once and gain access to all systems protected by the same SSO solution without being prompted to log in again.

In this section, we'll cover:

- OAM SSO login request flow
- OAM SSO cookies

OAM SSO login request flow

Applications protected by OAM SSO can use one of following three agents, OAM 11*g* WebGate—OAM 10*g* WebGate, or OSSO Agent—as a **policy enforcement point** (PEP). The login request flow for applications protected by OSSO is slightly different than the ones protected by 10*g*/11*g* WebGate. OSSO uses only authentication policies, whereas 10*g*/11*g* WebGate uses both authentication and authorization policies.

SSO login request flow with OAM 10*g*/11*g* agents (WebGate)

The following diagram represents the request flow when the user accesses a resource protected by the OAM agent (10*g* or 11*g* WebGate).

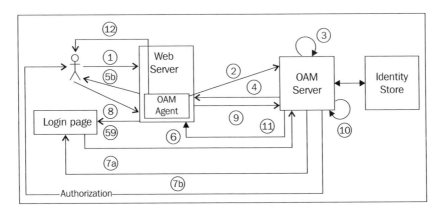

1. The user requests a resource on the web server, which is protected by WebGate

2. WebGate forwards the request to the OAM server

3. OAM checks:
    - Whether the SSO cookie is present in the request or not
    - The authentication policy, to determine if the resource is protected and how?

4. OAM logs and returns the decision to WebGate

5. WebGate responds as follows:
    - If the resource is protected, then user is presented with the login form based on the authentication policy (move to step 6)
    - If resource is unprotected, then the resource is presented to user

6. The sends their credentials

7. OAM server verifies the credentials.
    - If the credentials are correct, then OAM starts the session and creates SSO cookies (move to step 8)
    - If credentials are incorrect, then the login form is again presented to the user (move to step 6)

8. Credential collector redirects to WebGate and the authorization process begins

9. WebGate asks OAM to look for the authorization policy, compare them to the user's identity, and determines if the user is authorized to access the resource

10. OAM server checks the session, evaluates policies, and caches the result

11. OAM logs and returns the authorization policy decision to WebGate

12. WebGate responds as follows:
    - If the user is authorized to access, the resource is presented to them
    - If user is not authorized to access, the user is redirected to the URL mentioned in the Failure URL field of the authorization policy

SSO login request flow with OSSO agents

The following diagram represents the request flow when the user accesses a resource protected by the OSSO agent.

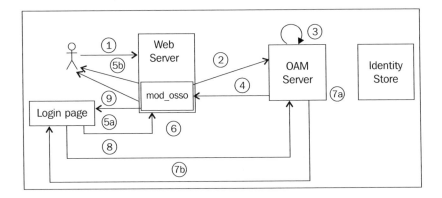

1. The user requests a resource on the Web server, which is protected by mod_osso.

2. mod_osso forwards the request to OAM server

3. OAM checks:

    ○   Whether an SSO cookie is present in the request or not

    ○   The authentication policy, to determine if the resource is protected and how

4. OAM logs and returns the decision to mod_osso

5. mod_osso responds as follows:

    ○   If the resource is protected, then the user is presented with the login form based on the authentication policy (move to step 6)

    ○   If the resource is unprotected, then the resource is presented to user

6. The user sends their credentials

7. OAM server verifies the credentials as follows:

    ○   If the credentials are correct, then OAM starts the session and creates SSO cookies (move to step 8)

    ○   If credentials are incorrect, then the login form is again presented to the user (move to step 6)

8. Credential collector redirects to mod_osso, which transmits header values that the application can use to authorize the user

9. If the user is authorized to access the resource (note the authorization is determined by application and not OAM), then the resource is served to the user

OAM SSO cookies

A **cookie** is a piece of text stored by a user's web browser. Cookie are used to maintain data related to the user during navigation across multiple visits. OAM maintains various cookies that can be set or cleared during user login. The cookies set or cleared by OAM are OAM_ID, OAMAuthn, ObSSO, OAM_REQ, OAMRequestContext, OHS-<host-port>, and GITO.

OAM_ID cookie

The OAM_ID is set by the OAM server and protected with keys known only to the OAM server. The cookie contains a Global user ID (GUID), creation time, and idle timeout. When a user attempts to access an application protected by the OAM server, the request comes to the SSO engine.

- If the cookie does not exist, user authentication begins. On successful authentication, the OAM_ID cookie is set by the SSO engine and encrypted with the SSO server key, and can be decrypted only by the SSO engine.

- If the cookie exists, then the cookie is decrypted and the sign-in process completes.

OAMAuthn cookie

The OAMAuthn cookie is set by each 11*g* WebGate when the user accesses applications protected by 11*g* WebGate and is authenticated successfully. If a user accesses two applications protected by two different 11*g* WebGates, then there will be two OAMAuthn cookies of the format `OAMAuthnCookie_<host:port>_<random_numnber>`. This cookie is protected by a key known to the respective 11*g* WebGate and the OAM server.

ObSSO cookie

The ObSSO cookie is set only when the user accesses applications protected by 10*g* WebGate. This cookie is protected with keys known only to the OAM server. This is a domain-based cookie.

OAM_REQ cookie

The OAM_REQ cookie is a transient cookie that is configured as a high-availability option to store the state of the user's original request to the protected resource, while their credentials are collected and the authentication is performed. This cookie is set by the OAM server if the authentication request context cookie is enabled. This cookie is protected by a key known to the OAM server only.

OAMRequestContext cookie

The OAMRequestContext, like OAM_REQ, is a transient cookie that is configured as a high-availability option to store the state of the user's original request to the protected resource, while their credentials are collected and authentication is performed. This cookie however, is set by 11*g* WebGate. This cookie is protected by a key known to the respective 11*g* Webgate and OAM Server.

OHS_<host-port> cookie

The OHS_<host-port> cookie is set only when the user makes a request to the resource protected by the OSSO agent (mod_osso) on the Oracle HTTP Server (OHS). This cookie is protected by a key known to the respective mod_osso agent and OAM server only.

GITO cookie

The Global Inactivity Time Out (GITO) cookie provides backward compatibility and interoperability between OSSO 10*g* and OAM 11*g*. This cookie is created by the OAM server, but accessed and modified by both the OAM server and the mod_osso agent.

SSO engine settings

The **SSO engine** is the controller of all user sessions. SSO engine settings are global and common to all OAM Managed servers in the WebLogic domain.

To access SSO Engine Settings:

1. Log in to the OAM Administration console. Click on **System Configuration | Server Instances** and then the OAM server name, such as **oam_server1**. Click on **Server Common Properties**:

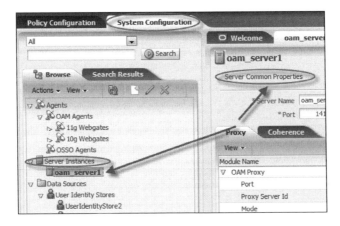

2. Next click the **SSO Engine** tab. You should see something like the following screenshot:

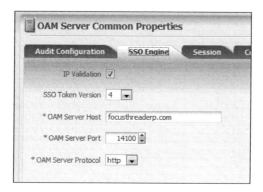

°   **IP Validation**: This is used to determine whether a client's IP address is the same as the IP address stored in ObSSO cookie generated for single sign-on

°   **SSO Token Version**: This is the drop-down list for SSO token version

°   **OAM Server Host**: This is the host on which OAM server is running

°   **OAM Server Port**: This is the port on which OAM server is listening

°   **OAM Server Protocol**: This is the protocol on which OAM server is listening (either HTTP or HTTPS)

For high-availability deployment with load balancer configuration, use load balancer details for Host, Port, and Protocol. For example, if you have two OAM Managed servers OAM_Server1 and OAM_Server2 running on `server1` and `server2`; with load balancer having URL `http://oamssoserver.com:80` forwarding requests to server1:14100 and server2:14100, then use OAM Server Host as `oamssoserver`, OAM Server Port `80`, and OAM Server Protocol `http`.

Managing application domain

As discussed at the beginning of this chapter, the application domain is a logical container for resources and the associated authentication and authorization policies, which dictates who can access these resources. In this section, we will see how to create an application domain to protect custom application with the following requirements:

- Users the access application via Oracle HTTP server 11g using the URL `http://myApplication.com` (protocol `http` and port `80`)
- The same application is also accessible via another URL `https://extApplication.com` (protocol `https` and port `443`)
- Users who are members of the LDAP group `group1` should be allowed to access URI `/protectedappgroup1`
- Users who are members of the LDAP group `group2` are allowed to access URI `/protectedappgroup2`, Monday through Friday, 9 A.M. to 5 P.M only
- Everyone (including unauthenticated users) should be able to access the URI `/unprotected`
- After successful authentication, OAM should also pass on the User ID to the application in the header variable `oamuserid`

Assumptions:

- OHS WebGate 11g is installed on OHS 11g server (check *Chapter 8, Install & Configure OAM Agents*)

Creating an application domain

To create an application domain with the above requirements, follow these steps:

1. **Create resource type**

   The first step to creating an application domain is to create the shared components of the policy model, namely, resource type, host identifiers and authentication schemes. Since the requirement is to protect the Web resource (HTTP and HTTPS), and OAM comes with the resource type HTTP that covers both HTTP and HTTPS, we will use the existing HTTP resource type in the application domain.

2. **Create host identifiers**

Log in to the OAM Administration console and click on the **Policy Configuration** tab. Select **Host Identifiers** and click on **Create** button on the toolbar.

Enter **Name** (HostIdent1), **Description** (Host Identifier for myApplication & extApplication) and add two hosts under **Operations** (myApplication.com, 80 and extApplication.com, 443) as this application can be accessed via two URLs). Then click **Apply**.

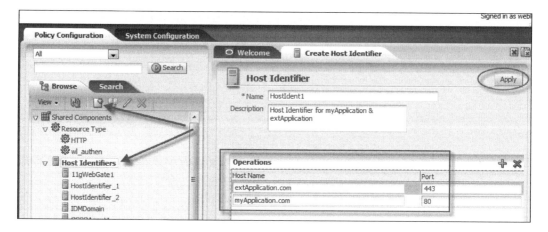

3. **Create Authentication scheme**

One requirement is to authenticate users based on userid/password from LDAP server. OAM comes with the LDAPScheme authentication scheme, which will be used here. Another requirement is allow to everyone (including unauthenticated users), which can be achieved with the pre-configured authentication scheme AnonymousScheme

4. **Create Application domain**

Log in to the OAM Administration Console and click on the **Policy Configuration** tab. Select **Application Domains** and click on **Create** button on the toolbar. Enter **Name** (AppDom1), **Description** (Application Domain to protect myApplication & extApplication), and click on **Apply**.

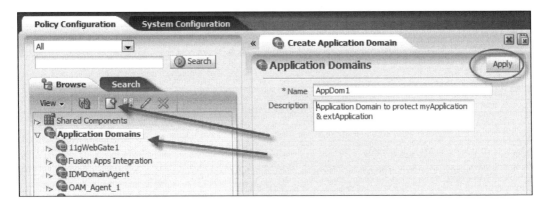

5. **Add resources to Application domain**

Login to the OAM Administration console. Click on **Policy Configuration | Application Domains | AppDom1** (created above). Select **Resources** and click on **Create** button on the toolbar. Enter **Type** (HTTP), **Description** (Resource allowed to LDAP group1), **Host Identifier** (HostIden1) and **Resource URL** (/protectedappgroup1/*) and click on **Apply**.

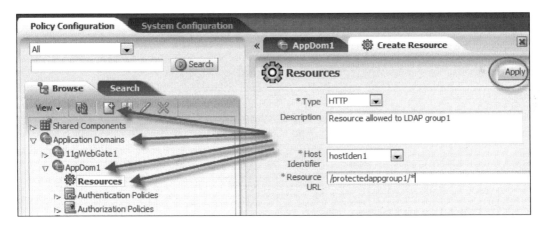

6. **Add two more resources with the following details:**

   Enter **Type** (HTTP), **Description** (Resource allowed to LDAP group2), **Host Identifier** (HostIden1), and **Resource URL** (/protectedappgroup2/*) and click on **Apply**.

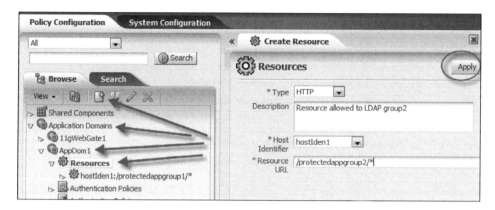

   Enter **Type** (HTTP), **Description** (Resource allowed to Everyone including unauthenticated users), **Host Identifier** (HostIden1), and **Resource URL** (/unprotected/*) and click on **Apply**.

   The final resource list should look similar to the following screenshot:

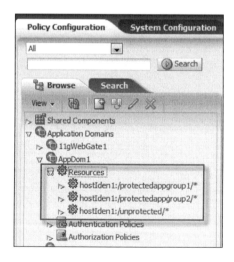

7. **Configure authentication policy to the application domain**

   Create two authentication policies under AppDom1, one using the LDAP authentication scheme for the resources protectedappgroup1 and protectedappgroup2, and another for the resource unprotected

- ○ Log in to the OAM Administration console. Select **Policy Configuration | Application Domains | AppDom1** (created above). Select **Authentication Policies** and click on the **Create** button on the toolbar.

- ○ Enter the **Name** (LDAPAuthen), **Description** (Authentication against LDAP Server), **Authentication Scheme** (LDAPScheme), and **Resources (hostIden1:/protectedappgroup1/*** and **hostIden1:/ protectedappgroup2/*)** and click on **Apply**.

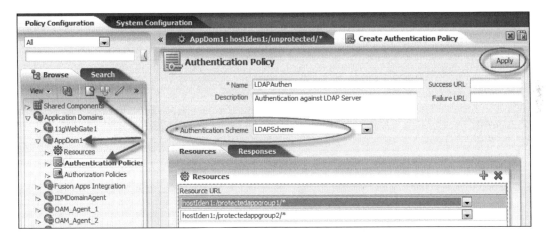

- ○ Create the second authentication policy with the **Name** (PublicPolicy), **Description** (Policy to allow access to everyone), **Authentication Scheme** (AnonymousScheme), and **Resources (hostIden1:/upprotected/*)** and click on **Apply**.

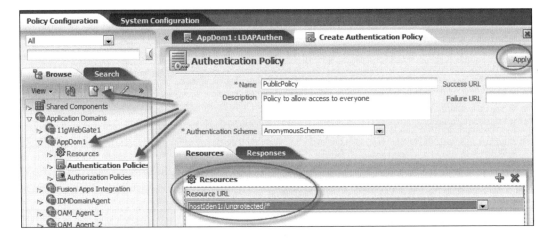

8. **Configure authorization policy to the domain**

Create two authorization policies, one to authorize if the user is a member of `group1` and the second to authorize if the user is a member of `group2`.

    ◦   Log in to the OAM Administration console. Click on **Policy Configuration | Application Domains | AppDom1** (created above). Select **Authorization Policies** and click on the **Create** button on the toolbar.

    ◦   Enter **Name** (LDAPGroup1Authorization), **Description** (Authorization based on LDAP Group1 against LDAP Server), and **Resources (hostIden1:/protectedappgroup1/*)** and click on **Apply**.

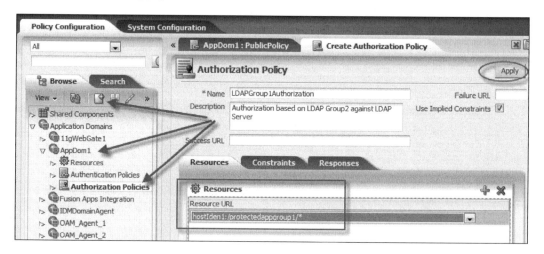

    ◦   Create a second authorization with **Name** (LDAPGroup2Authorization), **Description** (Authorization based on LDAP Group2 against LDAP Server), and **Resources (hostIden2:/protectedappgroup2/*)** and click on **Apply**.

9. **Define the SSO response to authentication policy**

    ◦   Log in to the OAM Administration console. Select **Policy Configuration | Application Domains | AppDom1 | Authentication Policies**. Select **LDAPAuthen** and click on the **Edit** button on the toolbar.

    ◦   Click on the **Responses** tab and add a response with **Name** (oamuserid), **Type** (Header), and **Value** ($user.userid).

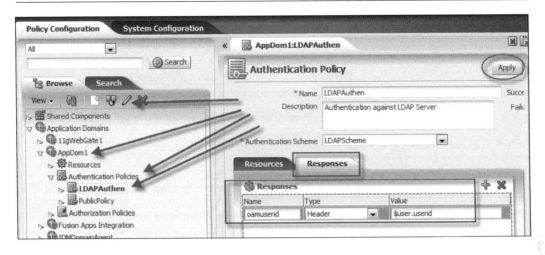

10. **Define authorization constraints**

Now define authorization constraints to the two authorization policies created above (LDAPGroup1Authorization and LDAPGroup2Authorization)

° Log in to the OAM Administration console. Click on **Policy Configuration | Application Domains | AppDom1 | Authorization Policies**. Select **LDAPGroup1Authorization** and click on the **Edit** button on the toolbar.

° Click on the **Constraints** tab. Add **Name** (LDAPGroup1), **Class** (Identity), **Type** (Allow) and click on **Add Selected**.

- ° Select the constraint **LDAPGroup1** and add the details **Name** (group1) and **Type** (Group).

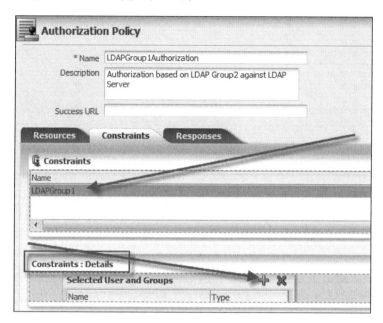

- ° On clicking **Save** you should see details of the constraints, as shown in the following screenshot:

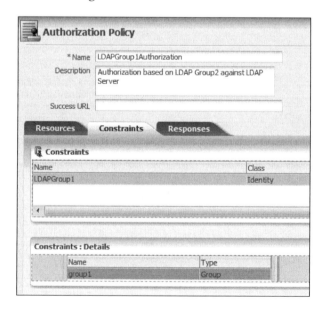

- ○ Similarly, edit `LDAPGroup2Authorization`'s constraints to allow `group2` of LDAP server.

- ○ Click on the **Constraints** tab and add **Name** (`LDAPGroup2`), **Class** (`Identity`), and **Type** (`Allow`), then click on **Add Selected**

- ○ Select constraint **LDAPGroup2** and add the constraint details **Name**(`group2`) and **Type** (`Group`)

- ○ Add a second constraint for LDAPGroup2Authorization with **Name** (`9to5`), **Class** (`Temporatl`), **Type** (`Allow`), then click on **Add Selected**

- ○ Select constraint **9to5** and add the constraint detail **Start Time** (`09:00`) and **End Time** (`17:00`). Check **Monday, Tuesday, Wednesday, Thursday, Friday** and click on **Save** and then **Apply**

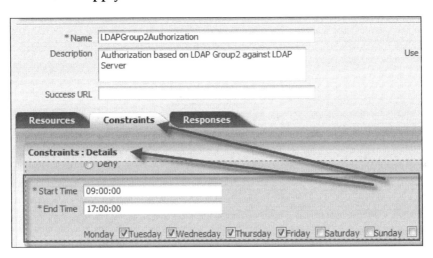

11. **Test the working of the Application domain**

- ○ The URLs `http://myApplication.com/protectedappgroup1` and `https://extApplication.com/protectedappgroup1` should be allowed only to users who are members of `group1` in LDAP server

- ○ The URLs `http://myApplication.com/protectedappgroup2` and `https://extApplication.com/protectedappgroup2` should be allowed only to users who are members of `group2` server and are logging in between 9 A.M. and 5 P.M. Monday to Friday

- ○ The URLs `http://myApplication.com/unprotected` and `https://extApplication.com/unprotected` should be allowed to anyone including unauthenticated users

Summary

In this chapter, we covered the various policy model components that make an Application domain. We also covered SSO request flow in OAM and the various cookies used in OAM. We finally created an application domain based on a real-life example.

In the next chapter, we are going to cover session management in OAM.

7

OAM Session Management

Oracle Access Manager **session management** refers to the process of managing the lifecycle of a user session. This chapter covers session, Session Management Engine, Session Data Store, User Lifecycle, and its settings. This chapter also covers the Session Management utility in OAM and configuring an independent database for Session Data.

Session in general refers to the interaction between user and website. In OAM 11*g*, an OAM session is created when a user is authenticated using Oracle Access Manager Authentication Service, or in other words, when the user successfully logs into an OAM protected resource.

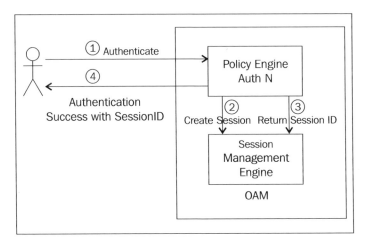

- When a user accesses an OAM-protected resource, OAM's Policy Engine checks the authentication policy that is configured for the resource and presents a **credential collection** form to the user where the user types in his username/password.

- OAM's Authentication (AuthN) Service validates the username and password and passes a request to create a session to OAM's Session Management Engine (SME).

- The SME creates a session and returns the session ID back to the Policy Engine.

- Policy Engine returns authentication success and Session ID back to the user.

OAM Session Management: This refers to the process of managing OAM Sessions which include tracking active user sessions, notification of session events to enable global logout, and limiting number of concurrent sessions a user can have at a time.

Session Management Engine (SME): This acts as controller for session events and notifications. SME enables the generation and updating of user session data. SME interfaces with the Single Sign-On (SSO) engine.

Oracle Coherence: A JCache-complaint, in-memory caching, and data management solution used for clustered Java EE applications and is used by Oracle Access Manager for session management. Coherence is installed automatically with WebLogic server during Fusion Middleware installation. For large OAM implementations, additional memory is required by Oracle Coherence for Session Management. If you are migrating from OAM 10*g* to OAM 11*g*, then extra memory is required at application server level for session management introduced as part of OAM 11*g*.

> Coherence Session cache size is defined in the file `oam-config.xml` under `$DOMAIN_HOME/config/fmwconfig` directory by parameter `DistributedCacheMaxSize` property. Default Coherence cache size is set to 100 MB.

Session Data Store: User's Session Data is stored in multiple tiers to balance latency, availability, and resource consumption. User Session Data store includes:

- Local in-memory cache of each OAM Managed server
- Distributed in-memory cache shared by all OAM Managed servers
- Optionally in Oracle database

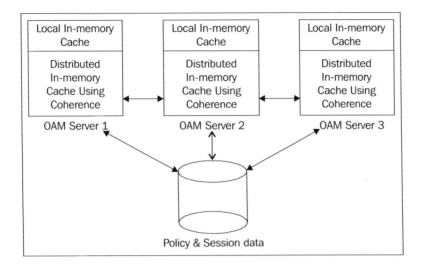

Policy & Session data

In clustered OAM environments (two or more OAM servers in cluster), Oracle Coherence is used to share a consistent session state among the clustered OAM servers. Oracle Coherence replicates and distributes session data across all Managed servers in the cluster. Coherence also performs failover and reconciliation, so if one OAM Managed server fails, Coherence automatically distributes data from the failed host to the in-memory cache of other OAM Managed server hosts. Oracle Coherence traffic is automatically encrypted.

- When a user is successfully authenticated, the session is created and session ID is assigned. The session data is stored in the local in-memory cache of OAM server which authenticated the user session.

- After a short period (approximately 3 minutes), session data in the local in-memory cache is transferred to distributed in-memory cache on the same host. If the distributed in-memory cache runs out of allocated memory space then the least recently-used sessions are evicted (and optionally stored in the database, if configured). If the database is not configured to use session store, then the sessions are stored in a flat file.

- Oracle Coherence updates, replicates, and distributes session data in the distributed cache of one more OAM Managed servers, whenever session information changes in the distributed in-memory cache.

- If the database is configured to store session data then Oracle Coherence also moves session data from distributed in-memory cache to the database.

 User Session data is stored in the OAM_SESSION table in the OAM schema in the database.

User session lifecycle

User session lifecycle refers to the period of user activity from the start of the user session to the end. There are three states in a user **lifecycle, namely ACTIVE, INACTIVE** and **EXPIRED**.

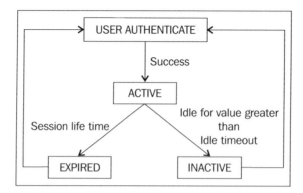

- Active: On successful authentication, a user session is created and remains active if the user continues to access OAM resources, until one of the following events occurs:
    a. The user logs out by clicking on the **logout** link (called explicit logout). The User Session on the OAM server gets destroyed in this case.
    b. The user implicitly logs out by closing the browser link (called implicit logout). The User Session stays on the OAM server which changes to inactive after idle timeout is reached.
    c. The user makes no request to the OAM-protected resource for the period defined by the `Idle Timeout` attribute. In this case, state changes to inactive.
    d. An administrator terminates the user's session by using the Session Management Utility from OAM Administration Console. The session is destroyed from the OAM server.
    e. Session's total duration exceeds the value configured for the `Session Lifetime` attribute. Session state changes to expired in this case.
- Inactive: Active state changes to **INACTIVE** when the user does not access OAM-protected content for the period defined by the `Idle Timeout` attribute. An inactive session can be activated by authenticating it again.
- Expired: Active state changes to **EXPIRED** when the duration of the session has exceeded the period defined by the `Session Lifetime` attribute. Expired sessions can't re-enter the active state. The user has to authenticate again and is given a new session ID.

A special purge process automatically purges expired sessions every 15 minutes.

User Lifecycle settings

Three parameters which control the user session lifecycle are **idle timeout, session life time**, and **maximum number of sessions per user**.

To manage these settings, follow these steps:

1. Login to OAM Administration Console.

2. Click on the **System configuration** tab. Under **Server Instances** select the OAM Server and then click on **Server Common Properties**.

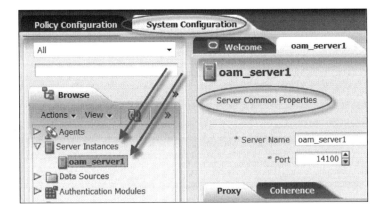

3. While on the Server Common Properties page, select the **Session** tab to view/edit user session lifecycle settings.

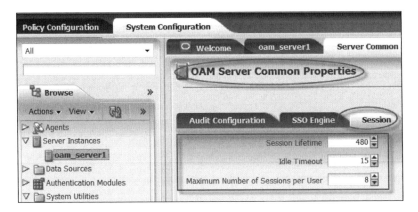

The following section contains parameters that control user lifecycle settings:

- Idle timeout
- Session life time
- Maximum number of sessions per user

Idle timeout

Idle Timeout represents amount of time (in minutes) that a user's session remains valid without accessing any OAM protected resources. When the user is idle for a period longer than the one defined in this setting, they are asked to re-authenticate. The default value is 15 minutes; a value of 0 disables the setting.

Session life time

Session life time represents the amount of time (in minutes) that a user's session remains valid. The user session expires after this limit is reached. The default value is 480 minutes, that is, eight hours, so the user session will expire eight hours after authentication.

Maximum number of sessions per user

A user can run multiple sessions by opening different browser sessions from the same machine or from browsers on different machines. This setting limits the number of sessions each user can have at one time. The default value is eight.

Managing active users' sessions

Active sessions can be managed from the OAM Administration Console. Login to OAM Administration Console and select the **System Configuration** tab then double-click on **Session Management** under **System Utilities**.

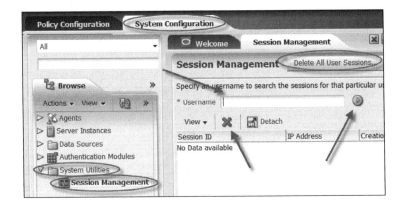

To view user session information, enter a User ID and click on the > button. This displays all active sessions for this user. To delete this user session ID, click on **Delete** button. All user sessions can be deleted by clicking on the **Delete All User Sessions** button.

Wildcards are not allowed in the **Username** field and Administrators can delete only an active user's session data.

Configuring a separate database for session data

You can use the following procedure to configure a separate database instance to store Session Data:

1. Install the database and then use Repository Creation Utility (RCU) to create an OAM-specific schema.

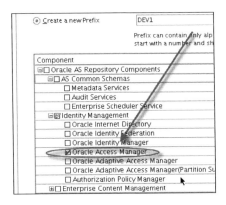

2. Login to Oracle WebLogic Server Console `http://serverName:7001/console` and go to **Domain Structure | Services | JDBC | Data Sources**.

3. Click on the **New** button to create a new Data Source.

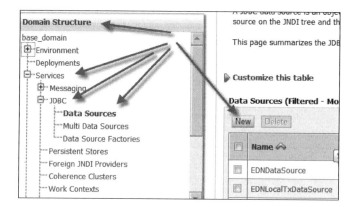

4. In the next few screens enter the following data:

Name: oamsessionds
JNDI name: jdbc/oamsessionds
Database Name: <Name of Database>
Host Name: <DNS/CNAME of server on which database is running>
Port: <Database Port>
Database User Name: <OAM schema created in step 1 above>
Password: <Database User Password>

5. Click on the newly-created oamsessionds and then on the **Targets** tab. Select the respective OAM Server and click on the **Save** button:

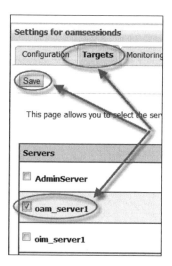

6. Stop WebLogic Admin server and OAM Managed server.

7. Update the `DataSourceName` attribute created above in `$DOMAIN_HOME/config/fmwconfig/oam-config.xml` from this:

```
<Setting Name="SmeDb" Type="htf:map">
<Setting Name="URL" Type="xsd:string">jdbc:oracle:thin://amdb.
example.com:2001/AM</
Setting>
<Setting Name="Principal" Type="xsd:string">amuser</Setting>
<Setting Name="Password" Type="xsd:string">password</Setting>
<Setting Name="DataSourceName" Type="xsd:string">jdbc/oamds</
Setting>
</Setting>
```

To this:

```
<Setting Name="SmeDb" Type="htf:map">
<Setting Name="URL" Type="xsd:string">jdbc:oracle:thin://amdb.
example.com:2001/AM</
Setting>
<Setting Name="Principal" Type="xsd:string">amuser</Setting>
<Setting Name="Password" Type="xsd:string">password</Setting>
<Setting Name="DataSourceName" Type="xsd:string">jdbc/
oamsessionds</Setting>
</Setting>
```

8. Start WebLogic Admin Server and OAM Managed Server.

Summary

In this chapter we covered the Session Management Engine, Session Data Store, and User Lifecycle and its settings. We also covered the Session Management utility in OAM and configured an independent database for Session Data.

In the next chapter we are going to cover installation and configuration of OAM Agents, that is, OAM 10*g*/11*g* Webgate, and their properties.

8

Installing and Configuring OAM Agents

Agents in OAM 11*g* are **policy enforcement points (PEP)** registered with OAM server that act as a filter for HTTP Requests. Each agent plays the role of a gatekeeper to secure the resource and manages all interactions with the user who is trying to access the resource. Agents receive request from users and contact the OAM server to find whatever authentication and authorization has been configured for the resource which the user is requesting. Each OAM server has two ports: a managed server port (default value 14100) which is the WebLogic server port on which the OAM server runs; and the OAM proxy server port (default value 5575) which listens for agent requests. Agents communicate via the OAM proxy server port. This chapter will cover agents in OAM and installation of 10*g*/11*g* agents (WebGate).

OAM 11*g* supports the following agents:

- **OAM 10g Webgate**: These are C-based agents that are intended to be deployed in the Web server.

- **OAM 11g WebGate**: These are Java-based agents that are intended to be deployed in the web server. Currently OAM 11*g* WebGate is available for Oracle HTTP server (OHS) 11*g* only. OAM 11*g* WebGates are an enhanced version of 10*g* Webgates, that support a per-agent secret key for SSO, that is, one shared secret key generated for each 11*g* WebGate.

- **OAM 10g AccessGates**: These are custom agents created by using the OAM Software Development Kit (SDK).

- **OSSO Agent** (mod_osso): These are C-based agents intended to be deployed in Oracle HTTP server (OHS) with mod_osso module.

Before installation, these agents must first be registered with OAM server. Registration can be done either from the OAM Administration console or by using the **Remote Registration Tool** (**RREG**). OAM agents communicate with the OAM server proxy-port over **Oracle Access Protocol** (**OAP**) also known as **Netpoint Access Protocol** (**NAP**). OAP channel communication (also known as agent transport mode) can be:

- **Open**: No encryption on data passed between OAM agent and OAM server.
- **Simple**: The data passed between OAM agent and OAM server is encrypted using self-signed certificates provided by OAM. Self-signed certificates are generated by default during OAM.
- **Cert**: The data passed between OAM agent and OAM server is encrypted using CA Signed (such as Verisign or Thawte) X.509 certificates.

Agent transport mode side can be configured either during registration or later. The transport mode at the OAM server side can be configured using OAM Administration Console.

Security Mode at Agent side must be the same as security mode configured at OAM Proxy.

1. To modify the mode via the OAM server proxy, login to OAM **Administration Console** | **System Configuration** | **Server Instances** | **oam_server1**, select the tab **Proxy**, and select the drop-down menu for Mode as shown in the following screenshot:

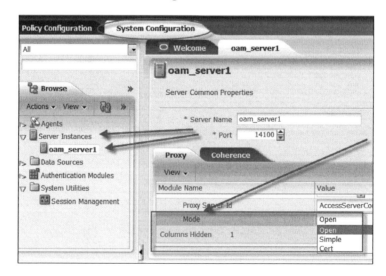

2. To modify the mode at the agent side, login to **OAM Administration Console | Agents** and select the respective Agents, and then modify **Security**:

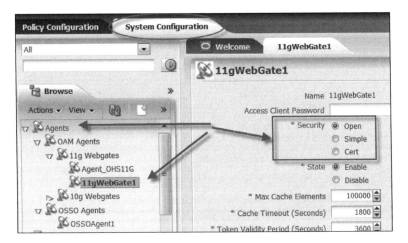

Installing OAM agents

Before OAM agents (10*g*/11*g* Webgate or OSSO agents) can communicate with OAM server, agents must be provisioned and installed.

Provisioning agent: Provisioning is the process of creating an agent profile in the OAM server. An agent can be provisioned in this way using either RREG or using OAM Administration console. Provisioning agents generate some artefacts/files on the server which must be copied to the agent instance's directory.

Installing agent: WebGate is installed using agent/WebGate software, during which binaries and common configuration files are installed in its own ORACLE_HOME (known as WebGate ORACLE_HOME).

The key steps to install OAM agents (11*g* or 10*g* Webgate) are:

- Download OAM agent software
- Provision agent
- Install WebGate

Downloading OAM agent software

The OAM agent (WebGate) can be installed against various Web servers such as Oracle HTTP Server (OHS), Apache HTTP Server, IBM HTTP Server (IHS), Microsoft Internet Information Server (IIS), and many more. The software you download and use will depend on the web server version and operating system on which that Web server is running. Let's assume you wish to configure OAM agent (WebGate) with Apache HTTP server version 2, running on a 64-bit Linux machine. You should use `Oracle_Access_Manager10_1_4_3_0_linux64_APACHE22_WebGate` executable. It is recommended to use the latest available version of WebGate for specific web servers. For example, for OHS 11*g* both Webgate 10*g* and 11*g* are available, so use 11*g* WebGate, whereas for OHS 10*g* only 10*g* (10.1.4.3) WebGate is available, so use 10.1.4.3 Webgate.

10g WebGates executables are available in the format of `Oracle_Access_Manager<Version>_<OS>_<WebServer>_WebGate`, so for Oracle HTTP server 10*g* R3 (built using Apache 2) on a Windows 32 bit machine use executable `Oracle_Access_Manager10_1_4_3_0_win_OHS2_WebGate`

> 11*g* WebGates are currently available only for Oracle HTTP server 11*g*. For all other web servers, use 10*g* WebGate.

WebGate installation on Linux/Unix also requires GCC libraries (`libgcc_s.so.1` and `libstdc++.so.5/6`) which are included in Linux/Unix distribution. Copy these GCC libraries into a directory of your choice and refer to it during WebGate installation.

Downloading 11*g* WebGate

To download 11*g* WebGate (available only for OHS 11*g*), go to `http://www.oracle.com/technetwork/middleware/downloads/oid-11g-161194.html` (if you are not already registered, then register yourself to download the software. OTN registration is required to download any software from OTN.) and click **Disk1** under **Oracle Access Manager WebGates (11.1.1.3.0)**:

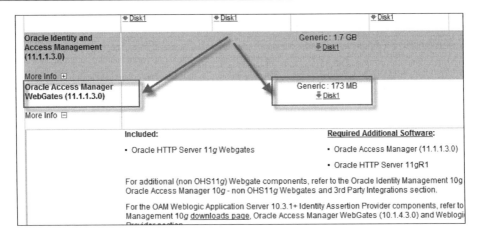

Downloading 10*g* WebGates

To download 10*g* WebGate, go to `http://www.oracle.com/technetwork/`
`middleware/ias/downloads/101401-099957.html` (if you are not already
registered, then register yourself to download software) and select the software for
the appropriate operating system against **Oracle Access Manager 10g - non OHS11g**
Webgates and 3rd Party Integrations:

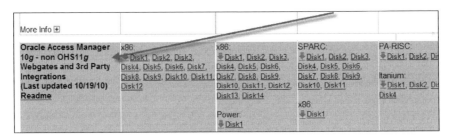

Downloading GCC libraries

GCC libraries are only required for Linux/Unix installations of WebGate.
To download GCC Library, go to `http://www.oracle.com/technetwork/`
`middleware/ias/downloads/101401-099957.html` and click on **Disk1** under **GCC**
Libraries for Oracle Identity Federation (these GCC libraries are compatible with
WebGate too.)

GCC Libraries for Oracle Identity Federation		x86: 1.5 MB ⏷ Disk1	
Metadata Repository Creation Assistant	x86: 629 MB ⏷ Disk1, Disk2	x86: 738 MB ⏷ Disk1, Disk2	S ⏷
	Itanium: 520 MB	Itanium: 543 MB	x8

Installing 11*g* WebGate for OHS 11*g*

This section covers provisioning and installation of 11*g* WebGate with OHS 11*g*:

- Download 11*g* WebGate as mentioned previously in the **Download** section.
- If OHS 11*g* is running on a non-Windows operating system (such as, Linux, Solaris, or HP-Unix) then download GCC libraries as mentioned previously in the **Download** section.

Provisioning and registering 11*g* WebGate with OAM server

Register 11*g* WebGate either using OAM Administration console or RREG. RREG can be used in either in-band mode or out-of-band mode (for more information check *Chapter 5, OAM Administration and Navigation*). The following sections use RREG in-band mode:

1. **RREG on an OAM server**:

   This is a one-time activity to be performed on an OAM server and only required for registering OAM agents from command-line tools like RREG. It is safe to ignore this step if you are registering WebGate from OAM Administration console, or if you have already setup the RREG utility in the past on an OAM server.

   ```
   Unix: cd $ORACLE_HOME/oam/server/rreg)
   Windows: cd $ORACLE_HOME\oam\server\rreg

   set OAM_REG_HOME & JDK_HOME in oamreg.sh (Unix) and oamreg.
   bat (Windows) where OAM_REG_HOME is full path to the directory
   $ORACLE_HOME/oam/server/rreg (where ORACLE_HOME is directory in
   which IDAM product was installed)
   ```

2. **Update OAM11gRequest.xml on server**:

   Update `serverAddress, agentBaseURL, agentName, HostIdentifier,` and `applicationDomain` in `$OAM_REG_HOME/input/OAM11GRequest.xml`,

   where:

   - `serverAddress` is the WebLogic Admin server URL, such as `http://serverName:7001`
   - `agentBaseURL` is the URL of WebServer which WebGate will protect, such as `http://WebServerHost:7777`
   - `agentName` is a unique name for WebGate, which will be used during WebGate installation. For example, `Agent_OHS11g`

- ° `HostIdentifier` is a unique name to define the host identifier. Registration will create host identifier with this name. For example, `HidOHS11gWG`

- ° `applicationDomain` is a unique name to create application domain in OAM. For example, `AppDomOHS11G`

> `OAM11GRequest.xml` and `OAM11GRequest_short.xml` are templates which can be used to register 11*g* WebGate.

3. Run the RREG tool to register 11g WebGate with OAM server:

    Windows: cd $OAM_REG_HOME/bin/
    Unix: cd %OAM_REG_HOME%\bin

    `/oamreg.sh inband input/OAM11GRequest.xml`

    When prompted for:

    - ° Your **agent username:** Enter the name of a user with OAM administrator access like WebLogic
    - ° Your **agent password:** Enter that user's password
    - ° Entering a **WebGate password? (y/n):** n
    - ° Importing a **URIs file?(y/n):** n

    On successful registration (WebGate provisioning) you should see a message saying that the agent was registered successfully, as shown in the following screenshot:

```
Enter agent password:                        Do you want to enter a Webgate
password?(y/n):
n
Do you want to import an URIs file?(y/n):
n


------------------------------------------
Request summary:
OAM11G Agent Name:Agent_OHS11G
Base URL:http://focusthreaderp.com:7780
URL String:HIdOHS11gWG
Registering in Mode:inband
Your registration request is being been sent to the Admin server at: http://focu
sthreaderp:7001
------------------------------------------

Inband registration process completed successfully! Output artifacts are created
 in the output folder.
[idam@focusthreaderp bin]$
```

On execution, RREG will create:

- An instance of WebGate under OAM Agents in the 11*g* WebGate container under **System Configuration** tab of **OAM Administration Console**:

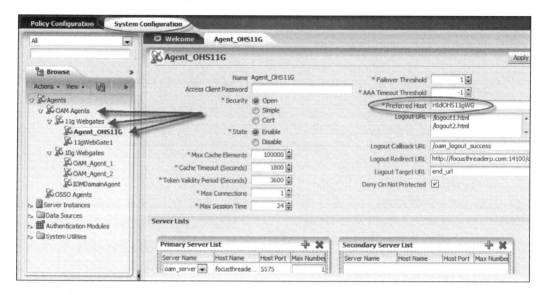

- A host identifier under **Shared Components** in the **Policy Configuration** tab:

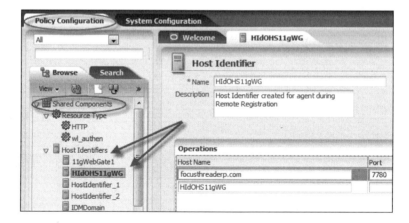

- An application domain under **Application Domains** in the **Policy Configuration** tab:

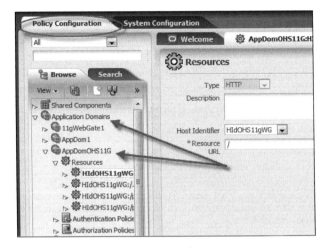

- The registration process will also create the following files under $OAM_REG_HOME/output/<AgentID> directory which must be copied to WebGate Instance directory after installation (the WebGate Instance directory is webgate directory under Oracle HTTP Instance directory, and is different from WebGate ORACLE_HOME):

  ○ cwallet.sso and ObAccessClient.xml files

  ○ If the WebGate to OAM server communication mode is set to **Simple** then three additional files are created: password.xml, aaa_key.pem, and aaa_cert.pem

  ○ If the WebGate to OAM server communication mode is **Cert** then it creates one additional file, password.xml

Installing WebGate 11*g* Software

11*g* WebGate must be installed on the same machine where the web server is running. WebGate 11g requires JDK 1.6, so you can use JDK 1.6 shipped with OHS 11*g* under Middleware Home ($MW_HOME/jdk160_XX). WebGate must be installed using the same operating system user who owns the web server executables:

1. Start WebGate installer:

    For Unix/Linux:

    ```
    $WebGate_Software/Disk1/runInstaller –jreLoc <jreLocation>
    ```

For Windows:

```
%WebGate_Software%\Disk1\setup.exe -jreLoc <jreLocation>
```

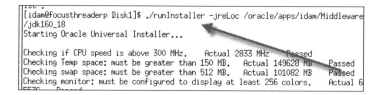

2. Click **Next** on the **Welcome** screen.

3. Ensure that prerequisite checks are successful and then click **Next**.

4. Select **Middleware & Oracle Home Directory** as shown in the following screenshot. WebGate Installer will create a directory (as mentioned in Oracle Home Directory) inside the directory mentioned by **Oracle Middleware Home**. According to the following screenshot, ORACLE_HOME for 11*g* WebGate will be /oracle/apps/idam/Middleware/Oracle_OAMWebGate1:

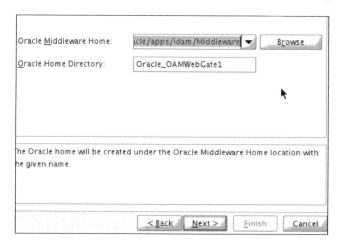

5. For Unix/Linux machines, select your GCC library location (the directory in which you have unzipped GCC libraries) and click **Next**:

6. Click **Install** on the **Installation Summary** screen as shown in the following screenshot:

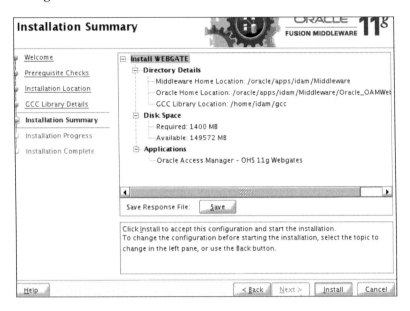

7. Finish installation by clicking on **Finish** as shown in the following screenshot:

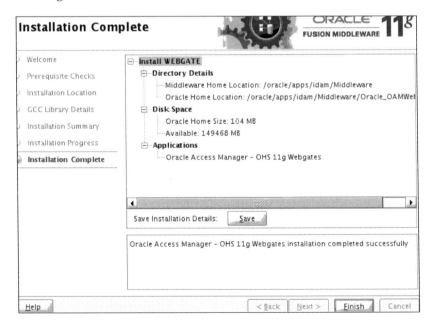

8. Deploy WebGate to the OHS instance directory:

   This step will copy WebGate configuration files to OHS instance directory:

   ○ **WebGate ORACLE_HOME**: This is the directory in which WebGate is installed.

   ○ **WebGate Instance Directory**: This is the OHS instance directory. The default location for Instance Directory in OHS 11*g* is `$OHS_ORACLE_HOME/instances/instance1/config/OHS/ohs1`

   ```
   cd <Webgate_Home>/webgate/ohs/tools/deployWebGate
   ```

   ```
   ./deployWebgateInstance.sh -w <Webgate_Instance_Directory>
   -oh <Webgate_Oracle_Home>
   ```

   ```
   ./deployWebGateInstance.sh -w /oracle/apps/idam/Middleware/
   Oracle_WT1/instances/instance1/config/OHS/ohs1 -oh /oracle/
   apps/idam/Middleware/Oracle_OAMWebGate1
   ```

   ```
   [idam@focusthreaderp deployWebGate]$ pwd
   /oracle/apps/idam/Middleware/Oracle_OAMWebGate1/webgate/ohs/tools/deployWebGate
   [idam@focusthreaderp deployWebGate]$ ./deployWebGateInstance.sh -w /oracle/apps/
   idam/Middleware/Oracle_WT1/instances/instance1/config/OHS/ohs1 -oh /oracle/apps/
   idam/Middleware/Oracle_OAMWebGate1
   Copying files from WebGate Oracle Home to WebGate Instancedir
   [idam@focusthreaderp deployWebGate]$
   ```

9. Edit the OHS configuration file:

   This step will edit the OHS configuration file `httpd.conf` and include WebGate configuration file `webgate.conf`:

   ```
   export LD_LIBRARY_PATH=$LD_LIBRARY_PATH:<Oracle_Home_for_Oracle_
   HTTP_Server>/lib
   ```

   ```
   export LD_LIBRARY_PATH=$LD_LIBRARY_PATH:/oracle/apps/idam/
   Middleware/Oracle_WT1/lib
   ```

   ```
   cd <Webgate_ORACLE_HOME>/webgate/ohs/tools/setup/InstallTools
   ```

   ```
   cd /oracle/apps/idam/Middleware/Oracle_OAMWebGate1/webgate/ohs/
   tools/setup/InstallTools
   ```

   ```
   ./EditHttpConf -w <Webgate_Instance_Directory> [-oh <Webgate_
   Oracle_Home>] [-o <output_file>]
   ```

```
./EditHttpConf -w /oracle/apps/idam/Middleware/Oracle_WT1/
instances/instance1/config/OHS/ohs1 -oh /oracle/apps/idam/
Middleware/Oracle_OAMWebGate1 -o /home/idam/output2.txt
```

```
[idam@focusthreaderp InstallTools]$ ./EditHttpConf -w /oracle/apps/idam/Middle
ware/Oracle_WT1/instances/instance1/config/OHS/ohs1 -oh /oracle/apps/idam/Middle
ware/Oracle_OAMWebGate1 -o /home/idam/output.txt
The web server configuration file was successfully updated
/oracle/apps/idam/Middleware/Oracle_WT1/instances/instance1/config/OHS/ohs1/http
d.conf has been backed up as /oracle/apps/idam/Middleware/Oracle_WT1/instances/i
nstance1/config/OHS/ohs1/httpd.conf.ORIG
[idam@focusthreaderp InstallTools]$
```

10. Copy files and artifacts generated during WebGate provisioning/registration to the WebGate instance directory.

    The registration process will create the following files/artifacts under the `$OAM_REG_HOME/output/<AgentID>` directory on OAM server:

    ° `cwallet.sso` and `ObAccessClient.xml` files.

    ° If the WebGate to OAM server communication mode is set to **Simple** then it creates three additional files `password.xml`, `aaa_key.pem`, and `aaa_cert.pem`

    ° If the WebGate to OAM server communication mode is **Cert** then it creates one additional file `password.xml`

    Manually copy the files generated in `$OAM_REG_HOME/output/<AgentID>` to `<WebGate_Instance_Home>/webgate/config` (that is `/oracle/apps/idam/Middleware/Oracle_WT1/instances/instance1/config/OHS/ohs1/webgate/config`).

11. Restart Oracle HTTP server 11*g*:

    Restart OHS 11*g* using `opmnctl`:

    $ORACLE_HOME_for_OHS11g/instances/<instance1>/bin/opmnctl stopall

    $ORACLE_HOME_for_OHS11g/instances/<instance1>/bin/opmnctl startall

12. Test 11*g* WebGate for OHS 11*g*:

    Access OHS 11*g* URL via a browser and you should be redirected to the OAM **Login** page.

     By default, all resources (URLs) in 11*g* WebGate are protected. To allow access to unauthenticated users, create a resource with Anonymous authentication scheme.

Installing and configuring 10*g* WebGate for OHS 10*g*

This section covers 10*g* WebGate installation and configuration with OAM 11*g*. 10*g* WebGate should be used for web servers where 11*g* WebGate is not available, such as OHS 10*g* R3 or lower, IHS, IIS, and Apache. Like 11*g* WebGate, 10*g* WebGate should be installed using the same operating system user and group as the web server. 10*g* WebGate can be installed in graphical mode, console mode (-console), or silent mode as follows:

- Download 10*g* WebGate as mentioned previously in the Download section
- If the web server is running on a non-Windows operating system (such as Linux, Solaris, HP-Unix) then download GCC libraries as mentioned previously in Download section.

Provisioning 10*g* WebGate for OAM 11*g*

10*g* WebGate can be provisioned/registered with OAM 11*g* using either the OAM Administration console or RREG with either in-band or out-of-band mode (For more information check *Chapter 5, OAM Administration and Navigation*).

1. **Setup RREG on OAM server**:

   This is a one-time activity to be performed on the OAM server, and is only required for registering OAM agents from command-line tools such as RREG. It is safe to ignore this step if you are registering WebGate from the OAM Administration console or if you have already setup RREG utility in the past on OAM server:

   ```
   cd $ORACLE_HOME/oam/server/rreg/bin    (Unix)
   cd %ORACLE_HOME%\oam\server\rreg\bin    (Windows)
   ```

   Set OAM_REG_HOME and JDK_HOME in oamreg.sh (Unix) and oamreg.bat (Windows) where OAM_REG_HOME is the full path to the directory $ORACLE_HOME/oam/server/rreg.

2. **Update OAMRequest.xml on server**:

   Update serverAddress, agentBaseURL, agentName, HostIdentifier, PrimaryCookieDomain, and applicationDomain in $OAM_REG_HOME/input/OAMRequest.xml

   Where

   ○   serverAddress is the WebLogic Admin server URL such as http://serverName:7001

- agentBaseURL is the URL of the web server which 10*g* WebGate will protect such as `http://focusthreaderp.com:7781`

- agentName is a unique name for the WebGate. This name will be used during WebGate installation. For example, `10GWG_OHS`

- HostIdentifier is a unique name to define the host identifier. Registration will create `HostIdentitfier` with this name. For example, `10GOHS`

- PrimaryCookieDomain is the domain name of your webserver. For example, `.com`

- applicationDomain is a unique name to create an application domain in OAM. For example, `10GOHS_AppDOM`

 OAMRequest.xml and OAMRequest_short.xml are templates which can be used to register 10*g* WebGate.

3. Run the RREG tool to register 11*g* WebGate with OAM server:

```
cd $OAM_REG_HOME/bin/
cd %OAM_REG_HOME%\bin\

./oamreg.sh inband input/OAMRequest.xml
```

 WebLogic Admin server should be running during RREG.

When prompted for

- Your **agent username:** Enter user with OAM Administrator Access like WebLogic

- Your **agent password:** Enter that user's password

- Entering a **WebGate password? (y/n)**: n

- Importing a **URIs file?(y/n)**: n

Finally, you should see a message saying that the agent registration was completed successfully, as shown in the following screenshot:

```
Enter agent password:                                                  Do you want to
password?(y/n):
n
Do you want to import an URIs file?(y/n):
n


--------------------------------------------------------------

Request summary:
OAM Agent Name:10GWG_OHS
Base URL:http://focusthreaderp.com:7781
URL String:10GOHS
Registering in Mode:inband
Your registration request is being been sent to the Admin server at: http://focusthreaderp.com:7001
--------------------------------------------------------------

Inband registration process completed successfully! Output artifacts are created in the output folder.
[idam@focusthreaderp bin]$
```

The execution of RREG will create:

- An instance of WebGate under OAM Agents in the 10*g* WebGate container under **System Configuration** tab of the OAM Administration console:

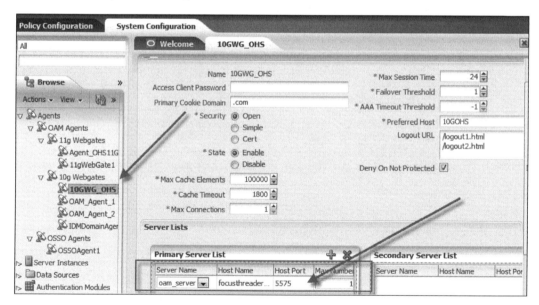

- A **Host Identifier** under **Shared Components** in **Policy Configuration** tab:

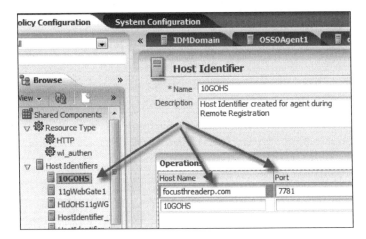

- An application domain under **Application Domains** in **Policy Configuration** tab:

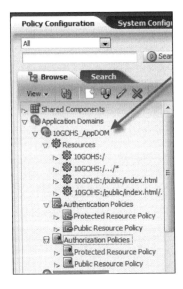

- The registration process will also create the following files under the
  $OAM_REG_HOME/output/<AgentID> directory, which must be copied
  to the WebGate instance directory after 10*g* WebGate installation:

    ○ ObAccessClient.xml files.

- ○ If the WebGate to OAM server communication mode is set to **Simple** then it creates three additional file `password.xml`, `aaa_key.pem`, and `aaa_cert.pem`

- ○ If the WebGate to OAM server communication mode is **Cert** then it creates one additional file `password.xml`

Installing 10*g* WebGate Software

10*g* WebGate must be installed on the same machine where the web server is running. WebGate must be installed using the same operating system user who owns the web server executables. 10*g* WebGate should already be provisioned/registered before you can install 10*g* WebGate.

OAM Proxy server: OAM Proxy server is installed with each managed server for OAM server. OAM Proxy is used for backward compatibility for 10*g* WebGate that is registered with 11*g* OAM server. OAM Proxy server listens on port 5575 by default. To view/modify this setting, login to **OAM Administration console | System Configuration | Server Instances | oam_server1**:

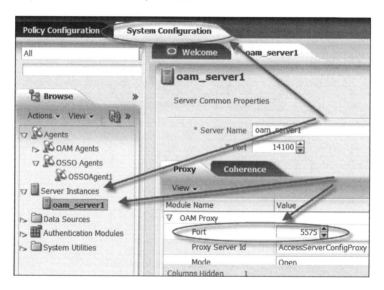

1. Start the 10*g* WebGate installer.

2. Click **Next** on the welcome page:

    - ○ For Windows: Click **Next** on the screen where you get the message to install WebGate with a user who has administrative privileges.

    - ○ For Unix: Select the username and group of the user who is running the web server.

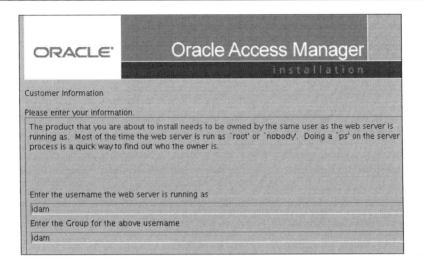

3. Enter the location of the WebGate installation directory:

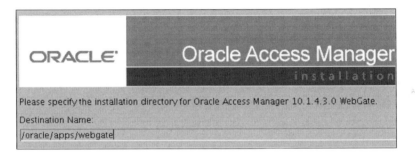

4. For Unix/Linux only, provide the location of GCC:

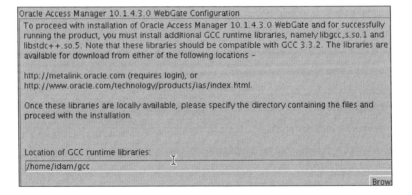

5. On the WebGate configuration screen, select transport security mode
   (Open, Simple, Cert)

   [Security Mode on WebGate should match with Security
   Mode of OAM Proxy server.]

6. Enter **WebGate ID**, **Access Server ID**, OAM server host, and port:

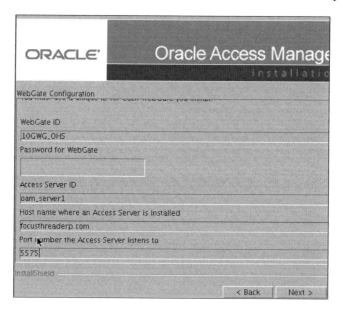

- ○ **WebGate ID**: Enter the agent name that you supplied during
  registration. That is, `10GWG_OHS`.
- ○ **WebGate password**: Enter the password supplied during
  registration, if any. If no password was entered, leave the field blank.
- ○ **Access server ID**: Enter the name of the OAM 11*g* server with which
  this WebGate is registered, if desired, or use any name you choose
  such as `oam_server1`.
- ○ **Access server hostname**: Enter the DNS hostname for the OAM 11*g*
  server with which this WebGate is registered.
- ○ **Port number**: Enter the port on which the OAM Proxy is running.
  (The default value is `5575`).

OAM Managed server `oam_server1` should be running and the OAM proxy port should be open across the firewall from the web server to OAM server.

7. In the next screen, you get an option to update your web server configuration file to include the WebGate plugin. This configuration can be updated later as well:

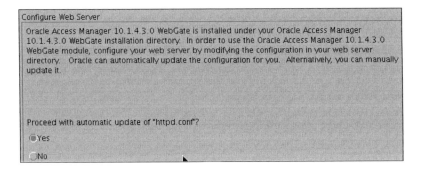

8. Enter the location of the Web server configuration file. For OHS 10*g*, configuration file location is `$OHS_INSTALL_DIR/Apache/Apache/conf/httpd.conf`.

9. Click **Finish**.

10. Copy the files/artifacts generated during WebGate provisioning/registration to the WebGate instance directory.

    Copy files generated during the registration process under `$OAM_REG_HOME/output/<AgentID>` directory from OAM server to `$WEBGATE_INSTALL_DIR/access/oblix/config`.

11. Restart the web server (OHS 10*g*) using OPMNCTL:

    `$OHS10G_INSTALL_DIR/opmn/bin/opmnctl stopall`

    `$OHS10G_INSTALL_DIR/opmn/bin/opmnctl startall`

12. Confirm the WebGate installation.

    Confirm the WebGate installation by accessing the following URL on your browser:

    ◦ For most Web servers (apart from IIS): `http(s)://hostname:port/access/oblix/apps/webgate/bin/webgate.cgi?progid=1`

    ◦ For IIS Web server: `http(s)://hostname:port/access/oblix/apps/webgate/bin/webgate.dll?progid=1`

If the WebGate diagnostic page appears as shown in the following screenshot, the WebGate is functioning properly:

OAM agent (WebGate/OSSO) properties

When you register an OAM agent either from the OAM Administrator console or using RREG, you get some default properties set for agent.

OAM agent, also known as WebGate is a pre-packaged web server plugin which communicates with OAM server. There are two versions of OAM Agents, namely 11*g* WebGates and 10*g* WebGates.

OSSO agent is an agent introduced in OAM 11*g* for applications protected by mod_osso (Oracle as 10g SSO).

Agent registration in OAM 11*g* is organized under the **System Configuration** tab of the OAM Administration console. To access agent properties, login to **OAM Administration Console | Administration Console | Agents** and then **OAM Agents** (for 10*g*/11*g* WebGate) or **OSSO Agent** (for OSSO Agents). The following section describes properties configured for:

- 11*g* WebGate
- 10*g* WebGate
- OSSO Agent

11*g* WebGate Properties

This section describes 11*g* WebGate properties, which can be edited from the OAM Administration console with the exception of **Name** and **Deny On Not Protected:**

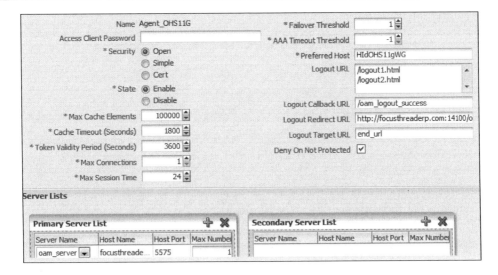

- Name: Name of the WebGate.

- Access **Client Password**: An optional parameter. When WebGate connects to OAM server, it uses the password to authenticate itself to the OAM server.

- Security: Transport mode between WebGate and OAM server. It can have three possible values **Open**, **Simple**, and **Cert**.

- State: Whether WebGate is enabled or disabled.

- Max **Cache Elements**: The number of elements (URLs, authentication schemes) maintained in the cache, including data such as whether a URL is protected or not.

- Cache Timeout (Seconds): Amount of time data is maintained in the cache before WebGate contacts OAM server for any changes.

- Token **Validity Period(Seconds)**: Maximum time period (in seconds) for an agent token (the content of `OAMAuthnCookie`) to remain valid.

- Max **Connections**: The maximum number of connections that this OAM agent can establish with the OAM server.

- Max **Session Time**: The maximum duration, in hours, for a connection between the WebGate and the OAM server. A value of **0** means WebGate maintains connection with OAM server until one of them dies.

- **Failover Threshold**: This is the number which determines when WebGate should failover to a secondary OAM server. When the number of live primary OAM servers drops below this value, WebGate will failover from OAM server listed in **Primary Server List** to the one listed in the **Secondary Server List**.

- AAA **Timeout Threshold**: Specifies how long (in seconds) the web component waits for a non-responsive OAM server before it considers it unreachable and attempts to contact another. **-1** value indicates that WebGate will use the default TCP/IP timeout figure.

- Preferred **Host**: This information is used to acquire web server host information. To support virtual hosts on Apache-based web servers (OHS, IHS, Apache) set this value to SERVER_NAME. To support virtual hosts on non Apache-based Web servers set this value to HOST_HTTP_HEADER. There should be a corresponding **Host Identifier** listed in the OAM Administration console (See *Chapter 6,* section on *Host Identifiers*).

- Logout **URL**: Triggers the logout handler, which removes the cookie (ObSSOCookie for 10*g* WebGates; OAMAuthnCookie for 11*g* WebGates) and requires the user to re-authenticate the next time he accesses a resource protected by OAM. If there is a match in the URL, the WebGate logout handler is triggered. If this field is left blank, the logout handler is triggered when users access a URL containing the text "logout" (except logout.gif or logout.jpg).

- Logout **Callback URL**: The URL to oam_logout_success, which clears cookies during the callback. This can be a URI format without host:port (recommended), where the OAM server calls back on the host:port of the original resource request. This can also be a full URL format with a host:port, where OAM 11*g* server calls back directly without reconstructing a callback URL. When the request URL matches the **Logout Callback URL**, WebGate clears its cookies and streams an image file (in GIF format) in the response. This is similar to OSSO agent behavior.

- Logout **Redirect URL**: This parameter is automatically populated after agent registration completes. By default, this is based on the OAM server host name with a default port of 14100 and a default value of http://OAM_Host:14100/oam/server/logout. When the WebGate logout handler is triggered, it redirects to the page specified by this parameter. If this is left blank, then 10*g* WebGate behavior is triggered, serving the local logout page instead of redirecting to another. The local logout page can have a customized script to redirect to the central logout page and can clear additional third-party cookies if desired.

- Logout **Target URL**: The value for this is the name of the query parameter that the OPSS application passes to WebGate during logout. This query parameter specifies the target URL of the landing page after logout. If this value is configured, WebGate searches for the value passed in the logout request's query parameter, and passes it as `end_url` query parameter in the redirect URL to OAM server. If left blank, WebGate searches for the default name `end_url` and passes that `end_url` query parameter along.

- Deny **On Not Protected**: Always selected in 11*g* WebGate and cannot be changed. Denies access to all resources to which access is not explicitly allowed by a rule or policy.

- Primary **Server List**: List of Primary OAM servers to which WebGate can connect.

- Secondary **Server List**: List of Secondary OAM server which WebGate can connect when the number of connections to primary OAM servers goes below the value defined in **Failover Threshold**.

10*g* WebGate Properties

This section describes 10*g* Webgate properties,which can be edited from the OAM Administration console with the exception of **Name**:

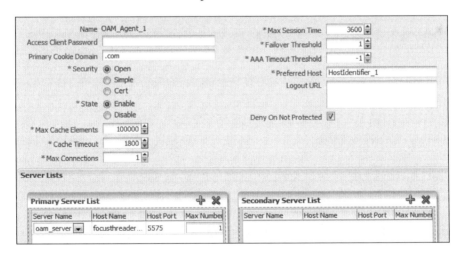

- **Name**: Name of the agent.

- **Access Client Password**: An optional parameter. When Webgate connects to OAM server, it uses the password to authenticate itself to the OAM server.

- **Primary Cookie Domain**: Describes the Web server domain (client domain) on which the OAM 10*g* agent is deployed. For example, onlineappsdba.com.

- **Security**: Transport mode between WebGate and OAM server. It can have three possible values: **Open**, **Simple**, and **Cert**.

- **State**: Whether WebGate is enabled or disabled.

- **Max Cache Elements**: Number of elements (URLs, authentication schemes) maintained in the cache, including data such as whether a URL is protected or not.

- **Cache Timeout**: Amount of time (in seconds) cached information remains in the OAM agent cache when the information is neither used nor referenced.

- **Max Connections**: The maximum number of connections that this OAM agent can establish with the OAM server.

- **Max Session Time**: Maximum amount of time in seconds that a user's authentication session is valid, regardless of their activity. At expiration of this session time, the user is re-challenged for authentication. This is a forced logout.

- **Failover Threshold**: This value determines when WebGate should failover to a secondary OAM server. When the number of live primary OAM servers drops below this value, WebGate will failover from the OAM server listed in **Primary Server List** to the OAM server listed in **Secondary Server List**.

- **AAA Timeout Threshold**: Specifies how long (in seconds) the Web component waits for a non-responsive OAM server before it considers it unreachable and attempts to contact another. A **-1** value indicates that WebGate will use default TCP/IP timeout figure.

- **Preferred Host**: This information is used to acquire web server host information. To support virtual hosts on Apache-based Web servers (OHS, IHS, Apache), set this value to SERVER_NAME. To support virtual hosts on non Apache-based Web servers, set this value to HOST_HTTP_HEADER. There should be a corresponding **Host Identifier** defined before setting preferred host.

- **Logout URL**: Triggers the logout handler, which removes the cookie (ObSSOCookie for 10*g* WebGates; OAMAuthnCookie for 11*g* WebGates) and requires the user to re-authenticate the next time he accesses a resource protected by OAM. If there is a match in the URL, the WebGate logout handler is triggered. If this field is left blank, then when the user accesses any URL containing the text logout (except logout.gif or logout.jpg), the logout handler is triggered.

- **Deny On Not Protected**: Denies access to all resources to which access is not explicitly allowed by a rule or policy. This can be disabled for 10*g* WebGate.

- **Primary Server List**: List of primary OAM servers to which WebGate can connect.

- **Secondary Server List**: List of secondary OAM servers to which WebGate can connect when the number of connections to primary OAM servers goes below the value defined in **Failover Threshold**.

OSSO agent properties

This section describes OSSO agent properties, which can be edited from the OAM Administration console with exception of **Name**, **Token Version**, and **Site Token**:

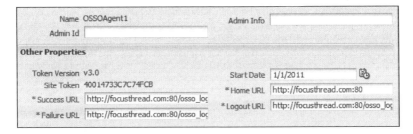

- **Name**: Name of the agent.

- **Admin Info**: Optional administrator details for this mod_osso instance. For example, OSSO Administrator.

- **Admin Id**: Optional administrator login ID for this mod_osso instance.

- **Token Version**: SSO token version.
    - v3.0 represents the most secure token, using the AES encryption standard for tokens exchanged between OAM 11*g* server and mod_osso. OSSO version 10.1.4.3 supports token v3.0.
    - v1.4 uses the DES encryption standard and is supported by OSSO 10*g* prior to OSSO 10.1.4.3 PatchSet.
    - v1.2 uses DES encryption standard and is used to exchange between OSSO partners prior to OSSO 10.1.4.0.1.

- **Site Token**: The application token used by the partner when requesting authentication. This cannot be edited.

- **Start Date**: First month, day, and year for which login to the application is allowed by the server.

- **Success URL**: The redirect URL to be used upon successful authentication.

- **Failure URL**: The redirect URL to be used if authentication fails.

- **Home URL**: The redirect URL to be used for the home page after authentication.

- **Logout URL**: The redirect URL to be used when logging out. This redirects the user to the global logout page on the server `osso_logout_success`.

Summary

In this chapter, we discussed about policy enforcement points in OAM, namely, 10*g*/11*g* Webgate and OSSO Agent. We covered step-by-step instructions to install 11*g* WebGate for OHS 11*g* and 10*g* Webgate for 10*g* OHS. We also covered properties/parameters of WebGate and OSSO Agent.

In the next chapter we are going to discuss Oracle Identity Manager (OIM) administration and navigation through the administration and design consoles.

9
OIM Navigation: Administration and Design Console

There are multiple ways in which users or other external systems can talk to the Oracle Identity Manager (OIM). In this chapter, we will cover various Oracle Identity Management interfaces, such as Oracle Identity Manager Administrative and User Console, Design Console, and SPML Web Service. Design Console can be used to configure system settings and allows you to perform user management, resource management, process management, and other administrative and development tasks.

This chapter covers the following topics:

- OIM Administrative and User Console
- Oracle Identity Manager Design Console interface
- SPML Web Service interface
- Installation of OIM Design Console

OIM interfaces

Oracle Identity Manager supports three interfaces to perform identity management tasks:

- Oracle Identity Manager Administrative and User Console
- Oracle Identity Manager Design Console
- SPML Web Service

Oracle Identity Manager Administrative and User Console

Oracle Identity Manager Administrative and User Console is a HTML-based interface accessible to both authenticated and unauthenticated users. The URL to access Oracle Identity Manager Administrative and User Console is `http://servername:<oim_port>/oim` (default OIM Port is 14000). The console provides four categories of user interface:

- Self-Service Console for unauthenticated users
- Self-Service Console for authenticated users
- Administration Console for authenticated users
- Advanced Administration for authenticated users

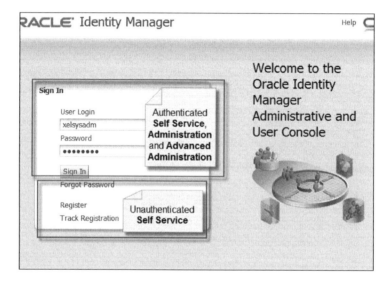

Self-Service Console for unauthenticated users

The self-service console for unauthenticated users (users who have not authenticated or logged into Oracle Identity Manager) provides the following functions:

- Reset a forgotten password
- Self-registration
- Tracking self-registration requests

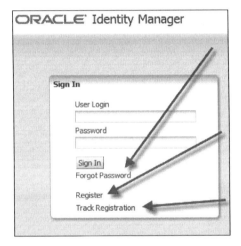

Reset a forgotten password

The **Forgot Password** link on Oracle Identity Manager Administrative and User Interface is used to reset a forgotten password. You must correctly answer the challenge questions set during user registration or by account creation workflow to successfully reset a password.

1. First click on the **Forgot Password** link, type the user ID in the **User Login** textbox, then click **Next**:

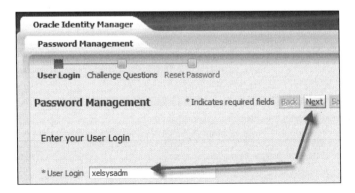

2. Answer the challenge questions set during account registration and click **Next**:

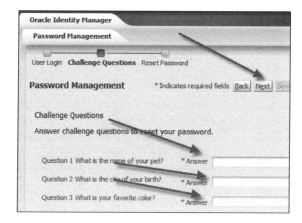

3. Type a new password, confirm it by typing the password again, then click **Save**:

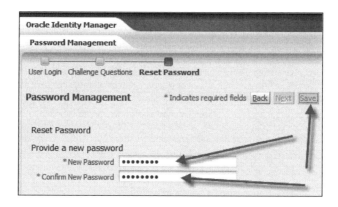

4. Finally, you should get a confirmation message "**Password has been reset**". You will be automatically logged in.

 In the previous version of OIM, you would be redirected back to the login page.

Self-registration

The **Register** link on Oracle Identity Manager Administrative and User Interface is used for self-registration.

1. To self-register, click on the **Register** link. Next, fill the mandatory attributes **Last Name** and **Email** and the optional attributes **First Name**, **Middle Name**, **Common Name**, and **Display Name**, and then click **Next**:

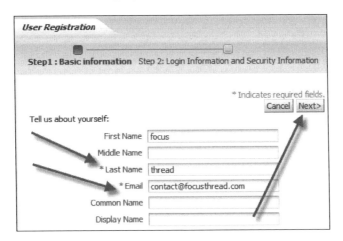

2. Set User ID, Password, challenge questions, and Password Policy (if configured) then click **Register**:

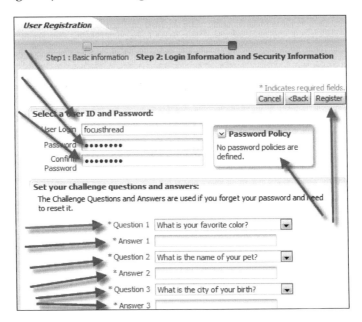

3. Finally you should get a confirmation message "Congratulations, <user id> Your registration request has been sent. Your registration tracking request number is : <tracking number>".

Note down tracking number to find the status of your registration number. User Registration request is sent to the SOA Server. If the SOA server is down your registration request will fail. Make sure the SOA server is up and running.

Track self-registration requests

The Track Registration link on Oracle Identity Manager Administrative and User Interface is used to track the status of self-registration.

1. To track status of self registration, click on the **Track Registration** link, type the **Tracking ID** (received during self-registration), and click on **Submit**:

2. You will get the status of the tracked request, which will be failed, pending, rejected, or approved.

 For a failed status, the reason for failure is not displayed. Administrators can check OIM Managed server log file to find reasons for the failed status.

Self-Service Console for authenticated users

This console is available to all users with an account in Oracle Identity Manager. When a non-administrator logs into Oracle Identity Manager Administrative and User Console, they are sent to the Self-Service Console by default. When an OIM Administrator (for example, XELSYSADM) logs in, they can switch between Self-Service, Administration, and Advanced Administration Console:

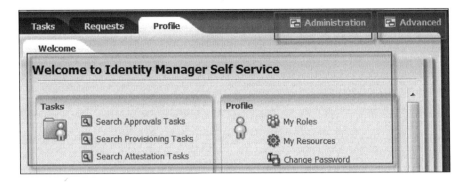

For authenticated users, the Self-Service Console provides following functions:

- Profile management
- Request management
- Task management

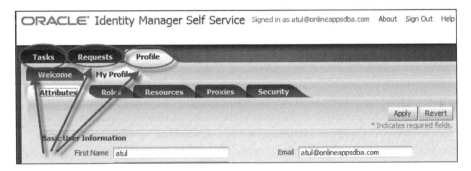

Profile management

An authenticated user can manage their profile by clicking the **Profile** tab on the Self-Service Console. Using the **Profile** page a user can:

- **Modify User Attribute**: Modify certain attributes for themselves such as First Name, Last Name, Telephone Number, and so on
- **Manage Roles**: Request or Remove Roles
- **Manage Resources**: Request or Modify Resource
- **Manage Proxies**: Add or Remove Proxies, that is, assign tasks or responsibilities to a delegated user
- **Manage Security**: Change Password or Security Questions

Request management

The **Request** tab in Self-Service Console is used to create requests for yourself or other users, view the status of requests, or withdraw a pending request. An example of a request includes requesting access to a resource (e-Business Suite or Active Directory) or role (Administrators or System Configuration Administrators)

Task management

The **Tasks** tab in Self-Service Console enables you to view tasks that have been assigned to yourself, to roles you have membership of, or to users you manage. The **Provisioning** tab under the **Tasks** tab, lists task pending manual provisioning or failed automatic provisioning tasks. The **Attestation** tab under Tasks, lists tasks pending an outstanding attestation process, including reviewing reports about provisioned resources.

In the previous versions of OIM, administrators were able to reassign provisioning tasks in this tab. In 11*g* you have to go to the **Resource Profile** tab within a user's account to reassign a provisioning task.

Administration Console

Oracle Identity Manager Administration Console is accessible by clicking the **Administration** link on the top-right corner of the screen. This console provides two tabs, **Administration** and **Authorization Policy** as shown in the following screenshot:

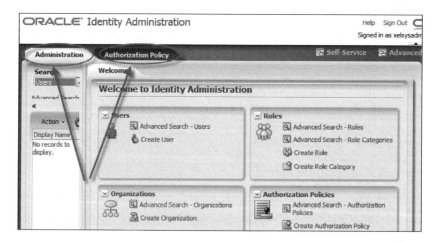

The **Administration Console** provides the following functions:

- **Users**: Enables users to search, create, or modify user accounts.

- **Organizations**: Enables users to search, create, or modify organizational records.

- **Roles**: Roles represents a logical grouping of users to which specific access rights can be assigned. This option enables users to search, create, or modify roles and roles categories.

- **Authorization Policies**: Oracle Identity Manager is integrated with **Oracle Entitlement Server (OES)** as authorization system and provides access control to Oracle Identity Manager application. This option enables users to create or modify authorization policies.

Advanced Administration Console

This console is accessible by clicking the **Advanced** link on the top-right corner of the screen. As shown in the following screenshot, there are five tabs available:

- **Administration**
- **Event Management**
- **Policies**
- **Configuration**
- **System Management**

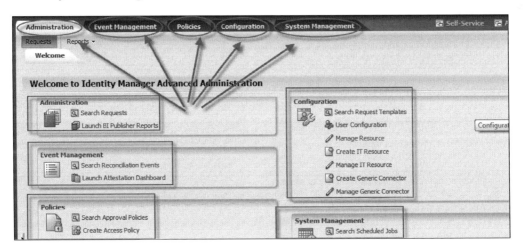

Oracle Identity Manager Design Console

The Oracle Identity Manager Design Console is a Java-based application which interacts directly with the business logic tier of Oracle Identity Manager architecture. Start OIM Design Console using:

```
cd %ORACLE_HOME%\designconsole\xlclient.cmd
```

Installing Design Console

Oracle Identity Manager Design Console is mainly used to configure system settings. To install Design Console on Windows:

1. Download and install JRE 1.6 or higher.

2. Install Oracle Identity and access Management Software on Windows:

   ```
   cd OIM_SOFTWARE_LOCATION/Disk1
   ```

   ```
   setup.exe -jreLoc <JRE_Location>
   ```

   where JRE_Location is a top-level directory for JRE installation. You can use JDK 1.6 too.

3. Installer will run all prerequisite checks. In the next screen specify the Oracle Middleware Home and Oracle Home (for IDAM) directory.

4. Click on the **Install** button to install Oracle Identity and Access Management Component.

5. Configure OIM Design Console:

   ```
   cd %ORACLE_HOME%\bin
   ```

   ```
   config.cmd
   ```

6. Select the **OIM Design Console** checkbox and click **Next**:

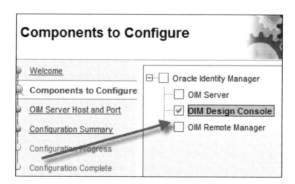

Enter **OIM Server Hostname** and **OIM Server Port** (default port is 14000) as shown in the following screenshot:

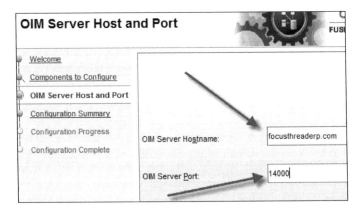

7. Select **Configure**.

8. Click **Finish**.

9. Create wlfullcleint.jar on the OIM Server. (Skip this step if file is already created on the OIM server.)

10. Copy wlfullclient.jar from the server to %ORACLE_HOME%\designconsole\ext

11. Start the OIM Design Console using:

```
cd %ORACLE_HOME%\designconsole
xlclient.cmd
```

12. Enter **UserID**(xelsysadm) and **Password** of OIM Administrator.

OIM Design Console navigation

This section contains navigation and key functionality supported by OIM Design console. The following figure displays the view when a users logs in to a Design Console as an OIM Super-user (for example, as user XELSYSADM).

 The folders and tools available in the Design Console will vary depending on the privileges of user used to login to the Design Console.

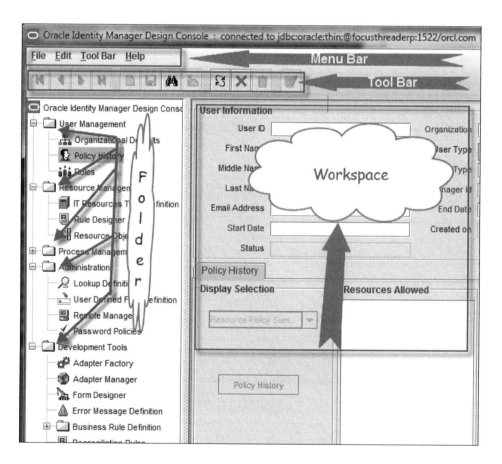

Menu Bar: The **MenuBar** is displayed at the top of the window and contains menus to perform operations in the Design Console.

Tool Bar: The **ToolBar** is displayed just below the menu bar and consists of buttons for frequently used actions like first record, next record, save, query, and so on.

Folders: Folders enables access to specific functions in OIM Design Console. These are arranged on the left-hand side of the Design Console and include User Management, Resource Management, Process Management, Administration, Development Tools, and Business Rule Definition.

Forms: Forms enable administrators to perform certain actions through the Design Console. Forms are arranged in folders, which will be displayed on the right-hand panel of the Design Console known as the **workspace**.

Workspace: Workspace is the region of the main screen that displays forms. This section contains:

- User Management
- Resource Management
- Process Management
- Administration
- Development Tools
- Business Rule Definition

User Management

The User Management folder provides tools to create and manage users, roles, and organizations. It contains the following forms:

- **Organizational Defaults**: Use this form to specify the default values that the organization users should have for certain resources.
- **Policy History**: Use this form to view resources that are allowed and disallowed for users through the policy system.
- **Roles**: Use this form to specify which Design Console forms are available for which roles.

Resource Management

The Resource Management folder provides tools to create and manage Resources. It contains the following forms:

- **IT Resources Type Definition**: Use this form to create resource types that are displayed as lookup values on the IT Resources form.

- **Rule Designer**: Use this form to create rules that can be applied to password policy selection, autogroup membership, provisioning process selection, task assignment, and pre-populating adapters.

- **Resource Objects**: Use this form to create and manage resource objects. These objects represent resources that you want to make available to users and organizations.

Process Management

The Process Management folder provides tools to create and manage processes and e-mail templates. IT contains the following forms:

- **Email Definition**: This form enables you to create templates for e-mail notifications.

- **Process Definition**: This form is used to create and manage approval and provisioning processes. It also lets you start the **workflow definition renderer** that displays your workflow definition in a graphical presentation.

Administration

The Administration folder provides tools to manage Oracle Identity Manager administrative features. It contains the following forms:

- **Lookup Definition**: Use this form to create and manage lookup definitions. A lookup definition represents a lookup field and the values you can access from that lookup field.

- **User Defined Field Definition**: Use this form to create and manage user-defined fields. A user-defined field enables you to store additional information, such as user, request, and resource information.

- **Remote Manager**: Use this form to display information about the servers that the Oracle Identity Manager uses to communicate with third-party programs. These servers are known as **remote managers**.

- **Password Policies**: Use this form to set password restrictions for users and view the rules and resource objects that are associated with a password policy.

Development Tools

The `Development Tools` folder provides tools to customize Oracle Identity Manager, and contains another folder, `Business Rules Definitions`. The `Development Tools` folder contains the following forms:

- **Adapter Factory**: You use this form to create and manage the code that enables Oracle Identity Manager to communicate with any IT Resource by connecting to that resource's API. This code is known as an **adapter**.

- **Adapter Manager**: You use this form to compile multiple adapters simultaneously.

- **Form Designer**: You use this form to create process and resource object forms that do not come packaged with Oracle Identity Manager.

- **Error Message Definition**: You use this form to create error messages that can be used for reporting when certain problems occur while using Oracle Identity Manager. This form also enables a system administrator or developer to define the error messages that users can access when they create error handler tasks using the Adapter Factory form.

- **Reconciliation Rules**: You use this form to create and manage reconciliation rules in Oracle Identity Manager.

The Business Rule Definition subfolder contains the following forms:

- **Event Handler Manager**: You use this form to create and manage the event handlers that are used with Oracle Identity Manager.

- **Data Object Manager**: Through this form, you can define a data object, assign event handlers and adapters to it, and map any adapter variables associated with it.

 There are additional steps for approval processes in 11*g* now that it is incorporated with SOA.

SPML Web Service

Oracle Identity Manager provides its identity management service to client applications, so they can manage users and roles. The service uses Service Provisioning Markup Language (SPML), which is an XML framework for exchanging user, resource, and service provisioning information. SPML Web Service supports inbound provisioning requests for creation, modification, deletion, and lookup of Oracle Identity Manager users, organizations, and roles. The interface also provides features for managing role membership, resetting passwords, and enabling/disabling user accounts. As per SPML specifications, interactions can be synchronous or asynchronous; Oracle Identity Manager supports only asynchronous interaction for add, delete, suspend, and resume requests. All username services in OIM are synchronous. To use SPML services, the application must create a web service client. WSDL for this client is available at `http://OIM_Server:OIM_PORT/ spml-xsd/SPMLService?WSDL`.

The following table lists default web services available in OIM:

Sl. No.	SPML Service	Description
1	addRequest	To create an identity with user or role attributes.
2	modifyRequest	To modify an existing role, user attribute, or to assign/revoke role membership from an existing user.
3	deleteRequest	To delete an existing role or user. To delete a role membership from an existing user.
4	statusRequest	Enables a requestor to determine whether a synchronous has failed, is pending, or is completed successfully.
5	listTargets	Enables a requestor to obtain the set of targets that the provider makes available for provisioning.
6	suspendRequest	Enables requester to suspend/disable an existing user.
7	resumeRequest	Enables requester to resume/enable a suspended user.
8	activeRequest	Enables requester to determine whether a specified user is active or has been suspended.
9	validateUsername	Enables requester to determine whether a username already exists or it is reserved.
10	suggestUsername	Enables requester to obtain a valid username for a given policy

Summary

In this chapter, we covered various interfaces to Oracle Identity Manager namely, Administrative and User Console, SPML Web Service and Design Console. We also covered various administrative and user consoles such as authenticated and unauthenticated Self-Service, Administration, and Advanced Administration Consoles.

In the next chapter we are going to cover OIM Connectors, their types, and events such as reconciliation and provisioning. We will also cover installation and configuration of three predefined connectors for Oracle Identity Manager.

10

OIM Connectors—Installation and Configuration

An OIM connector contains information and functionality to integrate OIM with heterogeneous targets, such as Oracle Internet Directory, Microsoft Active Directory, Oracle E-Business Suite, or SAP. This chapter covers:

- Integration solution available with OIM
- Reconciliation, provisioning, and predefined connectors
- Installation and configuration of predefined connector for MS-AD, EBS, and OID

Connector

A **connector** is a container that contains all the components used by OIM to communicate with a resource in order to provision or reconcile with that resource. OIM's Advanced Administration console provides two web-based wizards to install/configure a connector, namely **Connector Installer** and **Deployment Manager**.

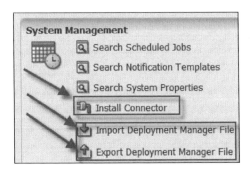

- **Connector Installer** is used to import and configure predefined connectors.
- **Deployment Manager** is used to export connectors and connector components. Deployment Manager is also used to import connectors and connector components not supported by the Connector Installer.

Connector Components

An OIM connector must have the following seven components:

- IT resource type
- IT resource
- Process form
- Process task adapter
- Resource object
- Provisioning process
- Process task

IT resource type

The **IT resource type** contains information about classification type, parameter fields, and settings associated with an external resource. Multiple IT resources are grouped together into this one category called IT Resource Type. Each connector has one and only one IT resource type associated with it. The Database or Directory Server resource represents a IT resource type.

IT resource

An **IR resource** contains values that OIM requires to communicate with a target system, such as Microsoft Active Directory or Oracle Database. The information stored includes hostname, username, and password of the target system. There must be one IT resource for each installation or instance of a target system. For example, if you have two Oracle databases (Database A and Database B) to provision then you must create two IT, resources each with the IT resource type set to database.

Process form

A **process form** captures data required to either provision a user to an external resource, or reconcile a user with this resource. Each process form consists of field definitions required by the standard connector. If you require additional fields, you can create another version of the form and add the required fields. For every provisioning process, there will be one process form. For example, there are 10 users provisioned with accounts in Database A, and 10 users provisioned with accounts in Database B; this will involve a single process form, but 20 instances of it.

Resource object

A **resource object** is a virtual representation of a target application to which you want to provision the account. A one-to-one relationship exists between the connector and the resource object. That is, each connector should have only one resource object associated with it.

Provisioning process

The **provisioning process** represents the flow or logic that OIM must complete to perform provisioning or reconciliation. Each connector contains a single provisioning process, but you can create additional provisioning processes.

Process task

A **process task** is a step contained in the provisioning process and represents the action that OIM performs in a resource. A one-to-many relationship exists between a provisioning process and its process tasks. Each provisioning process contains five predefined process tasks to create, disable, enable, update, and delete a user.

 Approval tasks in OIM 11*g* are also managed by SOA Suite.

Process task adapter

A **process task adapter** is the Java code used to automate completion of a provisioning task. Each adapter is predefined with certain mappings and functionalities. Each process task has one adapter associated with it, so there will be one adapter for each task such as enable user, disable user, or create user.

Types of OIM connectors

OIM provides three types of connector solution:

- Predefined connectors
- Custom connector using adapter factory
- Generic technology connector

Predefined connectors

OIM provides a broad range of predefined connectors for commercial applications and identity-aware systems. These predefined connectors are found in the OIM Connector Pack at `http://www.oracle.com/technetwork/middleware/id-mgmt/downloads/connectors-101674.html` and are currently available for Oracle e-Business Suite (Employee Reconciliation, User Management), Oracle Internet Directory, Oracle Retail Warehouse Management, SAP (CUA, Employee Reconciliation, User Management), PeopleSoft (Employee Reconciliation, User Management), Microsoft (Active Directory, Active Directory Password Sync, Microsoft Exchange), IBM (Lotus Notes/Domino, AS/400 Adv, RACF standard/advanced), JDEdward (EnterpriseOne), CA (ACF2 Advanced, Top Secret Advanced), RSA (Authentication Manager, Clear Trust), UNIX (SSH, Telnet), Novell (eDirectory, GroupWise), and BMC Remedy (Ticket Management, User Management).

 9.1.X OIM Connectors are compatible with Oracle Identity Manager 11*g*.

Custom connector using Adapter Factory

Adapter factory provided by OIM is a code-generation tool that enables you to create Java classes. You can create or modify integration connectors Adapter Factory's GUI, without programming or scripting.

Generic technology connector

If there is no predefined connector to integrate OIM with a target system, and if you do not need the customization features of the Adapter Factory, then you can create a connector using the generic technology connector feature of OIM.

 Predefined connectors are the preferred method of integration; use them if one is available.

Provisioning and reconciliation

This section covers two important processes: provisioning and reconciliation in OIM integration. The following figure shows that provisioning or reconciliation involves synchronization from OIM to the target system, or from the target system to OIM:

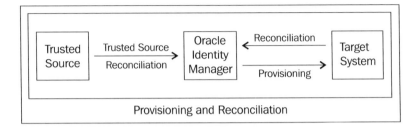

Provisioning and Reconciliation

In terms of flow, **provisioning** provides an outward flow of user information from OIM using a push model, whereas **reconciliation** provides an inward flow of user information into OIM by using either a push or a pull model.

Provisioning

Provisioning is the process by which operations such as user creation, modification, or deletion which start on OIM are communicated to the target system. Provisioning can be request-based, policy-based, or direct.

Request-based provisioning

A request can be manually created by the administrator, or by users themselves to provision the account in the target system. Approval workflows are started after the provisioning request is submitted, and after the approval, the account is provisioned in the target system.

Policy-based provisioning

In policy-based provisioning the user is provisioned in the target resource automatically, based on defined policies. Policies are used to define associations between the role and the target system. By default, each member of these roles gets a predefined account in the target system.

Direct provisioning

This type of provisioning is a special administrator-only function where an authorized administrator can create a user account on the target system without any approval process.

 When you install the OIM connector, the direct provisioning feature is automatically enabled.

Reconciliation

Reconciliation is the process by which operations such as user creation, modification, or deletion which start on the target system (OID, E-Business, SAP, and so on) are communicated to OIM. The reconciliation process compares the entries in the OIM repository and the target system repository, determines the difference between the two repositories, and applies the latest changes to the OIM repository. Reconciliation is of two types, trusted source reconciliation and account reconciliation.

Trusted source reconciliation

If data is reconciled from a system (for example, Active Directory) that drives the creation of users, roles, role memberships, or role hierarchies into OIM, then that reconciliation mode is called **trusted source reconciliation**. Trusted source reconciliation is also known as **authoritative source reconciliation**.

Account reconciliation

In **account reconciliation** mode, changes made to the user's access rights on an external resource are reconciled directly into OIM.

Installing predefined connectors

Predefined connectors are used to integrate OIM with heterogeneous IT systems for provisioning or reconciliation. All predefined connectors are installed using Connector Installer from the OIM Advanced Administration screen. To go to Connector Installer:

1. Login to the OIM Advanced Administration console at
    `http://server:14000/oim` and then click the **Advanced** link,
    as shown in the following screenshot:

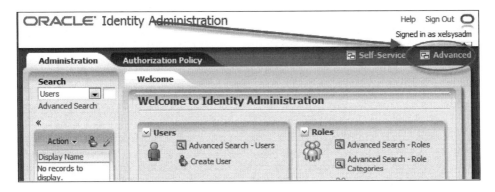

2. On the **Advanced Administration** console screen, select **Install Connector** under **System Management**, as shown in the following screenshot:

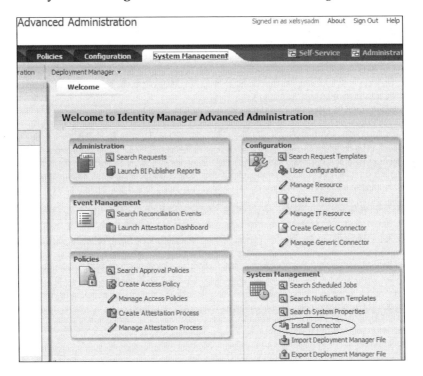

This section covers deploying three predefined OIM connectors:

- Deploying the OIM connector for Oracle Internet Directory

- Deploying the OIM connector for Microsoft Active Directory User Management

- Deploying the OIM connector for Oracle e-Business Suite User Management

Deploying the OIM connector for Oracle Internet Directory

Oracle Internet Directory(OID) is a **Lightweight Directory Access Protocol (LDAP)** version 3 compliant Directory Server from Oracle. Oracle Identity Manager Connector installation/configuration for Oracle Internet Directory OID for provisioning and reconciliation includes the following points:

- Preinstallation
- Installation
- Configuring IT resource for OID
- Using OIM-OID connector

Preinstallation steps

1. Download the connector file from `http://www.oracle.com/technetwork/middleware/id-mgmt/downloads/connectors-101674.html`.

2. Upload the connector software to the OIM server at:

   `$ORACLE_HOME/server/ConnectorDefaultDirectory`.

3. Unzip the connector file software uploaded on the server at:

   `$ORACLE_HOME/server/ConnectorDefaultDirectory`.

4. Download LDAP-1.2.4 from `http://java.sun.com/products/jndi/downloads/index.html` (Click on **Download JNDI 1.2.1 & More**) and then click on the **ldap-1_2_4.zip** link. Extract `ldap.jar` and `ldapbp.jar` from the lib directory of `ldap-1_2_4.zip`. Upload these two jar files to the `$ORACLE_HOME/server/ThirdParty` directory on the OIM server.

    In OIM Cluster deployment, copy connect media and all jar files on all the nodes of OIM cluster.

5. Create a user account on the target system for connector operations. (This is an optional step; you could use the existing user with proper privileges on the target OID instance). OIM connector will use this account to connect to the target system.

6. Upload external code files to the OIM Server at `$ORACLE_HOME/server/ThirdParty`.

Installing OIM-OID connector

1. Log in to the OIM Advanced Administration console at `http://server:14000/oim` and then click on the **Advanced** link.

2. On the **Advanced Administration** console screen, select **Install Connector** under **System Management**.

3. From the **Connector List** drop-down menu, select connector (**Oracle Internet Directory 9.0.4.12**) and click on **Load** and then **Continue**, as shown in the following screenshot:

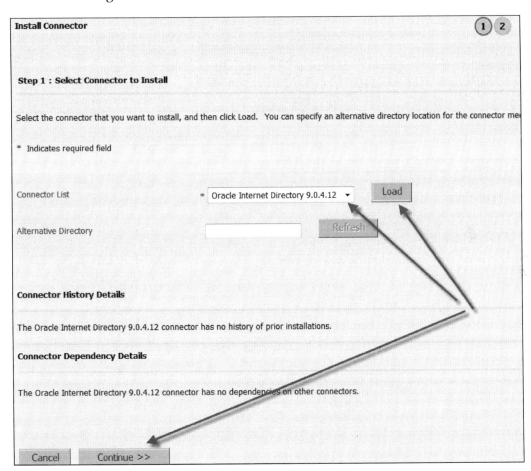

4. Click **Finish** after Connector Installation completes.

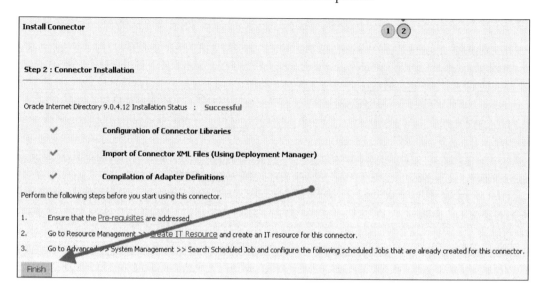

Configure IT Resource (OID)

After installation, we configure the connector's IT resource value so that OIM can connect to OID as follows:

1. Log into the **OIM Advanced Administration** console and under **Configuration** click on **Manage IT Resource**, as shown in the following screenshot:

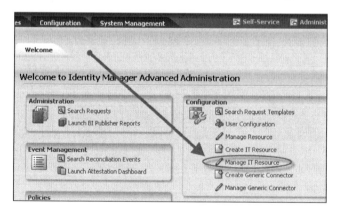

2. In the **Manage IT Resource** screen, from the **IT Resource Type** drop-down menu, select the name of the resource type and click on **Search**. From the search results, click on **Edit** next to **IT Resource type**, as shown in the following screenshot:

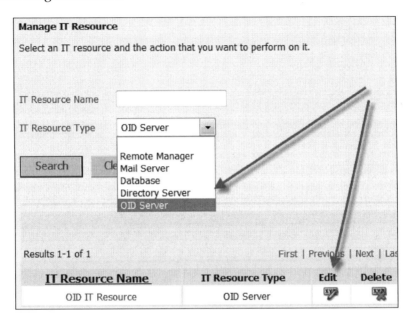

3. Enter OID details and click on the **Update** button:

   ○ **Admin ID**: Distinguished name of the user who has administrator rights on OID (for example, cn=orcladmin).

   ○ **Admin Password**: Password of the user

   ○ **Port**: OID port; the default for OID 11g is 3060 and for OID 10g it is 389.

   ○ **Root DN**: Base distinguished name on which all user operations are to be carried out. In OID, this is also called a **Realm**.

   ○ **SSL**: True or false, if set to true then use OID SSL port (3131 for OID 11g or 636 for OID 10g) in the **Port** field.

   ○ **Server Address**: Server name or IP address of the OID Server.

- ° **Use XL Org Structure**: True or false. An organization in OIM is the logical container to implement authorization and permission on data. A user in OIM must belong to one OIM organization only. OIM comes with a default organization, Xellerate. If set to `true`, then the OIM organization structure is used during provisioning and reconciliation. If the value is set to `false`, then all the users are provisioned and reconciled in the default OIM organization, Xellerate Users.

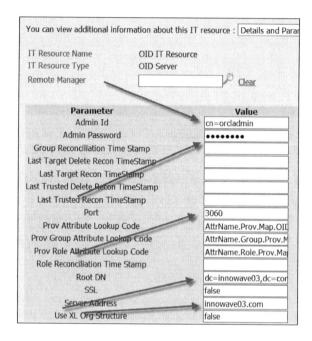

Using the OIM-OID connector

Depending on your requirement, you can then schedule or run reconciliation or provisioning tasks.

Performing reconciliation

Reconciliations are of two types; **target resource** (also known as account management) and **trusted source** (also known as authoritative source or identity reconciliation). During connector installation, scheduled tasks for user reconciliation are automatically created.

Reconciliation is a process-intensive activity and may take a considerable amount of time depending upon the number of accounts and the system configuration.

The following tasks are created for target resource reconciliation for OID:

- **OID User Target Recon**: To reconcile user data when OID is configured in target resource mode.
- **OID Target Delete Recon**: To reconcile deleted users in target resource mode. During a reconciliation run, for each deleted user on OID, the OID user resource is revoked from the corresponding OIM user.
- **OID Group Recon**: To reconcile the group's data from the target system (OID).
- **OID Role Recon**: To reconcile the role's data from the target system (OID).

The following tasks are created for trusted source reconciliation:

- **OID User Trusted Recon**: To reconcile user data when OID is configured as a trusted source.
- **OID Trusted Delete Recon**: To reconcile a deleted user. During a reconciliation run, for each deleted target system user account, the corresponding OIM user is deleted.

Performing provisioning

Provisioning involves creating or modifying a user's account information on the target system such as (Active Directory) through OIM. As discussed earlier in this chapter provisioning is of three types, namely direct provisioning, request-based provisioning, and policy-based provisioning. When you install OIM connector, direct provisioning feature is automatically enabled. If you enable request-based provisioning, direct provisioning is disabled.

Switching from direct provisioning to request-based provisioning

In order to switch from direct provisioning to request-based provisioning, follow the given steps:

1. Log in to the Design console.
2. Expand **Process Management** and then double-click **Process Definition**.
3. Search for the **OID User** process definition and open it.
4. Select the **Auto Save Form** checkbox and click on the **Save** icon.

5. If you wish to enable end users to raise request for themselves, then continue.

6. Expand **Resource Management** and double-click **Resource Objects**.

7. Search for the **OID User** resource object and open it.

8. Select the **Self Request Allowed** checkbox and click on **Save**.

Switching from request-based provisioning to direct provisioning

In order to switch from request-based provisioning to direct provisioning follow the given steps:

1. Log in to the Design console.

2. Expand **Process Management** and then double-click **Process Definition**.

3. Search for the **OID User** process definition and open it.

4. Deselect the **Auto Save Form** checkbox and click on the **Save** icon.

5. If the **Self Request Allowed** feature is enabled, then continue.

6. Expand **Resource Management** and double-click **Resource Objects**.

7. Search for **OID User** Resource Object and open it.

8. Deselect the **Self Request Allowed** checkbox and click on **Save**.

Provision resource using Direct provisioning

You can provision either an existing OIM user to Active Directory, or create a user in OIM and then provision the user to Active Directory. To provision a resource in Active Directory using direct provisioning, follow these steps:

1. Log in to the **OIM Administrative and User** console.

2. On the **Welcome to Identity Administration page**, search for **OIM User** by selecting **User** from the list on the left pane.

3. From the list of users displayed in the search result, select **OIM User**. The user details page is displayed on the right pane; click the **Resources** tab.

4. From the **Action** menu, select **Add Resource**. The **Provision Resource To User** page is displayed in a new window.

5. On the **Select a Resource** page, select **OID User** from the list and then click **Continue**.

6. On **Verify Resource Selection** page, click **Continue**.

7. On **Provide Process Data for OID User Details** page, enter details of the account that you want to create on the target system OID and then click **continue**.

8. On the **Provide Process Data for OID User Group Membership Details** page, search and select a group for the user on Active Directory and then click **continue**.

9. On **Verify Process Data** page, verify the data and click **Continue**.

10. A message is displayed saying that the provisioning has been initiated; close this window.

11. On the **Resources** tab, click **Refresh** to view the newly-provisioned resource.

Deploying OIM connector for Microsoft Active Directory User Management

OIM comes with four predefined connectors for Microsoft Products. They are as follows:

- **Microsoft Active Directory for User Management**: Use this connector to integrate Microsoft Active Directory (MS-AD) or Microsoft Active Directory Application Mode (ADAM) configured either as a managed (target) resource or as an authoritative (trusted) source for OIM.

- **Microsoft Active Directory Password Synchronization**: Use this connector to synchronize (or propagate) Microsoft Active Directory account passwords to OIM.

- **Microsoft Windows**: Use this connector to create folders or grant or revoke permission on folders in Microsoft Windows from OIM.

- **Microsoft Exchange**: Use this connector to provision mailbox operations from OIM to Microsoft Exchange. This connector can also be used reconcile mailboxes created or modified directly on Microsoft Exchange to OIM.

Installing and configuring the OIM connector for Microsoft Active Directory User Management includes the following points:

- Pre-installation
- Installation
- Configuring IT resource for Active Directory
- Setting up lookup definition in OIM
- Using OIM-AD connector

If you wish to include terminal services profile fields of Active Directory in reconciliation or provisioning operations, then you must install Remote Manager.

Pre-installation

1. Download the connector file from `http://www.oracle.com/technetwork/ middleware/id-mgmt/downloads/connectors-101674.html`.

2. Upload the connector software to the OIM server at `$ORACLE_HOME/server/ ConnectorDefaultDirectory`.

3. Download LDAP-1.2.4 from `http://java.sun.com/products/jndi/ downloads/index.html` (Click on **Download JNDI 1.2.1 & More**) and then click on the **ldap-1_2_4.zip** link. Extract `ldap.jar` and `ldapbp.jar` from the `lib` directory of `ldap-1_2_4.zip`. Upload these two jar files to the `$ORACLE_HOME/server/ThirdParty` directory on the OIM server.

 In OIM cluster deployment, copy connect media and all `jar` files on all nodes of the OIM cluster.

4. Upload the external code files to the OIM server at `$ORACLE_HOME/server/ ThirdParty`.

5. Create a user on the target system (Active Directory or Active Directory Application mode) for connector operations and grant the necessary access. This user is used during reconciliation and provisioning.

Installation

1. Log into the OIM Advanced Administration console at `http://server:14000/oim` and then click the **Advanced** link.

2. On the **Advanced Administration** console screen, select **Install Connector** under **System Management**.

3. From the **Connector List** drop-down menu, select connector (**ActiveDirectory 9.1.1.5**) and click on **Load** and then **Continue**. The connector installer will configure connector libraries, import the connector XML file, and finally compile the adapter.

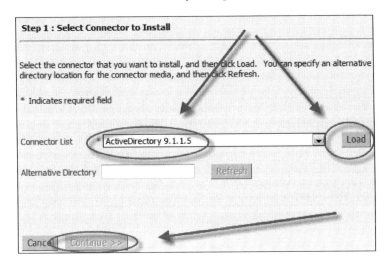

4. Click **Finish** after connector installation completes.

Configuring IT resource for Active Directory

An IT Resource for Active Directory is created during connector installation. You must configure this IT Resource so that OIM can connect to the target resource during provisioning and reconciliation.

1. Log into **OIM Advanced Administration** console and under **Configuration** click **Manage IT Resource**, as shown in the following screenshot:

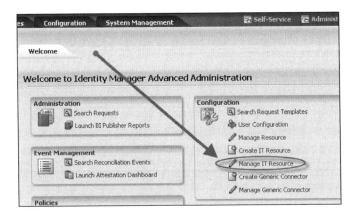

2. In the **Manage IT Resource** screen, from the **IT Resource Type** drop-down menu, select **AD Server** IT Resource Type and click **Search**. From the search results, click on **ADITResource** under **IT Resource Name**, as shown in the following screenshot:

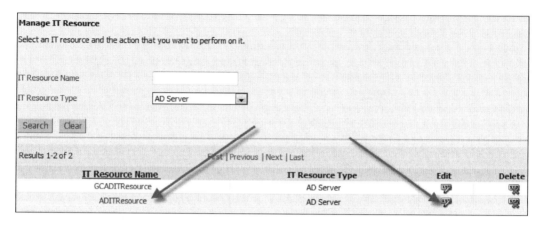

3. Enter values for parameters of the IT Resource and click **Update**:

    ○   **ADAM Lockout Threshold Value**: If the target resource is Microsoft Active Directory Application Mode (ADAM) comma then enter the number of unsuccessful login attempts allowed before a user's account is locked. If the target resource is Microsoft Active Directory then you need not enter a value.

    ○   **ADMIN FQDN**: Enter the fully qualified domain name of the Active Directory user account used during reconciliation or provisioning operations. This user account can be in the format `username@domainname` or `cn=username,OU=users,DC=domain,DC=com`.

    ○   **Admin Password**: Password of the admin user mentioned previously.

    ○   **Server Address**: Hostname or IP address of machine on which Microsoft Active Directory or Active Directory Application Mode is running.

    ○   **Root Context**: Enter base distinguished name on which provisioning and reconciliation of deleted user data are to be carried out. For example, `DC=domain,DC=com`.

    ○   **Use SSL**: Enter `yes` if communication between OIM and Active Directory will be SSL, otherwise enter `no`.

- ○ **Port**: Active Directory port; the default value port for is 389 or, for SSL connections, 636. For ADAM, default non-SSL port is 50001 and SSL port is 50000.

- ○ **isADAM**: Enter yes if target instance is Active Directory Application mode. Enter no if target instance is Active Directory.

- ○ **Allow Password Provisioning**: Enter yes if you want:

4. Password changes on Oracle Identity Manager to be propagated to the Active Directory

5. Password changes for an OIM user to be propagated to all resources allocated (provisioned) to the OIM user.

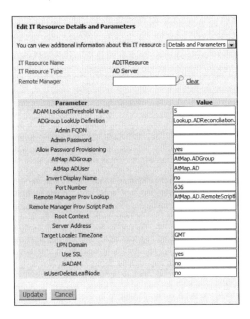

Setting up lookup definition in OIM

When you deploy a connector, the Lookup.AD.Configuration and Lookup.AD.Country **lookup definitions** are created in Oracle Identity Manager. The entries in lookup definition Lookup.AD.Configuration are used during both reconciliation and provisioning. To configure lookup definition, the Design console is used.

1. Log into the Design console.
2. Expand **Administration**, and double-click **LookUp Definition**.
3. Search and open lookup definition Lookup.AD.Configuration.
4. Enter **Decode** value for the parameter listed.

Using OIM-AD connector

Depending on your requirements, you can then use the OIM-AD connector for reconciliation or provisioning.

Performing reconciliation

Reconciliations are of two types target; resource (also known as account management) and trusted source (also known as authoritative source or identity reconciliation). During connector installation, the scheduled tasks for user reconciliation are automatically created.

The following tasks are created for target resource reconciliation:

- **AD User Target Recon**: To reconcile user data in target resource mode.
- **AD User Target Delete Recon**: To reconcile deleted users in target resource mode. During a reconciliation run, for each deleted user on Active Directory, the AD user resource is revoked from the corresponding OIM user.
- **AD Group Recon**: To reconcile group data from the target system.
- **AD Group Delete Recon**: To reconcile deleted groups in target resource mode. During reconciliation run, for each deleted group on Active Directory, the AD group resource is revoked from the corresponding OIM group.

The following tasks are created for trusted source reconciliation:

- **AD Organization Recon**: To reconcile organizations.
- **AD User Trusted Recon**: To reconcile user data.
- **AD User Trusted Delete Recon**: To reconcile a deleted user. During a reconciliation run, for each deleted target system user account, the corresponding OIM user is deleted.

Performing provisioning

Provisioning involves creating or modifying a user's account information on the target system such as (Active Directory) through OIM. As discussed earlier in this chapter, provisioning is of three types; direct provisioning, request-based provisioning, and policy-based provisioning. When you install the OIM connector, the direct provisioning feature is automatically enabled. If you enable request-based provisioning, then direct provisioning is disabled.

Switching from direct provisioning to request-based provisioning

In order to switch from direct provisioning to request-based provisioning:

1. Log in to the Design console.
2. Expand **Process Management** and then double-click **Process Definition**.
3. Search for the **AD User** process definition and open it.
4. Select the **Auto Save Form** checkbox and click on the **Save** icon.
5. If you wish to enable end users to raise request for themselves, then continue.
6. Expand **Resource Management** and double-click **Resource Objects**.
7. Search for the **AD User** resource object and open it.
8. Select the **Self Request Allowed** checkbox and click **Save**.

Switching from request-based provisioning to direct provisioning

In order to switch from request-based provisioning to direct provisioning:

1. Log in to the Design console.
2. Expand **Process Management** and then double-click **Process Definition**.
3. Search for the **AD User** process definition and open it.
4. Deselect the **Auto Save Form** checkbox and click on the **Save** icon.
5. If the **Self Request Allowed** feature is enabled, then continue.
6. Expand **Resource Management** and double-click **Resource Objects**.
7. Search for the **AD User** resource object and open it.
8. Deselect the **Self Request Allowed** checkbox and click **Save**.

Provision resource using direct provisioning

You can provision either an existing OIM user to Active Directory, or create a user in OIM and then provision the user to Active Directory. To provision a resource in Active Directory using direct provisioning follow these steps:

1. Log in to the **OIM Administrative and User** console.
2. On the **Welcome to Identity Administration** page, search for the OIM user by selecting **User** from the list on the left pane.
3. From the list of users displayed in search result, select **OIM User**. The user details page is displayed on the right pane; click the **Resources** tab.
4. From the **Action** menu, select **Add Resource**. The **Provision Resource to User** page is displayed in a new window.

5. On the **Select a Resource** page, select **AD User** from the list, and then click **Continue**.

6. On the **Verify Resource Selection** page, click **Continue**.

7. On the **Provide Process Data for AD User Details** page, enter details of the account that you want to create on Active Directory, and then click **Continue**.

8. On the **Provide Process Data for AD User Group Membership Details** page, search and select a group for the user on Active Directory and then click **Continue**.

9. On the **Verify Process Data** page, verify the data and click **Continue**.

10. A message saying the provisioning has been initiated is displayed; close this window.

11. On the **Resources** tab, click **Refresh** to view the newly-provisioned resource.

Deploying the OIM connector for Oracle e-Business User Management

OIM provides two types of predefined connectors for Oracle e-Business Suite. They are as follows:

- **Oracle e-Business Suite User Management**: Use this connector to integrate Oracle e-Business Suite users for provisioning (Create/Delete User, Enable/ Disable User, User Update, Password Update, Add/Remove Responsibility) and reconciliation (Update Apps Resource, Link with Oracle HR Employee)

- **Oracle e-Business Suite Employee Reconciliation**: Use this connector to integrate Oracle e-Business Suite with OIM for Employees reconciliation (Reconcile New/Deleted/Updated User).

This section covers the OIM connector for Oracle e-Business Suite(EBS) User Management and includes the following points:

- Pre-installation
- Installation
- Configure IT resource for Oracle e-Business Suite
- Using OIM-EBS connector for user management

Pre-installation steps

1. Download the connector file ORCL_EBS_UM_91050.zip from http://www.oracle.com/technetwork/middleware/id-mgmt/downloads/connectors-101674.html.

2. Upload the connector software to OIM server at $ORACLE_HOME/server/ConnectorDefaultDirectory.

3. Copy ojdbc14.jar from e-Business DATABASE_ORACLE_HOME/jdbc/lib to OIM_ORACLE_HOME/server/ThirdParty.

 In an OIM cluster deployment, copy media and jar files on all nodes of OIM cluster.

4. Create an account in EBS for the connector to use during reconciliation. Copy the scripts directory from the connector software to the EBS database. Run OIM.sh (Unix) or OIM.bat (Windows), semi colon when prompted, enter the system username/password, name of database, and APPS schema password.

Installation

1. Log in to the OIM Advanced Administration console at http://server:14000/oim and then click the **Advanced** link.

2. On the **Advanced Administration** console screen, select **Install Connector** under **System Management**, as shown in the following screenshot:

3. From the **Connector List** drop-down menu, select the connector (**Oracle EBS User Management 9.0.4.3**) and click on **Load** and then **Continue**. The connector installer will configure connector libraries, import connector XML files, and finally compile the adapter:

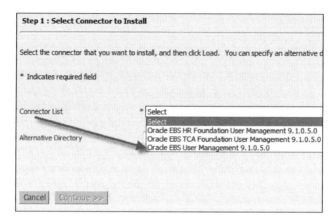

4. Click **Finish** after connector installation completes.

Configure IT resource for EBS

The IT resource for EBS is created during connector installation. To configure this IT resource so that OIM can connect to target resource (Active Directory) during provisioning and reconciliation, use the following steps:

1. Log in to the **OIM Advanced Administration** console and under **Configuration** click **Manage IT Resource**, as shown in the following screenshot:

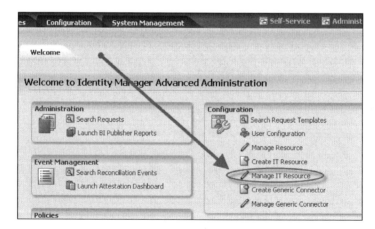

2. In the **Manage IT Resource** screen, from the **IT Resource Type** drop-down menu select **eBusiness Suite UM** and then click **Search**. Click on **Edit** against **IT Resource Name EBS-APPS12**:

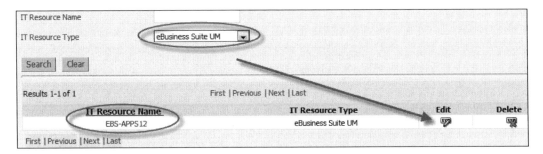

3. Enter values for parameter of IT resource and click **Update**:

   ○ **Admin ID**: User ID to connect to the EBS database created previously.

   ○ **Admin Password**: Password of Admin User

   ○ **Host**: Hostname or IP address of the EBS database server

   ○ **SID**: SID for the EBS database

   ○ **ResetPswdOnFirstLogon**: Yes or No, specifies whether or not users are to be prompted to change their passwords at first logon:

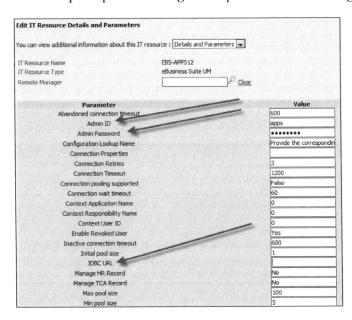

Using OIM-EBS User Management connector

Depending on your requirement, you can then use the OIM-EBS User Management connector for reconciliation or provisioning.

Performing reconciliation

Reconciliations are of two types; target resource (also known as account management) or trusted source (also known as authoritative source or identity reconciliation).

Configuring EBS as a trusted source

When you configure EBS as a trusted source, then during reconciliation:

- For each newly-created user on EBS, an OIM user is created
- Updates made to each user on EBS are propagated to the corresponding OIM user

To configure EBS as a trusted source for reconciliation comma, follow these steps:

1. Open the **OIM Administrative and User** console.
2. Click the **Deployment Management** link on the left navigation bar.
3. Click the **Import** link under **Deployment Management**. A dialog box for opening files is displayed.
4. Locate and open the XellUserOraApps.xml file, which is in the ORACLE_HOME/server/XLIntegrations/OracleEBiz/xml directory.
5. Click **Add File**. The **Substitutions** page is displayed.
6. Click **Next**. The **Confirmation** page is displayed.
7. Click **Import**.
8. In the message that is displayed, click **Import** to confirm that you want to import the XML file and then click **OK**.

The following task is created for trusted source reconciliation:

- EBS_TS_User: Used to reconcile the user in the trusted source mode.

Configuring EBS as target resource

When you configure EBS as a target resource, then during reconciliation:

- For each newly-created user on EBS, a resource is assigned to the corresponding OIM user.
- Updates made to each user on EBS are propagated to the corresponding resource in OIM.

The following task is created for target resource reconciliation:

- `EBS_TR_User`: It is used to reconcile the user in the target resource mode.

Transferring connectors from test to production

Deployment Manager is a Java application used for importing and exporting OIM configurations, including connectors. The Deployment Manager tool is available from the OIM Administrative and User console. An exported connector is stored in an XML file, which can then be imported into a different OIM environment. To access Deployment Manager follow these steps:

1. Log in to the OIM Advanced Administration console at `http://server:14000/oim` and then click the **Advanced** link.

2. On the **Advanced Administration** console screen, under **System Management** select the **Import Deployment Manager File** or **Export Deployment Manager File** link, as shown in the following screenshot:

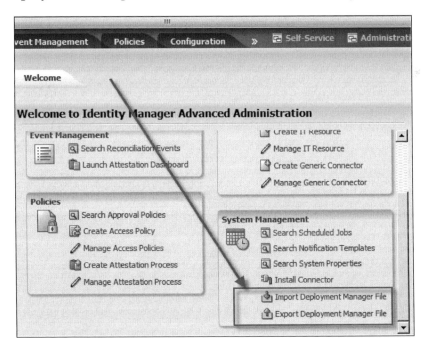

OIM connector components, entire connector or multiple connectors can be packaged in to a single Extensible Markup Language (XML) file and then migrated from one environment to another. Connector Installer and Deployment Manager are used to transfer connectors.

It is not possible to rollback connector or connector component import. If you want to go back to the previous version, a new import of the previous version of the connector/connector component is required. It is possible to transfer multiple connectors simultaneously across environments.

Summary

In this chapter, we covered OIM connectors, provisioning, and reconciliation, type of connectors and predefined connectors for various IT Systems such as Oracle, Microsoft, and SAP. We also covered installation and configuration of predefined connectors for Microsoft Active Directory user management, Oracle Internet Directory, and Oracle e-Business Suite user management.

In the next chapter, we are going to cover OIM configuration such as configuring attributes, password policies, updating passwords, and other key day-to-day task for administrators.

11

OIM Configuration and Tasks

In this chapter we will cover common Oracle Identity Manager configuration and key tasks including:

- Generating WebLogic Full Client
- Exporting/Importing/Deleting files using the MDS utility
- OIM password policy
- Purging the cache
- Managing OIM configuration
- Updating OIM server name, port, and password

WebLogic Full Client (WLfullclient)

WebLogic Full Client is a Java RMI client that uses Oracle's proprietary T3 protocol to communicate with the WebLogic server. The WebLogic Full Client requires the JAR file (`wlfullclient.jar`) under WebLogic Home at `WL_HOME\server\lib`. Various Oracle Identity Manager utilities like purgeCache, MDS utilities, and Design console use WebLogic Full Client JAR file, that is `wlfullclient.jar`.

How to Generate wlfullclient.jar

`wlfullclient.jar` must be created on a running WebLogic server using the following steps:

1. Set environment variable:

   ```
   cd $WL_HOME/server/bin
   . setWLSEnv.sh
   ```

2. Create wlfullclient.jar:

```
cd $WL_HOME/server/lib

$JDK_1.6/java -jar ../../../modules/com.bea.core.
  jarbuilder_1.3.0.0.jar
```

You should see a message such as **Created new jar file wlfullclient.jar** as shown in the following screenshot:

MDS utilities

Most of Oracle Identity Manager's configuration is stored in a MDS repository in the database. In order to view/update/delete these settings, you can use MDS utility weblogicExportMetadata, weblogicImportMetadata, and webLogicDeleteMetadata. WebLogic's MDS utilities can be found under the $ORACLE_HOME/server/bin directory and include:

- weblogicExportMetadata.sh: This script is used to export metadata files from MDS database to file system.

- weblogicImportMetadata.sh: This script is used to import metadata files from file system to MDS database.

- weblogicDeleteMetadata.sh: This script is used to delete metadata files from the MDS database.

WebLogic's MDS utilities properties file weblogic.properties serves as a parameter file. For MDS utilities to work, you should have already generated wlfullclient.jar on the OIM server as discussed in the previous section. Apart from weblogic.properties and wlfullclient.jar, the WebLogic Admin server and Managed server running OIM need to be running in order to use MDS utilities.

How to import/export/delete files using WebLogic MDS utilities

You can follow these steps to manage OIM files using MDS utilities:

1. Login to the OIM server (Window/Unix) as operating system user user that was used to install WebLogic/ OIM server.

2. Set the environment variable `OIM_ORACLE_HOME` to the IDM Oracle Home, for example `$MW_HOME/Oracle_IDM1` if `Oracle_IDM1` is the directory under Middleware Home in which Identity Management binaries are installed.

3. Set `weblogic.properties` file under `$ORACLE_HOME/server/bin` Update

   ○ `wls_servername=oim_server1`: OIM Managed server name

   ○ `application_name=oim`: for out-of-the-box event handlers, value in OIM) or `application_name=OIMMetadata` for custom data or any other out-of-the-box metadata apart from the one used by event handlers or values in OIM.

   ○ `metadata_from_loc = /directory_path_containing XML`: This parameter is used for import. Enter the full path of the directory from which XML file will be imported into MDS. For servers running on Windows use `//` as file or directory separator.

   ○ `metadata_to_loc = /directory_path`: This parameter is used for export. Enter the full path of the directory to which you want to export XML files from MDS. For servers running on Windows use `//` as file or directory separator.

   ○ `metadata_files=/file/<file>.xml`: This parameter is used for export and delete utility. Use comma-separated values for multiple XML files.

4. Run the command `$ORACLE_HOME/server/bin/weblogicXXXXXMetadata.sh` as shown in the following screenshot. When prompted enter your WebLogic admin username, password, and Admin server URL. (On successful completion you should see message such as **Transfer Complete** in OIM Managed server log file).

```
Starting export metadata script ...
Please enter your username [weblogic] :
Please enter your password [welcome1] :
Please enter your server URL [t3://localhost:7001] :
Connecting to t3://localhost:7001 with userid weblogic ...
Successfully connected to Admin Server 'AdminServer' that belongs to domain 'base domain'.

Warning: An insecure protocol was used to connect to the
server. To ensure on-the-wire security, the SSL port or
Admin port should be used instead.

Location changed to domainRuntime tree. This is a read-only tree with DomainMBea
n as the root.
For more help, use help(domainRuntime)


Disconnected from weblogic server: AdminServer
End of export metadata script ...


Exiting WebLogic Scripting Tool.
```

 Any error related to MDS will be reported in the OIM Managed server log file. To check the log file location check section *Domain Home* in *Chapter 3, IDAM Directory Structure and Files* or *Log Location* in *Chapter 13, Logging and Auditing for OIM/OAM*.

OIM password policy

Password policy is set of rules that dictate password restrictions for users such as password length, expiry time, minimum character, and more. Each password policy can be used by multiple resources. Password policy is managed by a form under the Administration folder in the OIM Design console.

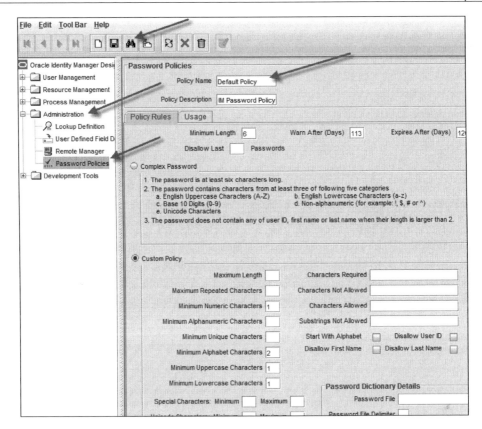

The **Policy Rules** tab in the previous screenshot shows password restrictions for password policy like **Maximum Length**, **Minimum Uppercase**, **Special Characters**, and so on.

The **Usage** tab shows rules and resource objects that are associated with this password policy.

Creating a password policy

To create a password policy in OIM:

1. Login to OIM Design console (refer *Chapter 9, OIM Navigation: Administration and Design Console* for details and double-click on the **Password Policies** form under the **Administration** Folder.

2. In the **Policy Name** field enter the name of policy and in the **Policy Description** field enter the description of this password policy.

3. Under the **Policy Rules** tab you can select either the **Complex Password** or the **Custom Policy**. Complex Password has a pre-defined set of rules whereas Custom Policy gives you an option to define your own password complexity.

4. Click on the **Save** button that is on the **Design Console** toolbar to save this password policy in the OIM database.

> At this stage the password policy is simply created and stored in the database, not applied to any resource.

Associate password policy with a resource

After a password policy is created, in order for that password policy to be applicable to a resource, the resource must be associated with it. In the **Resource Objects** form, use the **Password Policies Rule** tab to associate the password policy with a resource:

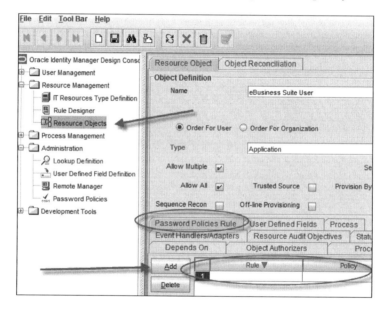

1. Login to OIM Design console (refer to *Chapter 9, OIM Navigation: Administration and Design Console* for details and double-click on the **Resource Objects** form under the **Resource Management** folder.

2. Search for the resource object for which you wish to apply password policy and click on the **Password Policies Rule** tab.

3. Click on the **Add** button and while under the **Rule** column, double-click to find a rule. Under the **Policy** column, double-click to find the password policy that you wish to apply. Set the rule to **Default** if you want it to apply for Self Registration.

4. Click the **Save** button on the Design console toolbar to save this password policy for specific resource object.

Purge OIM cache

Oracle Identity Manager caches metadata to reduce DB activity and increase performance. OIM caching is defined in file /db/oim-config.xml located in MDS. To check if caching for a particular component is enabled or disabled, export file /db/oim-config.xml using the MDS utility (explained earlier in this chapter) and look under the section *<cacheCategoriesConfig>*.

An entry such as <cacheCategoryConfig name="ProcessDefinition" enabled="false" expirationTime="14400"/> means caching is disabled for ProcessDefinition, whereas <cacheCategoryConfig name="ColumnMap" enabled="true" expirationTime="14400"/> means that caching is enabled for ColumnMap.

To purge the cache, use the PurgeCache.sh (Unix) or PurgeCache.bat (Windows) utility in the ORACLE_HOME/server/bin directory on OIM server. You can use the PurgeCache utility by executing the following command:

```
PurgeCache.sh|bat <category_name>
```

where category_name is the category/component for which you wish to clear cache. Use the category name All to clear every cache. So the complete sequence of steps is:

1. Run the command cd $ORACLE_HOME/server/bin.

2. Set WebLogic Home environment variable to WL_HOME.

3. Set JAVA_HOME environment variable to the JDK 1.6 directory under MW_HOME.

4. Ensure that wlfullclient.jar is available under $WL_HOME/server/lib (The steps to create wlfullclient.jar are discussed earlier in this chapter).

5. Run PurgeCache.[sh|bat] <category_name>; for example:

   ```
   PurgeCache.sh All
   ```

6. Enter OIM Admin username (xelsysadm) and password when prompted.

7. Enter OIM URL when prompted.

```
[idam11g@innowave03 bin]$ export WL_HOME=/oracle/apps/idm11g/mw_home/wlserver_10
.3/
[idam11g@innowave03 bin]$ export JAVA_HOME=/oracle/apps/idm11g/mw_home/jdk160_18
[idam11g@innowave03 bin]$ ./PurgeCache.sh All
[Enter the admin username:]xelsysadm
[Enter the admin password:]
[Enter the service url : (i.e.: t3://oimhostname:oimportno)]t3://innowave03.com:
14000
PurgeCache Login Success...
Purging the cache categories:[All] is successful
[idam11g@innowave03 bin]$
```

Managing OIM configuration

Oracle Identity Manager configuration files are stored in the database in MDS. Most of these configurations are exposed as MBeans, which can be managed via Enterprise Manager Fusion Middleware control. For some configurations (the ones not exposed as MBeans), you will have to export complete files from MDS, make changes, and import them back in using the MDS utility discussed earlier in this chapter.

How to manage OIM configuration using MBeans

To manage OIM configuration using MBeans, follow these steps:

1. Login to Fusion Middleware control application, which will be at http:// servername:admin_server_port/em (default Admin server port is 7001).

2. Right-click on **oim(11.1.1.3.0)** under **Identity and Access | OIM**, and then click on **System MBean Browser.**

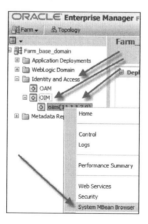

3. Next expand **Application Defined Mbeans | oracle.iam | Server: oim_ server1 | Application: oim | XMLConfig | Config**:

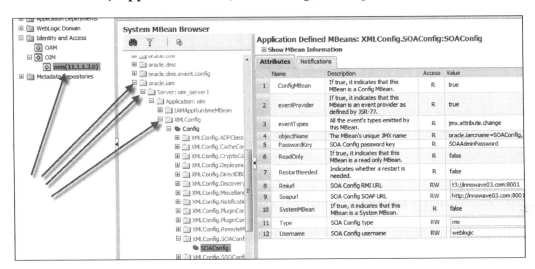

Managing system properties in OIM

OIM system properties define characteristics that control the behaviour of Oracle Identity Manager. System properties in OIM are managed from the **System Configuration** link in the **System Management** tab of OIM Advanced Administration console.

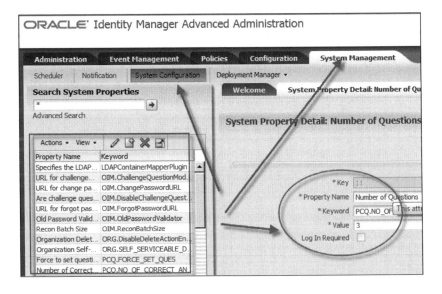

Changing OIM hostname and port number

If you change OIM host, port, or introduce a load balancer or HTTP server in front of your OIM server, then follow the next procedure.

OimFrontEndURL is the URL used to access the Oracle Identity Manager user interface. This URL is also used in notification e-mails and the URL for SOA calls. Change OimFrontEndURL to the load balancer URL, HTTP server URL, or WebLogic's OIM Managed server URL depending on your configuration. Use the MBean browser in Fusion Middleware Enterprise Manager Control as discussed in the *Managing OIM Configuration* section earlier in this chapter.

To update OimFrontEndURL, login to the Enterprise Manager console and click on **System MBean Browser** for oim(11.1.1.3.0). In System MBean Browser, expand **Application Defined MBeans | oracle.iam | Server: oim_server1 | Application: oim | XMLConfig | Config | XMLConfig.DiscoveryConfig | Discovery.**

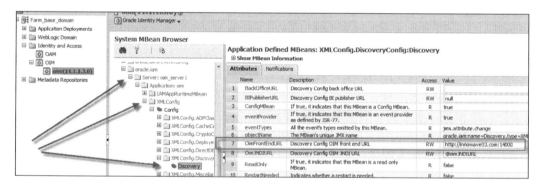

 When updating OimFrontEndURL for OIM, update OIM URL in SPML Client, OAM, OAAM, OIN, and any other application integrated with OIM.

Changing passwords related to OIM

Oracle Identity Manager creates an Administrator account (xelsysadm) and prompts for a password. You can use Identity Manager Self Service to change the xelsysadm password. To update the xelsysadm password:

1. Login to OIM Self-Service console, that is,
   `http://servername:<oim_port>/oim`.

2. Click on the **Change Password** link on **Profile**.

3. In the **Change Password** window, enter the old and new passwords, and click on **Apply**.

4. After a password change, you should get a message such as **Your Password has been changed successfully.**

Summary

In this chapter we covered common Oracle Identity Manager configuration and key tasks such as generating WebLogic Full Client, managing files using MDS utility, OIM password policy, purging caches, managing OIM configuration, and updating OIM server name, port, or password. In the next chapter, we are going to cover integrating OIM with OAM, including integrating OAM with other components like UCM or OBIEE for Single Sign-On.

12

OAM Integration with Fusion Middleware and EBS R12

In this chapter, we will cover OAM integration with Fusion Middleware applications (WebCenter, OBIEE) and the Oracle E-Business suite. Initially we will cover basic concepts of Fusion Middleware security such as users, groups, roles, authentication and identity assertion providers, and steps to integrate WebLogic (used to deploy Fusion Middleware application) with LDAP stores such as Oracle Internet Directory. Next we will cover integration with OAM for Single Sign-On (SSO). The last section of this chapter covers basic concepts for E-Business suite integration such as E-Business Suite Access Gate and high-level steps to integrate E-Business Suite with OAM for SSO.

OAM Integration with Fusion Middleware

Fusion Middleware (FMW) components (WebCenter, OBIEE, UCM, and SOA) by default, use WebLogic's embedded LDAP server to store users/groups and the WebLogic authentication engine (defined by security realm **myrealm**) to log in to these applications. Consider that while you have various FMW products deployed in their own WebLogic domain, you also have several other business applications such as Oracle EBS, Peoplesoft, or SAP. In order to access these applications, the user must log in to these applications individually, so for five applications users must log in five times. Moreover, these users must be provisioned into the WebLogic domain's embedded LDAP server of each FMW product.

It is possible to configure all FMW applications (WebCenter, UCM, OBIEE, and SOA) and applications such as EBS, Peoplesoft, and SAP with OAM's SSO solution. This way, each user has to log in just once and can then access any other application (even in a different WebLogic domain) without any further password prompts.

Following changes are done when a Fusion Middleware Application is integrated with OAM to provide Single Sign-On (SSO):

- An **authentication provider** is configured in the WebLogic domain that is hosting the FMW application. This authentication provider will point to the LDAP server where enterprise users and groups are stored. For example, Microsoft Active Directory (MS-AD) or Oracle Internet Directory (OID).

- OAM's UI store is also configured to point to the same LDAP server mentioned in the previous step. (Refer to the *User Identity Store* section in *Chapter 5, OAM Administration and Navigation*, to configure the identity store).

- The FMW application is configured for access via Oracle HTTP server (OHS), so instead of coming directly to WebLogic Managed server, any user request will always go via OHS. This is achieved using the module mod_wl_ohs in OHS. Direct access to WebLogic is blocked by using network channels in WebLogic server.

- OHS, which is configured as a proxy, is protected via WebGate so any request via OHS is evaluated by OAM server first.

- Application domain, that contains the policy which dictates public/protected URLs is created in OAM Server. Authentication scheme for each Fusion middleware application is defined in OAM server. This can be done either during WebGate registration (using RREG) or later using OAM console.

- An OAM **identity assertion** is configured in the WebLogic domain that hosts the FMW application. A cookie generated at OHS/WebGate (during successful OAM authentication) will be consumed (asserted) inside WebLogic server.

FMW security concepts

It is important that you understand the Fusion middleware (FMW) security building blocks such as users, groups, roles, policies, credential, and identity authentication/ assertion providers first before integrating FMW with Oracle Access Manager for Single Sign-On. The next section covers:

- User, groups, and application roles
- Identity, policy, and credential store
- WebLogic server authentication providers

Users, groups, application roles

Users are end-users accessing applications, and are stored in an identity store; the default identity store for FMW applications is WebLogic's embedded LDAP server. For a production environment it is recommended to move them to an enterprise level LDAP server such as Oracle Internet Directory (OID), Novell LDAP server, or Microsoft Active Directory.

Group is a collection of users and other groups. Groups are defined in the LDAP server and sometimes also referred as **Enterprise roles**.

An application role is a collection of users, groups, and roles. A **role** is the collection of application security (defining privileges and access control on an application) and can be assigned to a user, group, or another role. Application roles are specific to applications, for example, OBIEE, WebCenter, or UCM.

The following screenshot shows the four default application roles configured for OBIEE, namely. **BISystem**, **BIAdministrator**, **BIAuthor**, and **BIConsumer**.

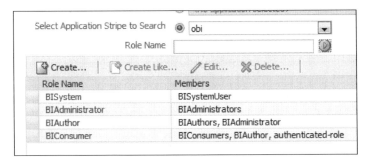

In the previous example, the application role BIAuthor has two members, BIAdministrator (another application role) and BIAuthors (a group).

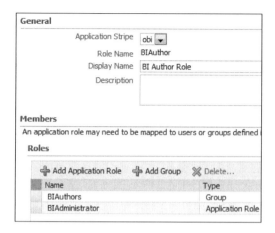

Seeded application roles for several FMW applications are defined in the policy store:

- **WebLogic**: Admin, Monitor, and Operator.

- **OBIEE**: BIAdministrator, BIPublisher, and BIConsumer.

- **UCM**: There are no seeded application roles defined in policy store. UCM uses its own store for roles, and the user whose group name is the same as the name of the UCM role is assigned that UCM role.

- **WebCenter spaces**: Administrator, Moderator, Participant, Viewer, Authenticated-User, and Public-User.

- **SOA**: SOAAdmin, SOAOperator, SOAMonitor, SOAAuditAdmin, and so on.

- **WebCenter**: Discussion Server-Administrator, and Moderator

Application roles in FMW applications such as OBIEE, WebCenter, and SOA can be defined by FMW Enterprise Manager Control (**Farm_<domain> | WebLogic Domain | <domain> | Security | Application Roles**) or WLST commands (grantAppRole). You can assign an application role directly to a user, but it recommended to assign roles to groups instead, and add users to those groups to assign them roles. To explain this, let's assume WebLogic is integrated with OID and you wish to make all users in the OID group **wladmingrp** into WebLogic administrators. You would need to add that group to the WebLogic role **admin**. Application roles in WebLogic can be assigned using the WebLogic console (**Security Realms | myrealm | Roles and Policies | Global Roles | Roles | Admin**).

In the following screenshot, the WebLogic admin role (application role) is mapped to three enterprise groups, namely wladmingrp, BIAdministrators, and Administrators.

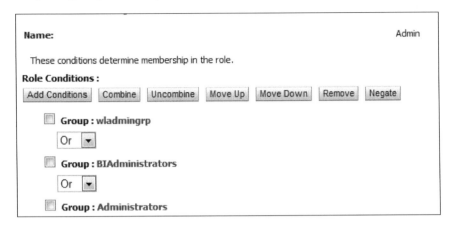

Similarly let's assume the WebLogic server that is hosting OBIEE is configured with LDAP server; to make all users in the OID group **biadmingrp** into OBIEE administrators, add that group to the BIAdministrator application role in application stripe `obi`.

Identity, policy, and credential stores

Identity, policy and credentials are the building blocks of FMW security. This section covers these components and their respective stores.

Identity store

An **identity store** is a repository of end-users, used by FMW applications such as WebCenter, UCM, OBIEE, and so on. By default, the identity store for FMW applications is WebLogic's embedded LDAP server (**Security Realms | myrealm | Providers | DefaultAuthenticator**). The following LDAP servers are supported for identity stores in FMW 11*g*: Oracle Internet Directory 11*g*, Oracle Virtual Directory, Oracle Directory Server Enterprise Edition 11.1.1.3.0, Active Directory 2008, Novell eDirectory 8.8, Tivoli Access Manager, Sun DS 6.3, 7.0, Oracle DB 10*g*, 11*g*R1, 11*g*R2, iPlanet Directory Server, and Custom Authenticator.

In FMW 11*g*, you can add additional Identity stores with the help of WebLogic's **Providers** screen by clicking on the **New** button, as shown in the following screenshot:

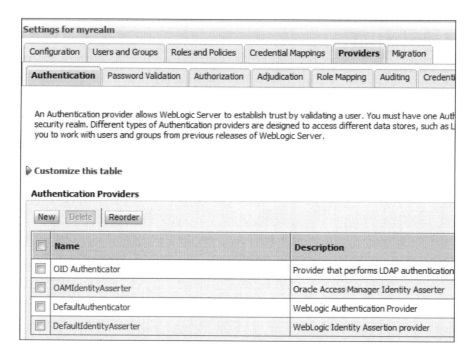

 To integrate FMW with OAM for SSO, both your WebLogic domain (hosting your FMW application) and OAM server should use the same LDAP server. Also this LDAP should be first (on top) in WebLogic authentication providers list as shown in the previous screenshot.

Policy store

Application policy is a collection of Java 2 and JAAS policies that are applicable to applications such as WebCenter Spaces or OBIEE analytics. The **policy store** is the repository where these applications and system policies are stored. This repository can be based on a file, an LDAP server or a database. There is only one policy store per WebLogic domain, and the default option is a file-based repository (XML file system-jazn.xml). In order to migrate policy store, you can either use FMW Enterprise Manager Control (go to **Farm_<domain> | WebLogic Domain | <domain> | Security | Security Provider Configuration**) or WLST (migrateSecurityStore). In the following screenshot, the policy store is configured in LDAP server. Click on **Change Store Type** button to change the policy store.

 In 11*g* R1 FMW policy store, Oracle Internet Directory is only supported ldap-based repository. Similarly only Oracle Database 10.2.0.4+, 11.1.0.7+, and 11.2.0.1+ are supported DB-based policy store.

Credential store

The **credential store** is the repository of security data (credentials) that certifies the authority of users, Java components, and system components. Credentials can be username/password, tickets, or public key certificates. Example of credentials stored in FMW (specifically, in OBIEE) are OracleBISystem user (`system.user`), BIScheduler password, or repository password. To view credentials in FMW using Enterprise Manager Controls go to **Farm_<domain> | WebLogic Domain | <domain> | Security | Credentials**.

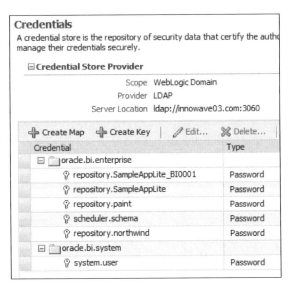

Like the to policy store, a credential store can be based on a file, LDAP server, or database. There is only one policy store per WebLogic domain and the default option is a file-based repository (wallet file `cwallet.sso`). In order to migrate the policy store you can either use FMW Enterprise Manager Control (EM) or WLST (migrateSecurityStore).

 Note that credential and policy stores are pointed at the same type of store, that is either file-based, ldap-based, or database-based. When you migrate policy or credential from file-based to LDAP, for example, both stores are migrated at the same time.

WebLogic server authentication providers

WebLogic server provides various authentication providers, which take username and password credentials and find a corresponding user in provider's user store. WebLogic comes with a default authentication provider called **"DefaultAuthenticator"** which accesses users and groups in WebLogic's embedded LDAP server.

There are various types of authentication providers (depending on the type of user store) such as LDAP, RDBMS, SAML, or Identity Assertion Provider. We are going to use two providers (Oracle Internet Directory Authentication Provider and OAM Identity Assertion Provider) to configure OAM SSO with Oracle FMW using Oracle Internet Directory as our user store.

JAAS flag

An authentication provider can have one of following four values:

- REQUIRED: This means that this provider must succeed; even if it fails, authentication proceeds down the list of other configured authentication providers (OAM Identity Assertion must be configured to REQUIRED for FMW integration with OAM).

- REQUISITE: This means that this provider must succeed; if it succeeds, authentication proceeds down the list of other configured authentication providers.

- SUFFICIENT: This means that this provider need not succeed; if it succeeds, authentication is considered successful. If this fails, authentication proceeds down the list of other configured authentication providers (OID Authentication Provider must be configured to SUFFICIENT for Fusion middleware integration with OAM).

- OPTIONAL: The user is allowed to pass or fail the authentication of this authentication provider. If all authentication providers are set to OPTIONAL, then for successful authentication at least one of the providers must be successful.

Oracle Internet Directory authentication provider

To configure OID as authentication provider in WebLogic server, follow these steps:

1. Log in to the Weblogic console
2. Select **Security Realms**
3. Click on **myrealm**
4. Click on **Providers**
5. Click on **New**
6. From the list of provider types, select **OracleInternetDirectoryAuthenticationProvider**
7. Click on **Save**
8. Click on newly-created OID authentication provider and select the **Provider Specific** tab.
9. Enter the following details related to OID:
    - **Host**: Hostname of the server where OID is running
    - **Port**: Port on which OID is listening
    - **Principal**: User ID of OID super user such as cn=orcladmin
    - **Credential**: Password of OID super user
    - **User Base DN**: Distinguished name in OID tree where users are stored such as cn=Users, dc=<domain name>
    - **Group Base DN**: Distinguished Name in OID tree where groups are stored such as cn=Groups, dc=<domain name>

> If login attribute is uid or mai,l then change cn to uid or mail in All User Filter and User From Name Filter respectively.

10. Select tab **Common** and change control flag to Sufficient
11. Click on **Save**

OAM identity assertion provider

An **identity assertion provider** is used where perimeter authentication (a system outside WebLogic server, such as OAM, is used to establish trust through tokens) is used. An identity assertion provider verifies the token and performs actions required to establish validity and trust in the token. **OAM Identity Asserter** (IA) is an identity assertion provider in WebLogic that uses the OAM's authentication service and validates already-authenticated OAM users though tokens, and also creates a WebLogic authentication session. To define OAM IA in your WebLogic server, follow these steps:

1. Log into the WebLogic console
2. Select **Security Realms**
3. Click on **myrealm**
4. Click on **Providers**
5. Click on **New**
6. From the list of provider types, select **OAMIdentityAsserter** and enter **Name**
7. Click on **OK**
8. Click on the newly-created OAM IA
9. Under the **Common tab, from the Active Type** field move **OAM_REMOTE_USER** to **Chosen**
10. Change control flag to REQUIRED
11. Click on **Save**

Integrating FMW with OAM for SSO

Single sign-on solutions enable the user to log in once, and access all integrated applications, without having to log in again till user logs off (or SSO server logs user out based on inactivity). With a default FMW installation and without SSO integration, the user accesses a FMW application directly or via a load balancer. FMW applications present their own authentication engine, which validate user credentials using WebLogic's default authenticator (pointing to WebLogic's embedded LDAP server). If authentication is successfulm the authenticator populates groups which the user belongs to and forwards the data to FMW applications such as WebCenter, UCM, or OBIEE. The FMW application then verifies whether the user is authorized to access the resource or not from the policy store.

An important point to note here is that without SSO, authentication takes place via WebLogic whereas with SSO (via OAM) integration, authentication is delegated to OAM server. In both cases, the application looks at the policy store's Application Role definition for authorization.

When FMW applications are integrated with OAM, all requests to those applications (such as OBIEE, UCM, and WebCenter) are routed via Oracle HTTP server (OHS) which acts as a reverse proxy server. This OHS is configured with Web Gate, which intercepts user requests and forwards them to OAM for authentication. OAM takes the credentials supplied by the user and validates them against its identity store (OID, AD, Novell, or other LDAP stores). On successful authentication, Web Gate generates a token (in the form of a cookie) and OHS forwards the request to WebLogic server on which the FMW application is deployed. WebLogic Server Security Service then invokes OAM Identity Asserter for SSO, which gets the token from the incoming request and populates the subject field with the WLSUserImpl principal. WebLogic server passes this subject (User ID) and its groups (WLSGroupIMpl) to the FMW application, which will then validate against the Application Role value in its policy store to see if user is authorized to access application.

Sentence case and hyphenate High-level for OAM with FMW

This section covers high-level steps to integrate FMW applications such as WebCenter, OBIEE, and UCM. This section assumes that Oracle Internet Directory (OID) is being used as the enterprise-wide identity store.

> OID is used for example, but you could have Active Directory or IBM Directory Server as the identity store instead.

1. Install OAM 11*g* R1
2. Install OID 11*g* R1 (11.1.1.2.0) and Select option **Install software- Do Not configure**
3. Install OID 11*g* R1 PS3 (11.1.1.4.0)
4. Configure OID by running:

    `$ORACLE_HOME/bin/config.sh`

> OAM 11.1.1.3 supports only one identity store, whereas OAM 11.1.1.5 supports multiple identity store.

5. Configure OIM's primary identity store to be `OID`

6. Install OHS 11gR1

7. Configure `mod_wl_ohs` to forward requests from OHS to the WebLogic Managed server running your FMw application such as WebCenter, SOA, OBIEE, or UCM.

8. Add OID as an authentication provider in the WebLogic domain that hosts your FMW application. Refer to section *Oracle Internet Directory Authentication Provider*.

9. Add OAM as the identity asserter for the WebLogic domain that hosts your FMW application. Refer to section *OAM Identity Assertion Provider*.

10. Provision an instance of Web Gate for an Oracle HTTP server installed previously via RREG or OAM console; see *Chapter 8, Install and Configure OAM Agents*.

11. Install Web Gate with Oracle HTTP Server (The only 11g Web Gate certified thus far is OHS, but OAM 11g is compatible with all 10g WebGates).

12. For OBIEE or Webcenter, complete the configuration with application-specific steps detailed next.

WebCenter-specific tasks

After the steps in *High-level integration steps* section, follow these steps to complete WebCenter configuration:

1. Set the system property `oracle.webcenter.spaces.osso` to `true`. Under `$DOMAIN_HOME/bin/setDomainEnv.sh`, set this property to the `EXTRA_JAVA_PROPERTIES` variable:

   ```
   "EXTRA_JAVA_PROPERTIES="-Doracle.webcenter.spaces.osso=true -
   noverify ${EXTRA_JAVA_PROPERTIES}""
   ```

2. Add the OAM SSO provider by running WLST:

   ```
   addOAMSSOProvider(loginuri="/${app.context}/adfAuthentication",log
   outuri="/oamsso/logout.html")
   ```

3. Configure a WebCenter Spaces administrator by creating a group called `wcspcadmingrp` in OID and adding this group to the role `s8bba98ff_4cbb_40b8_beee_296c916a23ed#-#Administrator` via FMW control or via WLST (`grantAppRole`). Add any existing user in OID to the group `wcspcadmingrp` and this user will then become a WebCenter administrator.

4. Configure WebCenter Discussion Server administrators by creating a group called `wcdisadmingrp` in OID and add this group to the Discussion Server administrator role using WLST (`addDiscussionsServerAdmin`).

5. Configure WebCenter Discussion Server to use OAM by setting the system property `owc_discussions.sso.mode` to `true` and add `jiveURL` to SSO server base URL.

OBIEE-specific tasks

After the steps in the *High-level integration steps* section, follow these steps to complete OBIEE configuration:

1. Login to EM and select **Security | Lock & Edit Configuration | Enable SSO**. From the drop-down box select **OAM**. Configure the **Login** and **Logout** pages to the OAM Login and OAM Logout URLs).

2. Update `instanceconfig.xml` (Presentation server `config`) to allow access from OHS, all BI Scheduler instances, BI Presentation Service Plug-In instance, and Oracle BI Java Host instances.

Integrate Oracle E-Business Suite with OAM

Oracle has two single sign-on solutions which can be integrated with Oracle E-Business Suite; Oracle Single Sign-On server (OSSO) and OAM with SSO is installed as part of Oracle application server 10*g*'s infrastructure. For OAM, there are two versions *10gR3* (10.1.4.X) and *11gR1* (11.1.1.X) certified with Oracle E-Business Suite R12. OAM is the recommended single sign-on solution for E-Business Suite.

This book covers integration of Oracle E-Business Suite R12 with OAM 11*g*. If you are integrating Oracle E-Business Suite R12 with OSSO then refer to My Oracle Support (MOS) note 376811.1. If you are integrating Oracle E-Business Suite R12 with OAM *10gR3* then refer to MOS note 975182.1, and if you are currently using OSSO and wish to migrate to the 11*g* R1 OAM then refer to MOS note 1304550.1.

E-Business Suite—OAM integration component

In order to understand OAM integration with the Oracle E-Business Suite, let's first understand the key components involved in this integration.

Profile option

Profile options are used in E-Business Suite to update the behavior of the environment. Two profile options which are used in Oracle E-Business Suite are Application SSO Type and Application Authentication Agent.

- **Application SSO Type** (APPS_SSO): This site-wide profile option can be set to one of the four values SSWA, Portal, SSWA w/SSO, or Portal w/SSO. To inform E-Business Suite that SSO is configured and to redirect users there rather than a local login page, set this profile option to either SSWA w/SSO or Portal w/SSO.

Oracle HTTP Server

Oracle HTTP Server (OHS) is a web server from Oracle on which Web Gate is deployed. OHS acts as a proxy server to the WebLogic server on which Access Gate is deployed. This OHS server also has mod_wl_ohs configured to forward requests to WebLogic server if the server hosts Oracle E-Business Suite Access Gate (EBS AG). The profile option Application Authentication Agent is set to point to the OHS.

> E-Business Suite R12 comes with its own OHS server. The OHS server mentioned here is a different OHS server than the one shipped with the EBS R12 technology stack.

Web Gate

Web Gate is a **policy enforcement point** (PEP), which is a plug-in deployed with web servers such as Apache, OHS, and IHS. It intercepts user requests and sends them to OAM to check if the user is authenticated/authorised to access the requested resource. For Web Gate to work, an instance of it must be configured in OAM server using RREG or OAMConsole, and Web Gate must be installed with OHS using the same user as OHS. Refer to *Chapter 8, Install and Configure OAM Agents*

mod_wl_ohs

This is a module in Oracle HTTP Server (OHS) which forwards request to WebLogic server from OHS as defined in `mod_wl_ohs.conf` under `$ORACLE_INSTANCE/config/OHS/<ohs1>/`.

WebLogic server

WebLogic server is application server where Oracle EBS AG is deployed. The Access Gate communicates with the EBS database using JDBC that is defined during deployment. For the database to allow communication from a machine where WebLogic server is deployed, you must register the machine hosting WebLogic server (and EBS AG) with the EBS database using Oracle E-Business Suite Java Development Kit (EBS JDK) to generate a DBC file. For more information on EBS SDK refer to node 974949.1.

> If the WebLogic server that hosts EBS AG is on the same machine as part of EBS middle tier, then there is no need to register the node in the database and you can use an existing DBC file from `$FND_SECURE` directory.

Oracle E-Business Suite Access Gate

EBS AG (`fndauth.war`) is a Java EE application which maps a SSO user (authenticated via OAM) to an Oracle EBS user (stored in `FND_USER` table), and creates EBS session for that user. EBS AG is deployed on WebLogic Server using ANT which creates a web application and JDBC connection to EBS database. The login page for EBS displayed after OAM integration is also configured as part of EBS AG.

There are currently two versions of EBS AG: 1.0.2, which is certified with OAM 10*g* R3; and 1.1.0.0, which you should use with OAM 11*g* R1. EBS AG 1.1.0.0 is available via patch 10124068.

> EBS AG must be deployed on a machine which has the same Internet domain as the EBSe middle tier servers.

Request flow for EBS integrated with OAM

The following diagram depicts the request flow when an unauthenticated user accesses EBS integrated with OAM.

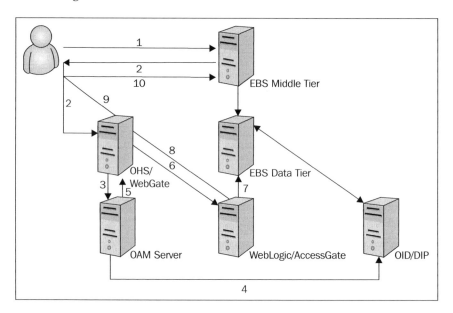

1. The user accesses EBS at L `http://<ebs_mid_tier>:<ebs_ohs_port>`. EBS checks that profile option `Application SSO Type` is set to `Portal w/SSO` or `SSWA w/SSO` (`w/SSO` signifies that EBS is integrated with SSOS).

2. EBS then checks the value of the profile option `Application Authentication Agent` (value is set to `http://<ohs_with_wg>:<ohs_with_wg:port>/<context_root>/`, where `<context_root>` is the value that is set during EBS AG deployment) and redirects the user to set value for `Application Authentication Agent`.

3. Web Gate (deployed with OHS server) then checks if any token/cookie is available in the user session and forwards this request to OAM server for validation.

4. OAM server then checks authentication URL configured for Web Gate (Host: Port or Host Identifier) and redirects the user to the authentication page configured by authentication URL. When the user enters a username/password, OAM will validate them against its identity store (Oracle Internet Directory). OID will validate username and password against `UID` (login attribute) and `userPassword` (password attribute).

5. On successful authentication, OAM will forward the response back to WebGate along with a cookie.

6. Web Gate will then redirect the user to EBS AG for validation or mapping.

7. EBS AG will take this user ID and map/validate it against the user in EBS (FND_USER).

8. On successful validation, a response is returned to Web Gate.

9. Web Gate will forward the response to the user.

10. The user, with their cookie, moves from Web Gate/Access Gate to EBS middle tier.

11. EBS middle tier will generate an EBS-specific cookie for the user. From this point onward, the user talks directly to Oracle EBS until explicit logout or timeout.

 The user in EBS (FND_USER) is synchronized with OID using Directory Integration Platform's Provisioning framework.

High-level steps to integrate EBS R12 with OAM SSO

High-level steps to integrate Oracle E-Business Suite with Oracle Access Manager are as follows:

1. Install OAM 11*g* R1 (11.1.1.3.0).

2. Apply BP02 for OAM 11*g* R1 that is 11.1.1.3.2.0.

3. Install OID 11*g* R1 (11.1.1.2.0).

4. Patch OID to 11*g* R1 PS2+ (11.1.1.4.0+).

5. Configure OAM's primary identity store to OID.

6. Integrate EBS with OID.

7. Install OHS 11*g*R1 (an authentication server for EBS requests).

8. Install Oracle WebLogic server (This will host EBS AG).

9. Generate a DBC file for WebLogic server on which Access Gate is to be deployed and installed.

10. Deploy EBS AccessGate using the ANT script. This script will deploy the web application and JDBC data source in WebLogic server.

11. Configure `mod_wl_ohs` in OHS for the Access Gate web application deployed on Web Logic server.

12. Register Web Gate for Oracle HTTP Server installed in Step 7 with OAM console.

13. Install Web Gate with Oracle HTTP server. installed in Step 7 with OAM console.

14. Define authentication module, authentication policies, and authorization response in OAM.

15. Configure Profile Option in EBS.

16. Test EBS – OAM Integration.

For step-by-step instructions refer to My Oracle Support (MOS) note 1309013.1 or check my e-Book *Oracle E-Business Suite R12 integration with OID/OAM for Single Sign-On* (`http://onlineappsdba.com/index.php/book/`).

Summary

In this chapter, we discussed Fusion middleware security concepts such as users, groups, roles, authentication and Identity assertion provider, and integration of Oracle Fusion middleware applications such as WebCenter and OBIEE. We also covered integration of Oracle E-Business Suite with Oracle Access Manager. In next chapter, we are going to cover logging and auditing in OAM/OIM.

13
Logging and Auditing for OIM/OAM

Logging is mainly used to diagnose problems and is a very useful tool for OAM and OIM administrators. Auditing answers the question *who has done what and where?* Auditing helps to evaluate adherence to policies, user access controls, and risk management procedures. It also conforms with regulatory requirements such as Sarbanes-Oxley (SOX) or Health Insurance Portability and Accountability Act (HIPAA). This chapter covers lower-case including:

- Logging methods in OAM and OIM
- Logging levels
- How to enable logging in OAM, OIM, and WebLogic server
- Important logfile locations
- Auditing in OAM including steps to configure auditing
- Auditing in OIM including log levels
- Remote Diagnostics Agents

Logging methods

Following are the logging methods available in Oracle FMW 11*g*:

- Oracle Diagnostic Logging (ODL) framework
- Apache log4j
- WebLogic Logging Service

Not all logging methods are used by OIM and OAM. For example, WebLogic Logging Service is used only by WebLogic server.

Oracle Diagnostic Logging (ODL) framework

The **Oracle Diagnostic Logging** (**ODL**) framework is the logging framework used by OIM and OAM. ODL extends the Java EE logging framework and consists of two components:

- Loggers
- Log handlers

Loggers

The logger component of the ODL framework is called when events require logging. Examples of logger components are SSO controller logger, Credential collector logger, and so on. The following table lists some of ODL loggers from OIM and OAM:

Sl No.	Components	Logger Name
1	Protocol binding	oracle.oam.binding
2	SSO controller	oracle.oam.controller.sso
3	OAM proxy	oracle.oam.proxy.oam
4	OSSO proxy	oracle.oam.proxy.osso
5	Credential collector	oracle.oam.credcollector
6	Remote Registration of partners	oracle.oam.engine.remotereg
7	Admin-console	oracle.oam.admin.console
8	Admin-Service config	oracle.oam.admin.service.config
9	Diagnostics and monitoring	oracle.oam.diag
10	Authentication engine	oracle.oam.engine.authn
11	Policy Service engine	oracle.oam.engine.policy
12	Session Management engine	oracle.oam.engine.session
13	Token engine	oracle.oam.engine.token
14	SSO engine	oracle.oam.engine.sso
15	PartnerTrustMetadata engine	oracle.oam.engine.ptmetadata
16	Authorization engine	oracle.oam.engine.authz
17	Session access	oracle.oam.session.access
18	Session Access implementation	oracle.oam.session.accessimpl

Sl No.	Components	Logger Name
19	Policy Access	`oracle.oam.policy.access`
20	Logs events related to request and request dataset management.	`oracle.iam.request, oracle.iam.requestdatasetgeneration, oracle.iam.requestactions,`
21	Logs events related to request template management.	`oracle.iam.requesttemplate`
22	Logs events related to authenticated and unauthenticated self-service operations.	`oracle.iam.selfservice`
23	Logs events for the password change functionality UI.	`oracle.iam.ChangePasswordtaskflow`
24	Logs events for the "forgot password" functionality UI.	`oracle.iam.forgotpasswordtaskflow`
25	Logs events for the administrative UI identity operations.	`oracle.iam.identitytaskflow`
26	Logs events related to the organization manager service operations.	`oracle.iam.identity.orgmgmt`
27	Logs events related to the user manager service operations.	`oracle.iam.identity.usermgmt`

An OAM logger name begins with the string `oracle.oam` whereas an OIM logger name begins with `oracle.oim` and `xellerate`.

Log handlers

Log handlers receive messages from loggers and write the messages to files. By default OAM uses `odl-handler` log handler and writes to file `$DOMAIN_HOME/servers/<OAM Server>/logs/<OAM_Server-diagnostics.log>`.

Log level

The log level determines the amount of logging output. These are the log levels for ODL format:

- `INCIDENT_ERROR:1`: This logging level produces least logging output and records only serious problems that may be caused by a bug.

- `ERROR:1`: A serious problem that requires immediate attention from the administrator and is not caused by a bug in the product.

- `WARNING:1`: A potential problem that should be reviewed by the administrator.

- NOTIFICATION:1: This generates log records for system error and notifications only, and major lifecycle events such as the activation or deactivation of a primary sub-component or feature.
- NOTIFICATION:16: A finer level of granularity for reporting normal events.
- TRACE:1: Trace or debug information for events that are meaningful to administrators, such as public API entry or exit points.
- TRACE:16: Detailed trace or debug information that can help Oracle Support diagnose problems with a particular subsystem.
- TRACE:32: Very detailed trace or debug information that can help Oracle Support diagnose problems with a particular subsystem. This logging level produces the most logging output.

The log level can be set at various levels, and uses an inheritance model. To understand this inheritance model, let's take an example of logger diagnostics and auditing oracle.oam.diag. Logging for the oracle.oam.diag logger be set at either oracle.oam.diag, oracle.oam, or oracle level. To determine the level, the logging system first looks to see if a log level has been explicitly set for that logger, that is, at the oracle.oam.diag level. If no explicit log level is found, the logging system strips the right-most string from logger name and looks for next logger up the hierarchy, that is oracle.oam and so forth.

 The default log level for OAM/OIM components is NOTIFICATION:1.

How to change log level

To change the logging level in OAM/OIM components, the following methods are supported:

- WLST command **setLogLevel**
- Fusion Middleware Control

Changing the log level using WLST

To change The log level using WLST carry out these steps:

1. Set environment variable by running setWLEnv.sh.
2. Start WLST using wlst.sh.
3. Connect to WebLogic Domain:

   ```
   connect(''weblogicUser'',''password'',''AdminServerHostName:
   AdminPort'')
   ```

4. Set Log Level for a logger:

```
setLogLevel(target="serverName", logger="logerName",
level="LogLevel")
```

For example, to set Log Level TRACE:32 for logger SSO Engine (oracle.oam.engine.sso) for OAM server oam_server1 run:

```
setLogLevel(target="oam_server1", logger=" oracle.oam.engine.
sso",level="TRACE:32")
```

To learn more on WLST commands for logging, check Logging Custom WLST commands at http://download.oracle.com/docs/cd/E14571_01/web.1111/e13813/custom_logging.htm.

Changing the log level using FMW Control

To change the log level using FMW Control, follow these steps:

1. Log in to Enterprise Manager Fusion Middleware Control using http://servername:admin_port/em where servername is the server on which the Admin server is running and the Admin_port is admin server port (default value 7001).

2. Navigate to OAM or OIM under **Identity and Access**, right click on **oam_server** (or **oim_server**), and then select **Logs | Log Configuration**.

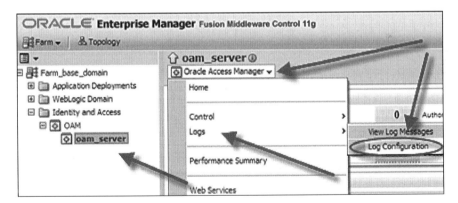

3. On the right-hand panel, under the tab **Log Levels**, and under the column **Logger name** expand **oracle.oam** (for OAM) or **oracle.oim** (for OIM). Under the specific logger, change and select the level from the drop-down menu **Oracle Diagnostics Logging Level**.

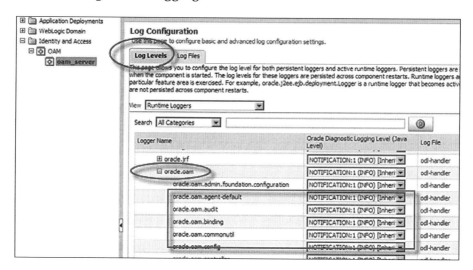

Logging Configuration for OAM/OIM is stored in file $DOMAIN_HOME/ config/fmwconfig/servers/<serverName>/logging.xml.

Changing Log Location/Log Rotation policy using FMW Control

To change the log location using FMW Control, follow these steps:

1. Login to Enterprise Manager Fusion Middleware Control using `http://servername:admin_port/em` where `servername` is the server on which the Admin server is running and `admin_port` is the Admin server port (default value `7001`).

2. Navigate to OAM or OIM under **Identity and Access**, right click on **oam_server** (or **oim_server**), and then **Logs | Log Configuration**.

3. On the right-hand panel, under the tab **Log Files**, under **logger**, select log handler and click on **Edit Configuration**.

4. Change parameter `Log Path` to change log location.

Change fields under `Rotation Policy` to change properties like size-based or time-based log rotation.

 Default log rotation is size-based, a new logfile is create when the size of the current log becomes 10 MB.

Apache log4j

OIM 11*g* uses Apache's **log4j** mechanism to log third party tools. As discussed earlier, ODL is used for the majority of OIM functionalities while Apache log4j is being used only for a few third party applications such as Nexaweb for deployment management and workflow design, and OSCache for caching. You should use the ODL way of setting logging, if you are not dealing with debugging of third party applications as mentioned previously, using the Apache log4j will not work in that case. For debugging custom adapters use ODL framework. Apache log4j is configured using configuration file at `$ORACLE_HOME/server/config/log.properties`.

Log level

Log level determines the amount of logging output. These are the available log levels for log4j format:

- `OFF`: No logging.
- `ERROR`: This records error events that might allow the application to continue running.
- `WARN`: This records potentially harmful situations.
- `ALL`: This level is intended to turn on all logging.
- `INFO`: This level designates informational messages that highlight the progress of the application at coarse-grained level.
- `DEBUG`: This level designates fine-grained informational events that are useful to debug an application.

How to configure log4j

To configure log4j for third party applications such as Nexaweb or OSCache, open the log4j configuration file at `$ORACLE_HOME/server/config/log.properties` and update the log level against the relevant logger, that is `log4j.logger.com.nexaweb.server` or `log4j.logger.com.opensymphony.oscache`.

WebLogic logging service

Oracle WebLogic server (on which OIM and OAM are deployed) uses its own logging service which is explained in detail at `http://download.oracle.com/docs/cd/E14571_01/web.1111/e13739/logging_services.htm`.

How to enable debugging in WebLogic server

WebLogic's debugging tool can be enabled on Admin or Managed servers using in multiple ways, one of which is the WebLogic console. To debug logging in WebLogic server, follow the given steps:

1. Login to WebLogic Console `http://serverName:adminPort/console` where `serverName` is the name of the server on which the WebLogic Admin server is running and `adminPort` is Admin server port (default value `7001`).

2. From the left-hand panel, under **Environment** click on **Servers**.

3. On the right-hand panel, click on the server (Admin or Managed) for which you wish to enable logging and click on the **Debug** tab.

4. Expand **WebLogic** and select the component for which you wish to enable debug. For example, to enable debug for authentication and authorization, expand **WebLogic | Security | atn** or **atz** (select checkbox) and click on the **Enable** button on top or at the bottom.

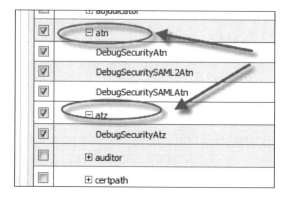

5. WebLogic server will start generating DEBUG messages in the respective server logfile as mentioned in the next section.

Log location

Logs for various components are located by default at the following places:

- WebLogic domain logs are at: $DOMAIN_HOME/servers/[AdminServer]/logs/[DomainName].log.

- Admin server logs are at: $DOMAIN_HOME/servers/[AdminServer]/logs/[AdminServer].log.

- OAM server logs are at: $DOMAIN_HOME/servers/[oam_server1]/logs/[oam_server1].log and $DOMAIN_HOME/servers/[oam_server1]/logs/[oam_server1]-diagnostic.log.

- OIM server logs are at: $DOMAIN_HOME/servers/[oim_server1]/logs/[oim_server1].log and $DOMAIN_HOME/servers/[oim_server1]/logs/[oim_server1]-diagnostic.log.

- Fusion middleware control logs are at: $DOMAIN_HOME/sysman/log/emoms.log and $DOMAIN_HOME/sysman/log/emoms.trc.

Auditing

Auditing is a process of collecting specific information related to administrative and run-time events. Auditing provides a measure of accountability and answer to *who has done what and where*. Auditing helps to evaluate adherence to policies, user access controls, and risk management procedures. Auditing may also be required for enterprise to conform with regulatory requirements such as Sarbanes-Oxley (SOX) or Health Insurance Portability, and Accountability Act (HIPAA). Auditing in OAM uses the FMW common audit framework whereas OIM uses its own audit engine.

Oracle Business Intelligence Publisher (BIP), another product from FMW can be used to generate audit reports on OAM auditing database as well as from audit tables in OIM schema. The following section covers:

- Auditing in OAM
- Auditing in OIM

Auditing in OAM

Auditing in OAM uses the FMW common audit framework where database is used to store audit events (audit database must include audit schema). The audit schema is created using the Repository Creation Utility (RCU) by selecting **Audit Services – XXX_IAU** from component **AS Common Schemas**.

 Audit schema for OAM and OAM schema which contains policy data can co-exist in the same database. However, for performance reasons it is recommended to configure audit schema in its own dedicated database.

Audit configuration for OAM components is stored in OAM configuration file, `oam-config.xml` whereas event configuration (which dictates auditing various OAM events to different levels) is stored in `component_events.xml`.

 Auditing in OAM 10g is based on OAM policies. However, auditing in OAM 11*g* is based on configuration parameters set in OAM console which enables data capture on a particular user, or set of users, or on all users of OAM.

Not all events or all components of OAM can be audited. All OAM events that can be audited fall under two categories:

- **OAM Administrative Events**: Administrative events are those generated when the OAM console is used. Administrative events which can be audited are OAM console login success/failure, authentication policy creation, authentication scheme modification, authentication scheme removal (Delete), server domain removal, server domain modification, server domain creation, constraints removal, constraints modification, constraints creation, partner removal, partner modification, partner addition, response removal (Delete), response modification, response creation, and server configuration change.

- **OAM Run-Time Events**: These are those events that are generated during actual functioning of OAM components such as when a user is authenticated using OAM. Run-time events which can be audited are authentication attempt, authentication success, authentication failure, session creation, session destroy, login success, login failure, logout success, logout failure, credential collection, credential submit, authorization success, authorization failure, server startup, and server shutdown.

OAM uses FMW's **audit framework**, which consists of the following components:

- **Audit bus-stop**: These are simple text files containing audit data records before they are pushed to the audit store. If no audit store is configured for a FMW component (such as OIM/OAM) then audit data remains in these bus-stop files; otherwise, it acts as an interface to load audit data into audit store. There is one bus-stop file for each OAM Managed server. These files are stored in `$DOMAIN_HOME/servers/<OAMserverName>/logs/auditlogs/OAM/audit.log`.

- **Audit Store**: This is a database with audit framework schema (`XXX_IAU`). The audit loader loads data here periodically from the bus-stop.

- **Audit loader**: This loads data from the audit bus-stop into the audit store. For OAM auditing, audit loader is a startup class that is part of WebLogic Managed server startup.

- **Audit configuration Mbeans**: These are used to configure/manage audit configuration. These MBeans are present in the WebLogic domain Administration server.

- **Audit APIs**: These APIs are provided by the FMW audit framework for any audit-aware component integration with the framework. OAM may call these APIs to audit the necessary information about a particular event in application code.

- **Oracle BI Publishers**: This is product from Oracle Business Intelligence (BI) family and is used to expose audit data (from Audit Store) using pre-defined reports. Enterprise can create their own reports from Audit Store using BI Publisher.

Auditing flow in OAM

The following diagram represents how auditing works in OAM, where two boxes on the left and right represent WebLogic servers, both running OAM server in Active-Active deployment. When any event (configured under audit policy) is generated by the system or the user, an audit call is invoked which will write events to the audit Bus-Stop. Audit Loader will then upload these Audit events to Audit database. BI Publisher is then used to generate/view reports on OAM audit events.

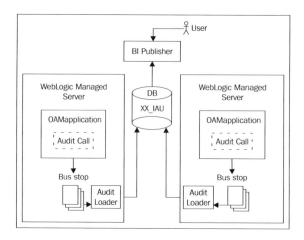

Configuring auditing for OAM

In order to configure auditing for OAM components follow the given steps:

- Prepare the audit store
- Configure WebLogic domain to connect to audit store
- Configure OIM/OAM to use audit store
- Configure audit policies in WebLogic domain for OIM/OAM
- Restart WebLogic servers
- Test events that are logged in audit database

Prepare the audit store

The first step to configure auditing in OIM/OAM is to create a database for the audit store. Though it is possible to use database containing OAM/OIM schema, for performance reasons it is recommended to use a dedicated database instead. Use RCU to load audit schema (XX_IAU) into the audit store database. RCU is covered in *Chapter 2, Installing Oracle Identity and Access Manager* of this book.

Configure WebLogic domain to connect to audit store

To configure WebLogic domain to connect to the audit store, follow these steps:

1. Create a data source in the WebLogic domain running OAM to point to the audit schema (`XX_IAU`) using WebLogic console.

2. Log in to WebLogic console
   `http://weblogicserver:<admin_port>/console`.

3. Expand **Services | JDBC | Data Sources** and click on the **New** button.

4. Enter **Name** and **JNDI Name** in the **JDBC Data Source Properties** page and click on **Next**.

   Name: `AuditStore`

   JNDI Name: `jndi/AuditStore`

5. Leave **Database Driver** with default values and click on **Next**.

6. Click **Next** on the **Transaction Objects** screen.

7. On the **Connection Properties** page, enter:

   Database Name: <name of your database in which audit schema is available>

   Hostname: <Hostname of machine where audit database is running>

   Port: <Database listener port of audit database>

   Database User Name:

   Password:

   Confirm Password:

   Click on **Next**

8. Click on the **Test Configuration** button to verify the connection to the audit schema and then click on **Next**.

9. Target this data source to the Admin server and the OAM server.

10. Click on **Finish**.

Configure OAM to use the audit store

Update your WebLogic domain configuration so OIM/OAM use the audit store to audit events.

1. Login to Enterprise Manager `http://weblogicserver:<admin_port>/em`

2. Expand **WebLogic Domain**. Right click on <domain_name>. Then click on **Security | Audit Store**.

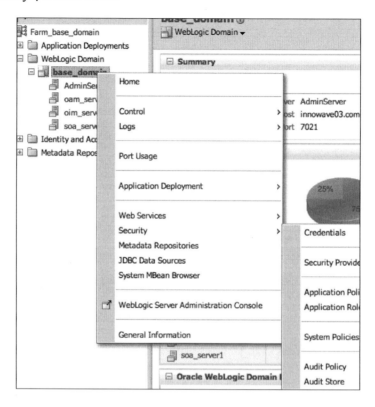

3. Click on the searchlight icon next to **Data Source JNDI Name** and select the data source created above, that is `jndi/AuditStore`

4. Click on **Apply**, you will see a confirmation as shown in the following screenshot:

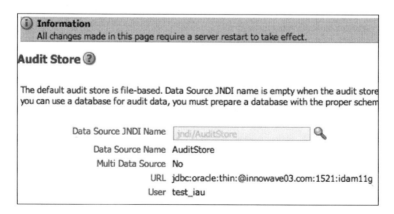

Configure audit policies

To configure audit policies, follow these steps:

1. Login to Enterprise Manager `http://weblogicserver:<admin_port>/em`.

2. Expand **WebLogic Domain**. Right click on the concerned domain name. Then click on **Security | Audit Policies**.

3. Expand **Oracle Access Manager** and select the component for which you wish to enable auditing, and from **Audit Level** select **Custom** as shown in the next screenshot:

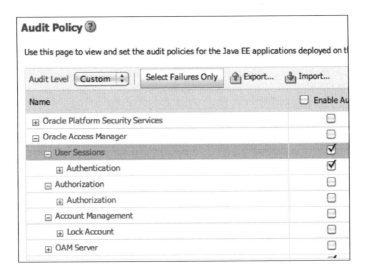

4. Click on **Apply**.

Restart WebLogic server

Restart WebLogic's Admin and Managed server for these changes to take effect. Refer to *Chapter 3, IDAM Directory Structure and Files* for startup and shutdown.

Test working of auditing

To test the working of auditing:

1. Execute any action which generates an event for which you have configured auditing (for example, authentication).

2. Login to the audit store database using audit schema (`XX_IAU`) using SQLPLUS.

3. You should see audit events registered in audit schema under query tables `OAM` and `IAU_BASE`.

Auditing in OIM

Auditing in OIM uses its own auditing engine and audit tables in OIM schema (XX_OIM) as audit repository. The audit engine in OIM captures the change (delta) and new values in XML format. The audit engine processes the components, then populates audit tables with relevant tables. OIM's audit engine performs these tasks in an asynchronous and offline manner using Java Messaging Service (JMS) as provided by WebLogic server.

The audit level defines what information will be audited and can be set to one of following levels:

- Process Task: This level audits entire all user profile changes, including changes in resource lifecycle.

- Resource Form: This level audits user records, role membership, resource provisioned, and form data associated with resource.

- Resource: This level audits user records, role membership, and resource provisioning.

- Membership: This level audits user records and role membership.

- Core: This level audits only the user records.

- None: No audit is performed.

 Audit level is case-sensitive and set using the OIM system property User profile audit data collection level (XL. UserProfileAuditDataCollection).

When OIM is first installed, the audit level defaults to Resource Form. This can altered by changing system property XL.UserProfileAuditDataCollection, under the System Configuration section in the OIM Advanced Administration console. If you change the audit level, then you must run the GeneratSnapshot.sh (Unix) or GeneratSnapshot.bat (Windows) from ORACLE_HOME/server/bin directory. This script generates a new snapshot for all users in the OIM database, based on a new audit level.

Tables UPA, UPA_USR, UPA_RESOURCE, UPA_GRP_MEMBERSHIP, and AUD are some of the key tables under OIM schema (XXX_OIM) to store audit data.

Remote Diagnostic Agent (RDA)

Remote Diagnostic Agent (RDA) is a command-line diagnostic tool that captures data and provides a comprehensive picture of your environment. RDA is a useful tool for Oracle support to identify your system configuration and dump all logfiles so that these files can be used to diagnose issues. RDA does not update or modify system configuration, it simply gathers required configuration. RDA is clearly explained in *My Oracle Support* (MOS earlier Metalink).

- 314422.1: Remote Diagnostic Agent (RDA) 4 Getting Started
- 853437.1: Running RDA Against Oracle Fusion Middleware 11*g*
- 1306020.1: How to Use Remote Diagnostics Agent (RDA) to collect Oracle Access Manager (OAM) 11*g* information.

In the next section, I am going to cover how to configure RDA and generate a zip file containing all required configuration and logfiles.

Configuring RDA

Generating RDA consists mainly of two steps, first configuring it and then running it to generate required files into zip file. You will need *My Oracle Support* access to download RDA files. Currently RDA is available for the OAM only; there is no RDA for OIM 11*g* component yet.

The following section contains the list of tasks required to configure RDA and gather required information:

1. Download RDA (4.23 or higher) using My Oracle Support (MOS, earlier Metalink). Download link for all available platforms is mentioned under the Download section in note 314422.1.

2. Upload RDA software (`pXXXX_4XX_<OS>.zip`) to a temporary location on the server such as `/tmp/rda`.

3. Unzip the uploaded file on server. This will extract files under folder `rda`.

4. Setup RDA using the following command:

   For Unix: `rda.sh -Sp FM11g_AccessManager`

   For Windows: `rda.batcmdbat -Sp FM11g_AccessManager`

   Here, `-S` is to setup specific module in RDA and `-p` is to specify setup profile (`FM11g_AccessManager` in this case).

When prompted for Oracle Home, Middleware Home, and Domain Home provides values as per your setup. For more information on these parameters refer *Chapter 3, IDAM Directory Structure and Files*. This step will complete the configuration of RDA.

5. Run RDA to gather required information:

    For Unix: `rda.sh`

    For Windows: `rda.batcmdbat`

    This will create the file `RDA.<prefix>_<hostname>.zip` under the output directory (default value `output`) mentioned during the RCA setup step using the `-Sp` option.

6. Upload the created zip file to the Oracle Support Analyst. You can also unzip the file generated via RDP and open `RDA__index.htm` to view the configuration and logfile.

For Windows the files are mainly `.cmd` files not `.bat` files.

Summary

In this chapter, we covered logging in OAM and OIM. We also covered the ODL framework including steps on how to change logging level, log properties such as filename, and log rotation method. We covered enabling debugging in the WebLogic server and the location of logfiles which you must look at during troubleshooting. We also covered the auditing framework and its components, including steps to configure auditing in OAM as well as the various audit levels supported by OIM. At the end of the chapter, we covered Remote Diagnostic Agent, which is a diagnostic tool to generate configuration and logfiles.

Appendix

This appendix will cover common "how-to" questions for OIM and OAM, such as how to find version/port numbers or install patches. We will also cover basic troubleshooting and common issues reported on the Internet, including solutions.

FAQ

This section covers frequently asked questions related to OAM and OIM.

Q: How do I find out which version of WebLogic server OAM/OIM is deployed on?

A: There are multiple ways to check the WebLogic server version number:

- Open `$MW_HOME/registry.xml` and search for "component name="WebLogic Server"" version="10.3.3.0" (variable version next to this will tell you the WebLogic version).

- Find the WebLogic Admin server logfile at `$DOMAIN_HOME/servers/AdminServer/logs/AdminServer.log` and search for "WebLogic Server". Output such as, "**WebLogic Server 10.3.4.0 Fri Dec 17 20:47:33 PST 2010 1384255 Copyright (c) 1995, 2009, Oracle and/or its affiliates. All rights reserved.**" will tell you the WebLogic server version (10.3.4.0 as per output).

- Execute:

  `$WL_HOME/server/lib/java -cp weblogic.jar weblogic.version`

  You should see something like, "**WebLogic Server 10.3.4.0 Fri Dec 17 20:47:33 PST 2010 1384255 Use 'weblogic.version -verbose' to get subsystem information**"

Q: How do I find the version number of OIM/OAM?

A: To find the version numbers of OIM or OAM software (binaries) and list of patches applied, run:

```
$MW_HOME/oracle_common/OPatch/bin/opatch lsinventory
```

To find the OIM schema version, run the following SQL query:

```
SQL> SELECT XSD_CODE,XSD_VALUE FROM <oim_schema>.XSD WHERE
xsd_code='XL_ADE_LABEL';
```

 To find a list of bundle patches of OIM, refer to MoS Note # 1275998.1 Document Title Version and Bundle Patch Cross Reference for OIM 11*g*R1.

To find list of bundle patches of OAM, refer to MoS Note # 736372.1 OAM Bundle Patch Release History.

Q: Where can I find the OAM/OIM certification matrix (list of supported OSs)?

A: Fusion Middleware, including an OIM/OAM certification matrix is available at:

http://www.oracle.com/technetwork/middleware/ias/downloads/fusion-certification-100350.html (Fusion middleware certification matrix).

http://www.oracle.com/technetwork/middleware/id-mgmt/identity-accessmgmt-11gr1certmatrix-161244.xls (OAM and OIM 11*g* Certification Matrix).

Q: I can only see OAM/OIM 11.1.1.3 or 11.1.1.5, where do I find OIM/OAM 11.1.1.1.2 or 11.1.1.4?

A: There is no version 11.1.1.2 or 11.1.1.4. The first release of 11*g*R1 was 11.1.1.3.0, and the next release was 11.1.1.5.0.

Q: I am using RCU 11.1.1.3.0, why can't I see schema for OAM or OIM?

A: OAM and OIM 11.1.1.3 schema are not available in 11.1.1.3.0 RCU, use RCU version 11.1.1.3.2 or higher.

Q: How do I upgrade from OAM/OIM 11.1.1.3 to 11.1.1.5?

A: Follow the instructions on patching Oracle Identity and Access Management at http://download.oracle.com/docs/cd/E21764_01/doc.1111/e16793/patch_oam.htm#BGBIJEHJ. For OAM, follow MoS Note# 1318524.1 Procedure to upgrade OAM 11.1.1.3.0 to OAM 11.1.1.5.0. In addition you should also patch WebLogic to the supported version (10.3.5).

Q: How do I change the port for OAM/OIM?

A: OAM/OIM servers are deployed on WebLogic server. To change the WebLogic server port, follow the link: `http://download.oracle.com/docs/cd/E21764_01/core.1111/e10105/ports.htm#CIHCBAAA` (Changing Oracle WebLogic Server Listen Ports). To change OIM database port, OIM frontend URL, or OIM back office URL, follow this link: `http://download.oracle.com/docs/cd/E21764_01/doc.1111/e14308/handlinglcm.htm` (Handling Lifecycle Management Changes).

Q: Does OAM support single identity store or multiple identity stores?

A: OAM 11.1.1.3 supports only single identity store whereas OAM 11.1.1.5 supports multiple identity stores for authentication. More information is available at `http://download.oracle.com/docs/cd/E21764_01/doc.1111/e15478/datasrc.htm#BHCJHHFD` (About Identity Stores).

Q: I would like to implement OAM's Admin server (and only the Admin server) on machine1 and OAM Managed server on machine2. Is it supported/certified?

A: As of version 11.1.1.3 and 11.1.1.5, this is not possible. You should have OAM's Admin server on the same machine as OAM Managed server. You can, however deploy Admin server and one Managed server are on machine1 and a second Managed server is on machine2.

Q: How do I implement a custom , externally-hosted login form for OAM?

A: Follow my Oracle support note: 1281026.1 How To Configure An External Custom Login Page For OAM 11*g*

Q: How do I apply a bundle patch in OAM/OIM?

A: Bundle Patches in OAM 11*g* are applied using opatch available under `$COMMON_ORACLE_HOME/OPatch/opatch`. Check the readme of each patch and also the Fusion Middleware patching guide at `http://download.oracle.com/docs/cd/E21764_01/doc.1111/e16793/opatch.htm#PATCH181`

Q: How do I create an OAM Administrator?

A: For OAM 11.1.1.5, to make a user into an administrator, add the user to the "Access System Administrators" role, or assign the user to a group which is a member of the role "Access System Administrators". Follow the steps at `http://download.oracle.com/docs/cd/E21764_01/doc.1111/e15478/datasrc.htm#BHCIBHIA`. For OAM 11.1.1.3, assign the user to a group which is mapped to the role OAM Administrator (default value Administrators). Follow the steps at `http://download.oracle.com/docs/cd/E14571_01/doc.1111/e15478/datasrc.htm#CHDDJCIB`.

Q: How do I integrate OAM with OIM?

A: Follow my Oracle Support (MOS) note # 1285124.1 How to integrate Oracle Access Manager 11*g* (OAM) with Oracle Identity Manager 11*g* (OIM) and Oracle Adaptive Access Manager 11*g* (OAAM). OIM/OAM integration is also covered in the chapter, *Integrating Oracle Access Manager with Oracle Identity Manager* `http://download.oracle.com/docs/cd/E21764_01/doc.1111/e15740/oim.htm#CACJDIDD`.

Common issues

This section covers issues commonly encountered during the installation and configuration of OIM/OAM components.

Start/Stop issues

- Error starting Admin server on IBM AIX.

  For issues related to startup, check WebLogic Server log file. In this case issue is during Admin server startup, so check the server's own log file at:

  $DOMAIN_HOME/servers/AdminServer/logs

  Error reported is:

  ```
  [2011-05-05T12:42:53.075+01:00] [AdminServer] [ERROR] []
  [Coherence] [tid: Logger@1751148640 3.5.3/465p2] [userId:
  <anonymous>] [ecid: 0000IyzxvQKBDCSMyENa6G1Dkcmh000001,0]
  [APP: oam_admin#11.1.1.3.0] 2011-05-05 12:42:53.075/276.984
  OracleCoherence GE 3.5.3/465p2 <Error> (thread=[ACTIVE]
  ExecuteThread: '1' for queue: 'weblogic.kernel.Default (self-
  tuning)', member=n/a): Error while starting cluster: (Wrapped)
  java.net.SocketException: No buffer space available[[ at com.
  tangosol.coherence.component.net.socket.UdpSocket.initializeDatagr
  amSocket(UdpSocket.CDB:28)
  ```

  Fix: Set parameter for coherence as documented in the following link:

  `http://wiki.tangosol.com/display/COH33UG/Performance+Tuning`

- Error starting OAM server on IBM AIX

  For issues related to startup, check WebLogic server log file. In this case issue is during OAM Managed server (oam_server1) startup, so check the server's own log file at:

  $DOMAIN_HOME/servers/oam_server1/logs

Error reported is:

```
####<05-May-2011 13:58:03 o'clock BST> <Error> <HTTP> <servername>
<oam_server1> <[ACTIVE] ExecuteThread: '1' for queue: 'weblogic.
kernel.Default(self-tuning)'> <<WLS Kernel>> <1304600283378> <BEA-
101216> <Servlet: "AMInitServlet" failed to preload on startup in
Web application:"oam".java.lang.ExceptionIn Initializer Error at
java.lang.ExceptionInInitializerError.<init>(ExceptionInInitialize
rError.java:72)
```

Fix: Ensure that the JDK used by OAM Managed server is certified with OAM server. In the above case JDK version was IBM 1.6 Service Release 3; the fix is to use the latest certified JDK version with OAM 11*g* R1, that is, IBM JDK 1.6 Service Release 8.

- Error starting OAM Managed server from the WebLogic console.

  For issues related to startup, check WebLogic Server log file. In this case the issue is during OAM Managed server (oam_server1) startup, so check the server's own log file at:

  `$DOMAIN_HOME/servers/oam_server1/logs`

  Error reported is:

```
<21/12/2010 8:36:58 AM EST> <Error> <Security> <BEA-090870>
<The realm "myrealm" failed to be loaded: weblogic.security.
service.SecurityServiceException: com.bea.common.engine.
ServiceInitializationException: com.bea.common.engine.
SecurityServiceRuntimeException: [Security:097533]SecurityProvider
service class name for IDMDomainAgent is not specified
```

  Fix: Ensure that NodeManager is running with option `StartScriptEnabled=true`. Configure NodeManager with this option.

  Execute `setNMProps.cmd` (Windows) or `setNMProps.sh` (Unix) located under (oam_home\oracle_common\common\bin).

  Restart NodeManager.

  Now start the oam_server1 from Weblogic Console.

User registration in OIM

1. Error during user registration in OIM, "**The registration request has failed. Please contact the help desk.**" as shown in the following screenshot:

User registration requests are handled by OIM Managed server (oim_server1) so check the server's log file at:

`$DOMAIN_HOME/servers/oim_server1/logs`

```
<Mar 13, 2011 10:19:24 AM GMT> <Error> <oracle.iam.request.
impl> <IAM-2050050> <Exception thrown oracle.iam.platform.
workflowservice.exception. IAMWorkflowException: Tasklist mapping
failed for workflowdefinition: default/DefaultRequestApproval!1.0
due to javax.naming.CommunicationException [Root exception
is java.net.ConnectException: t3://innowave03.com:8001/soa-
infra: Destination unreachable; nested exception is: java.net.
ConnectException: Connection refused; No available router to
destination]>
```

Fix: The previous error means SOA server is not available, so start SOA server or check for error message in SOA Managed server (soa_server1) at:

`$DOMAIN_HOME/servers/soa_server1/logs`

Error while running MDS utility

1. Error after supplying server URL during MDS utility execution.

Error message after supplying server URL for MDS utility execution is:

```
javax.security.auth.login.LoginException: unable to
find LoginModule class: weblogic.security.auth.login.
UsernamePasswordLoginModule
```

Fix: Create `wlfullclient.jar` file as described in *Chapter 11, OIM Configuration and Tasks*. This jar file contains class LoginModule

Unable to log in to OIM design console

2. Error during login to OIM design console at client machine:

    Error Message after typing username/password in OIM design Console as shown in the following screenshot:

```
D:\Oracle\Middleware\Oracle_IDM1\designconsole>xlclient.cmd
Exception in thread "main" java.lang.NoClassDefFoundError: javax/ejb/CreateExcep
tion
        at java.lang.Class.getDeclaredMethods0(Native Method)
        at java.lang.Class.privateGetDeclaredMethods(Class.java:2427)
        at java.lang.Class.getDeclaredMethod(Class.java:1935)
        at java.awt.Component.isCoalesceEventsOverriden(Component.java:5948)
        at java.awt.Component.access$500(Component.java:169)
        at java.awt.Component$3.run(Component.java:5902)
        at java.awt.Component$3.run(Component.java:5900)
        at java.security.AccessController.doPrivileged(Native Method)
        at java.awt.Component.checkCoalescing(Component.java:5899)
        at java.awt.Component.<init>(Component.java:5868)
        at java.awt.Container.<init>(Container.java:251)
        at java.awt.Window.<init>(Window.java:431)
```

Fix: Ensure that `wlfullclient.jar` is generated on server as explained in *Chapter 11, OIM Configuration and Tasks*. The jar file `wlfullclient.jar` should be copied (from the OIM server machine to the client machine from where OIM design Console is executed) under folder:

`$ORACLE_HOME\designconsole\ext`

3. The following screenshot shows an Invalid Login in OIM design console at client machine despite entering the correct password:

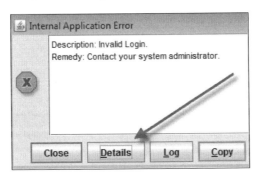

If you hit such an error in OIM design console then click on the **Details** button. If you get a message like "**No available router to destination**" as shown in the following screenshot, then this could be because of a number of reasons:

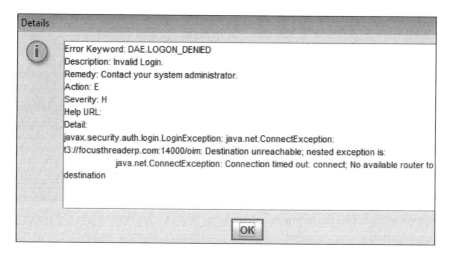

Fix:

- ° **Check 1**: Ensure that OIM Server is up and running and there are no errors in the OIM Managed server log file at:

  `$DOMAIN_HOME/server/oim_server1/`

- ° **Check 2**: Ensure that OIM Server port (`14100`) is open from design console machine to OIM Server.

Summary

In this chapter, we covered common queries such as finding the version number or changing a port. We also covered some common issues in OIM/OAM Server. If your query is not answered in this chapter, drop a mail to ebook@onlineappsdba.com with the subject line "*OAM OIM Book Query*".

Index

Thank you for buying
Oracle Identity and Access Manager 11*g* for Administrators

About Packt Publishing

Packt, pronounced 'packed', published its first book "Mastering phpMyAdmin for Effective MySQL Management" in April 2004 and subsequently continued to specialize in publishing highly focused books on specific technologies and solutions.

Our books and publications share the experiences of your fellow IT professionals in adapting and customizing today's systems, applications, and frameworks. Our solution based books give you the knowledge and power to customize the software and technologies you're using to get the job done. Packt books are more specific and less general than the IT books you have seen in the past. Our unique business model allows us to bring you more focused information, giving you more of what you need to know, and less of what you don't.

Packt is a modern, yet unique publishing company, which focuses on producing quality, cutting-edge books for communities of developers, administrators, and newbies alike. For more information, please visit our website: www.packtpub.com.

About Packt Enterprise

In 2010, Packt launched two new brands, Packt Enterprise and Packt Open Source, in order to continue its focus on specialization. This book is part of the Packt Enterprise brand, home to books published on enterprise software – software created by major vendors, including (but not limited to) IBM, Microsoft and Oracle, often for use in other corporations. Its titles will offer information relevant to a range of users of this software, including administrators, developers, architects, and end users.

Writing for Packt

We welcome all inquiries from people who are interested in authoring. Book proposals should be sent to author@packtpub.com. If your book idea is still at an early stage and you would like to discuss it first before writing a formal book proposal, contact us; one of our commissioning editors will get in touch with you.

We're not just looking for published authors; if you have strong technical skills but no writing experience, our experienced editors can help you develop a writing career, or simply get some additional reward for your expertise.

Oracle Database 11g—Underground
Advice for Database Administrators

Beyond the basics

A real-world DBA survival guide for Oracle 11g database
implementations

April C. Sims

Oracle Database 11g–Underground Advice for Database Administrators

ISBN: 978-1-849680-00-4   Paperback: 348 pages

A real-world DBA survival guide for Oracle 11g
database implementations

1. A comprehensive handbook aimed at reducing
   the day-to-day struggle of Oracle 11g Database
   newcomers

2. Real-world reflections from an experienced
   DBA—what novice DBAs should really know

3. Implement Oracle's Maximum Availability
   Architecture with expert guidance

EJB 3.0 Database Persistence with
Oracle Fusion Middleware 11g

A complete guide to EJB 3.0 database persistence with
Oracle Fusion Middleware 11g

Deepak Vohra

EJB 3.0 Database Persistence with Oracle Fusion Middleware 11g

ISBN: 978-1-849681-56-8   Paperback: 448 pages

A complete guide to building EJB 3.0 database
persistent applications with Oracle Fusion
Middleware 11g

1. Integrate EJB 3.0 database persistence with
   Oracle Fusion Middleware tools: WebLogic
   Server, JDeveloper, and Enterprise Pack for
   Eclipse

2. Automatically create EJB 3.0 entity beans from
   database tables

3. Learn to wrap entity beans with session beans
   and create EJB 3.0 relationships

Please check **www.PacktPub.com** for information on our titles

Printed in Great Britain
by Amazon.co.uk, Ltd.,
Marston Gate.